An AMERICAN *Original*

"I consi... ...n. My
ancestors ...sh two
hundred ... . I got
angry du... ...e been
angry eve...

Only ten years ago, Jane Fonda was despised and resented as a "Commie pinko slut"; even the U.S. Congress sought to indict "Hanoi Jane." As an actress, she'd been "Hank's daughter" who did nudies.

"People's ability to change is what's of greatest importance, not what used to be."

Jane Fonda learned from the North Vietnamese that a person's ability to change was of greatest importance. She transformed by being angry, by asking what our country means and what we were doing, by crying for America and trying to communicate the horror of war. Jane Fonda—a fighter with "guts"—a survivor. She grew to become the consummate actress—sensitive, honest, strong, intelligent. Today she is a powerhouse in the Hollywood industry, an exceptional woman at the height of her power.

Her life story is no fairytale.

JANE FONDA

THE ACTRESS IN HER TIME

Fred Lawrence Guiles

PINNACLE BOOKS NEW YORK

JANE FONDA: THE ACTRESS IN HER TIME

Copyright © 1981, 1982 by Fred Lawrence Guiles

A Pinnacle Books edition, published by arrangement with Doubleday and Company, Inc.

First printing, April 1983

ISBN: 0-523-41994-5

Cover illustration by

Printed in the United States of America

PINNACLE BOOKS, INC.
1430 Broadway
New York, New York 10018

Dedicated to the memory of Dorothy Brewster
(1883–1979)

Don't let the things I say against myself
Betray you into taking sides against me,
Or it might get you into trouble with me.
I'm not afraid to prophesy the future,
And be judged by the outcome, Meliboeus.
Listen and I will take my dearest risk.
We're always too much out or too much in.
At present from a cosmical dilation
We're so much out that the odds are against
Our ever getting inside in again.
But inside in is where we've got to get.
My friends all know I'm interpersonal.
But long before I'm interpersonal
Away 'way down inside I'm personal.
Just so before we're international
We're national and act as nationals.

ROBERT FROST

PREFACE

You probably have to be an American to appreciate fully the current power and popularity of Jane Fonda. A series of complicated maneuvers was needed to bring her safely through the white waters of political daring, mob hatred, career blacklisting and governmental surveillance to the safe harbor of general acceptance. The constant shower of awards might be stultifying to someone other than Jane, but every Golden Globe, every Oscar, is an answer to those critics who are still vocal; the awards make her present preeminence that much more secure.

You doubtless have to be an old Hollywood hand to understand the nature and depth of her power within the industry. Jane has total control of her career: she recently got rid of her agent as superfluous; why pay a man 10 percent of your earnings when you set it all up yourself? To speak ill of Jane Fonda in the Hollywood of 1981, if you are in the studio hierarchy of any of the major studios, is to risk professional suicide. And why should you? Jane is savvy, charming, fairly original, a commanding personality but infrequently demanding, direct, loyal, courageous beyond belief, and only interested in making movies with big themes that entertain and make money. If her former prole stance was offputting, don't knock it; Jane easily could become tomorrow's *grande dame* of the cinema, and does anyone really want that?

This book was written without Jane Fonda's permission or nod of approval. And yet when I had to have access to those persons in her life who witnessed severe traumas or breakthroughs the way was always clear. Divine nonintervention perhaps?

There would have been no book had I not spent several hours with director Sydney Pollack, a man as pivotal to Jane's career as John Ford was to her father's. Fortunately I had spent an equal amount of time several years ago with Actors Studio guru and one of the most influential acting teachers in the world, Lee Strasberg, so the background supplied by Pollack meshed perfectly with that supplied, in another context, by Strasberg. Through a series of doors opening up one after the other I was able to spend some time with acting teacher and director Andreas Voutsinas, who explained what Strasberg was doing for Jane.

In still another context, I managed to spend part of an afternoon in Bel Air with Jane's father, Henry Fonda. I did not yet know that I would undertake to write a book on his daughter, but those hours with Hank Fonda were invaluable to an understanding of both the man and the milieu of the Fondas, aristocrats of the film world, equally at ease in the enclaves of Benedict and Coldwater Canyons and on Cap Ferrat. My hope is that in these pages this legendary Fonda has been kept within human dimensions.

In attempting to trace the eventually tragic life of Frances Seymour Brokaw Fonda, Jane's mother, I especially want to thank her closest confidants, Eulalia Chapin and J. Watson Webb, Jr. Of Jane's stepmothers, Baronessa Afdera Fonda Franchetti has been the most helpful.

Among Jane's directors beyond Pollack I owe most to Elliot Silverstein, who filled me in on *Cat Ballou* and made me wonder why the work of this greatly gifted filmmaker is so infrequently seen on the screen. I am grateful, too, to Josh Logan, Alan Myerson and George Cukor for discussing Jane's talent at the beginning of her career and further along the road.

My research took me far from my Pennsylvania farm and wherever I happened to be queries about Jane Fonda brought forth instant interest and opinions. "What is she up to now?" someone in England inquires. "I have no idea," I tell them. She is finally developing something of a mystique, and to do that successfully you cannot be always available or totally accessible. And, alas, you cannot, if you are a screen star, make too many films. Overexposure chases mystique right off the film stock of movie history.

In their various corners of the world, I wish to send my thanks to Alexander Whitelaw, Alla Peigoulevskaya, Count Rudi Crespi and Countess Consuelo Crespi, Annabella Power, David Healy, Robert J. Allen, Hope Ryden, Seymour St. John, Theodore Gostas, Mary Kling, Maryel Locke, Felizia Seyd—again for her brilliant research—and two of the finest performers anywhere, Anne Baxter and Jack Lemmon. For background on Jane's political and antiwar activities I owe much to the office of columnist Jack Anderson, especially Joseph Spear, the Department of the Army, and Jane's own writings on the subject as well as her extraordinary documentary, *Introduction to the Enemy*. I am grateful to John Andrew of the American Studies Department and Sidney Wise of the Government Department at Franklin and Marshall College for reading the book in manuscript and making valuable suggestions, and to Carlos MacMaster for his encouragement and support. And once again I must acknowledge my debt to the staff of the Margaret Herrick Library of the Academy of Motion Picture Arts and Science and to Paul Myers, curator of the Billy Rose Library of the Performing Arts, Lincoln Center Branch of the New York Public Library, as well as to the Helen Ganser Library staff at Millersville State College.

Fred Lawrence Guiles

Lancaster County, Pennsylvania
1981

JANE FONDA:

The Actress in Her Time

PART I

Troubled Paradise

1

A hurricane blew north out of the tropics during the week that Henry Fonda married Frances Seymour Brokaw. It was a killer storm, but on their wedding day, September 17, 1936, most of its force had been spent and even if the day was damp nothing could have stopped Frances.

She had been a widow for a year and four months. At twenty-eight, she was a very young widow: her aging, alcoholic husband George had died of a heart attack in a Hartford sanatorium where he had gone to dry out. There was a great deal of Brokaw money, several million dollars, left in trust for their daughter Frances de Villers, known as Pan. Brokaw's first wife, Clare Boothe (later Luce), received only $425,000 in her divorce settlement back in 1929. And now Frances was marrying a movie star who was building a fortune of his own and not dissipating it. It is important to realize that our heroine, yet to be born, always knew wealth from the moment of her birth.

The Seymours were an old Canadian family,* and

*There was a Seymour family "festival" at Penhow Castle in South Wales on May 19, 1979, attended by over three hundred members of the family from both sides of the Atlantic. The Norman family name was derived from the Latin St. Maurus. The original Maurus was raised by St. Benedict at the monastery at Subiaco; the name was turned into French, which was then corrupted into an English version, Seymour, by the fourteenth century. The Seymours, however named, built their fortress castle in the twelfth century, eight miles from Newport. From this line Lady Jane Seymour, the Duke of Somerset, and, in our time, Jane Fonda descended.

Frances was born in Brockville, Ontario, in 1908. Except for one cousin, Henry Rogers, they were not known for their money, but they did have a firm base in society. Frances's father, Eugene Ford Seymour, was a part-time poet, with delicate, refined features which he passed on to his daughter. He was reserved and rather shy, but Frances was not. When one of her friends once confided to her that she had been jilted, Frances replied, "When a woman really wants a man, she should be the one who pursues him and gets him. Let him know that you care for him. Lots of women are just shrinking violets and the men don't know a thing about it." She said that she had done something to prod George Brokaw:

I went to Tiffany's and I bought a gold wedding ring and tied it onto a little pink ribbon, tied with a bow. We were having lunch and I took that out of my purse and I held it like this and displayed it like this and I said, "George, don't you think it's about time?" He said, "By George it is! When do you want to get married?"

Clearly the new Frances Fonda had a quality of control that would prove of inestimable value in preserving her new marriage long after the honeymoon was over. Hank Fonda's first wife, the actress Margaret Sullavan, had very little control; she suddenly would blaze up, her jaw would set and everyone would run for cover. Frances had a dashing confidence that overran and conquered all obstacles, including any resistance Hank Fonda might have had. His shyness was notorious, and many years later he was to say: "Christ knows there's nobody in the world more shy than I, but this [acting] is therapy for a shy man."

Frances's maneuvers in his case were subtler than with George Brokaw. On a European trip with her brother, she had gone to the London studio where Hank was starring in *Wings of the Morning* accompanied by two old friends who were sisters, Lillian Kent (wife

4

of Twentieth Century-Fox president Sidney Kent) and Ruth Kane (wife of the producer of the film, Robert Kane). She had been told that Hank and his costar, Annabella, were having "a little affair." That piece of news did not upset Frances unduly, although she had made up her mind upon first seeing him from a distance of about twenty yards that she was going to marry him. Following a couple of dinners in London, Frances suggested that Hank join her brother, named Roger,* and herself in Paris for a long weekend. "We have a lovely flat," she told him. "Why don't you come over and have some fun? We can go to Maxim's and we'll do the town." Frances's best friend, Eulalia "Euke" Chapin, recalls how she must have seemed to Hank: "She was very gay. She was flirtatious and adorably so. Hank used to tease her about it. And she would get some friend in a corner—she always had plenty of things to talk about—and they couldn't get away."

Frances had a remote, patrician kind of beauty, and yet on closer view she was very accessible. Hank's friends in the movies and theater thought that she was very little interested in show business. His best man at the wedding, director Josh Logan, remembers that she was "a practical kind of girl. I always used to say that she could talk on four subjects and on these she was great; outside of those subjects, it was just disaster. Money, babies, sex and clothes. I never heard Hank's career mentioned by her."

From all that is known of Hank and Frances at this time, it is probable that Frances knew, as perhaps Josh Logan did not, that her husband did not want to talk shop around the house. Hank had a healthy dislike for his frequent employer, Darryl F. Zanuck, and felt equally strongly about Jack Warner. It is possible that his distaste for film moguls made him more valuable to them. These men honestly believed that money could buy anything, perhaps in time Hank Fonda's goodwill, but in that they were mistaken.

*Some accounts insist that it was Roger's fiancée, and not Roger, who accompanied Frances.

Frances and Hank went to Hollywood in October; it was her first visit there. They found a home at 255 Chadbourne Drive in Brentwood. It was a small, Colonial-style house very close to the street, and Frances planted plumbago to ensure privacy. Less than two blocks away on Evanston were the Leland Haywards. She, of course, was Hank's first wife, Maggie Sullavan, now the queen of the Universal lot and soon to be lured over to the most elite of the studios, Metro-Goldwyn-Mayer. There was much visiting back and forth; their daughter Brooke remembered the closeness in her memoir:

> The Fondas went back forever in time as we knew it, and were to go forward forever in time to come. Our families were united in the most abstract but intricately woven patterns. The Haywards and the Fondas: our mother had been married to their father and, after they had divorced, almost remarried him; our father was their father's agent and eventually, with *Mister Roberts*, his producer.

Hank was to appear before the cameras of the gifted Fritz Lang, director of *M*, in a picture produced by a film mogul whom Hank truly admired, Walter Wanger. Wanger had a college degree (Hank had dropped out in his second year), which was almost unheard of among the heads of studios; his compromises were relatively small ones and his aim was a good film rather than just a commercially successful one. He and Hank gravitated toward the same kind of people, including more than a sprinkling of the socially acceptable. The movie they were making together, *You Only Live Once*, in which Hank would play opposite the fragile but nearly always triumphant Sylvia Sidney, was to have been shot in Mussolini's new, immense studio facility near Rome, Cinecittà, but it was not ready.

Hank Fonda did not go along with Wanger's dalliance with Il Duce. Hank had been a liberal nearly all of his adult life, and he could not appreciate Wanger's fond-

6

ness for the Italian dictator, despite the fact that Mussolini was, in Wanger's words, "a real movie fan with a fine projection hall in his palace." Wanger's flirtation with the Fascists was blessedly brief and he did not in fact make a film at Cinecittà until 1964, nearly twenty years after the killing of Mussolini by his own people near the end of the Second World War. Then at last Wanger set up a huge production there, *Cleopatra*, which was to prove so disastrous in every way that it must have been brought home to him that the place had a jinx on it.

The retakes on *You Only Live Once* were shot very quickly, and Hank went to Warner Bros. on a three-picture deal that gave him practically no refusal of roles. He and Frances had found some land they liked as a homesite in Brentwood and he needed to accumulate as much capital as he could in a short time. There was something modestly rewarding about his first Warner film, *Slim*, the sort of blue-collar melodrama in which the studio excelled, but Hank was considerably demoralized by the second of his assignments, *That Certain Woman*, a Bette Davis vehicle and an unholy mess for which both stars received bad notices. His friend and former roommate Josh Logan, then in Hollywood trying to succeed as a film director, was by this time as depressed as Hank, having been dialogue director on a 1936 Marlene Dietrich vehicle, *The Garden of Allah*.

Walter Wanger, who considered Hank Fonda the finest young leading man in Hollywood, managed to catch him between pictures at Warners and cast him in *I Met My Love Again*, a romantic comedy that he had built around the actress Joan Bennett, whom Wanger was to marry in 1940. Josh Logan was brought in as codirector. It was the by now familiar story, so often cast to type with Cary Grant, of the handsome professor dogged by an eccentric young woman. The only stir it caused was in the casting of the second female lead, a cool-headed brunette named Louise Platt. Unfortunately, Miss Platt's plaudits were overlooked by Wanger, whose obsession throughout this period was with Miss Bennett. Hank

7

would remember her, however, and recommended her as second female lead in *Spawn of the North*, a gesture doomed since the movie's director, Henry Hathaway, had to favor the big Paramount star Dorothy Lamour throughout the film.* It was a great pity, since Louise Platt had the same throaty wonder in her voice that had helped make Margaret Sullavan a star.

The Fonda image had been set by now. He *was* the American innocent whose eyes were open, who could not be deceived, who would trounce the evildoers of this world. That he could be young Abe Lincoln at one moment and young Frank James at another did not prove his versatility; it simply proved that the world's moviegoers would believe anything Henry Fonda wanted them to believe. His astonishingly blue eyes and the determined set of his jaw balanced each other neatly. One of these physical traits dared you to defy him, while the other melted you down to size, and at the same time persuaded you that they had looked upon vast spaces, the Great Plains, dust-swept and barren. No one really cared very much that he had in fact been born the son of a printer in a fair-sized American town in the Midwest, Grand Island, Nebraska, and had grown up in a major city, Omaha.

Once again Bette Davis had asked for Hank, but this time she and everyone else at Warners knew that the picture could only be successful. *Jezebel* was adapted from an earlier play that had starred Tallulah Bankhead, and they all realized that Warners had decided at last to film it because its central role was so close to the Southern vixen-Scarlett O'Hara mold. David O. Selznick had originally wanted Bette for *Gone With the Wind*, but Jack Warner had insisted that Selznick take Errol Flynn, too, as Rhett Butler; Selznick had balked and Warners had rushed *Jezebel* into production. Happily, the Warners

*Louise Platt would be given the female lead in John Ford's *Stagecoach* (1939), destined to become a classic, but hers was one of half a dozen fine performances and she was not singled out for praise.

factory was better equipped for such crises than almost any other studio. In Jack Warner's eagerness to exploit the nation's preoccupation with the preliminaries of making *Gone With the Wind*, the typical Warners budget was nearly doubled. It was, of course, Bette Davis's picture throughout, but the Fonda performance was among his finest during this period before *The Grapes of Wrath*. Miss Davis won her second Academy Award and even the film was nominated as best picture, although it lost out to *You Can't Take It with You*.

Working for the Warner Bros. made Hank extremely angry: he had no real dislike for Bette Davis, and if anything admired her spunk; but once on the lot she was the queen and this was brought home to the highest-paid (male) star and lowliest messenger boy. It is possibly a tribute to Fonda's integrity that, no matter how high he rose among the Hollywood elite, he never once lorded it over anyone on the set of a film. He would argue and disagree violently sometimes over a scene or a piece of business, but that, he felt, was only his right as star of the film.

Frances read his moods better than anyone and attempted to cope by always having a quiet sanctuary ready for his return at the end of the day. If only those critics who faulted her for never discussing his present work could see his anger when he got out of the car each evening!

The Fondas temporarily uprooted themselves and went back to New York in July. For six weeks Hank toured on the summer theater circuit, and then in August began rehearsals for *Blow Ye Winds* by Valentine Davies. Frances, who always spent part of her mornings studying stock market reports, saw that they lost no money on their rented California house, which was sublet, and in the East took all of her elegant furnishings from the Brokaw mansion out of storage and auctioned them off. Not incidentally, she was three and a half months pregnant at the time. In October, *Blow Ye Winds* opened and closed rather quickly. Although later Hank's stage and screen reputation rose to such a high level that even mediocre plays could be kept running just by his presence, in 1937 that was not so. The critics praised his calm, understated performance but blasted the play.

Hank was in no hurry to return to Hollywood and neither was Frances. She delighted in seeing old friends again and showing off her handsome, youthful-appearing husband; at thirty-two Hank still had the soft-focus male beauty of a twenty-one-year-old. He was waiting for his favorite producer, Walter Wanger, to iron out preproduction problems on his next picture, *Blockade*, which was to be an important statement *against* the Fascist armies under Franco, at that very moment engaged in battle with the Loyalists outside Madrid. Wanger's sympathies shifted quickly. Neither Hank nor Wanger could then foresee the troubles and vilification that lay ahead for everyone involved in this production of John Howard Lawson's screenplay.

2

Jane Seymour Fonda was born at Doctors' Hospital in New York City on December 21, 1937. Although a Cesarean section, there were no complications and within a week both mother and daughter were at home in their apartment, where Pan Brokaw's nanny doubled as nurse for a time. Almost at once the child was called "Lady Jane," after Lady Jane Seymour, third queen consort of Henry VIII, one of the few to keep her head on her body, although she died young.

Jane was born into a world closer to world war than it knew, for relations between the United States and Japan had been deteriorating for months. During the Japanese invasion of China the flagship of the U.S. Asiatic Fleet, the U.S.S. *Augusta*, was struck twice, with nineteen casualties including one killed. On December 12, the U.S.S. *Panay* was bombed by Japanese Navy warplanes and sunk. Neither an imposing nor a formidable target, the small double-decker gunboat looked a little like a showboat without the paddle wheel and was used by the American Government to patrol the Yangtze River to guard American life and property. President Roosevelt's anger was awesome and the American ambassador, Joseph Clark Grew, was grave in his warnings to the Japanese foreign minister. *Life* magazine, then a one-year-old pictorial weekly, reported that Japanese people went about the streets of Tokyo individually apologizing to Americans whom they encountered.

In Europe, Austrian shops were selling little Christ-

11

mas tree ornaments that consisted of miniature gallows bearing a hanged Jew topped by two vultures waiting to swoop down on the corpse. Such grim exotica was not lost on Hank Fonda, yet despite his visit to Washington that year with other screen stars to urge the President to take a strong anti-Nazi stand, most of America was still carefree and absorbed in its own concerns. The Big Apple, the dance craze of the moment, was a sort of jitter-bug square dance; swing music was ubiquitous and often thrilling, as when played by Benny Goodman and the Dorsey brothers, who now ran two different bands; New York City added to its list of attractions another notable museum, the Frick; and after child stardom Mitzi Green made an exciting comeback at seventeen to introduce a memorable song in the Broadway musical *Babes in Arms:*

> I go to ballgames,
> the bleachers are fine.
> I go to Coney,
> the beach is divine.
> I follow Winchell
> and read every line.
> That's why the lady is a tramp.

The day after Jane's birth, an engineering marvel was opened to traffic between New Jersey and Manhattan— the Lincoln Tunnel.

"Lady Jane" was unmistakably a Fonda: within a few months the contours of her face would take the shape they would have throughout her life: slightly bulging high forehead, a good American nose on the snub side, ample upper lip and generous mouth, strong and prominent jawline. There seemed to be little of her mother visible except for her golden hair, which would darken with the years. All of Frances's patrician beauty seemed to have gone to Jane's half-sister, Pan, who at nearly six had her mother's long, classically shaped nose and perfect oval face, as well as the golden hair. Pan also had her father George Brokaw's rather inscrutable eyes with

12

delicate and not unattractive pouches under them, and his mouth, smallish and good for quizzical smiles. The span of more than five years that separated the girls must have seemed an impossible barrier then, but they grew closer as they got older. Pan had come from a union saved from probable dissolution by the timely death of her father, but she trailed after her money and servants as well as good breeding from both sides.

Blockade was first bought by Wanger as a collaborative effort by leftist playwright Clifford Odets and veteran director Lewis Milestone, who called it *Castles in Spain*. By early February 1938, both of these men were out of the picture and, following a series of compromises by Wanger, the film had veered from the left to the middle of the road. Catholic, American State Department and Spanish rebel forces were all very much involved with the film's mutilation. Wanger, for example, received a cable from London reading: "Understanding here from authentic source Franco will bitterly resent any adverse criticism in your Spanish picture *Blockade*. Fear retaliation in Spain and Italy on future films after war is over."

If Henry Fonda, as a Loyalist soldier, had been so identified, and if Madeleine Carroll, as a spy and the daughter of a man working for the Fascists, had been clearly shown as such, and if the horrors unleashed upon innocent Spanish civilians had been left in the film, *Blockade* could have survived as a major statement against war and totalitarian inhumanity, but the pressure groups forced Wanger to make changes in both the script and the editing. What director Bill Dieterle and leading man Henry Fonda managed to salvage from the tatters of their film was a quiet plea from Henry to stop the oncoming carnage before it was too late. For the first time on the screen his voice quietly spoke up for the helpless:

There's no safety for old people and children.
Women can't keep their families safe in their houses.
They can't be safe in their own fields.

Churches, schools, hospitals are targets.
It's not war. War's between soldiers.
It's murder—murder of innocent people. There's no sense to it.
The world *can* stop it.
Where is the conscience of the world?

Audiences recognized that it was right up there on the screen in the person and voice of Henry Fonda, and in the years ahead it would become a familiar one. What was wrong with *Blockade* was that by stripping all identificaton of armies from the picture, it had become too abstract to make much impact on anyone. No one in the audience could possibly know just which country was being torn apart by civil war. What the film did for Hank Fonda was to emphasize the fact that he lived and worked in a place where compromise was the name of the game.

It is difficult to trace just when fame and high status begin to shift toward iconography, but surely something like that happened to Henry Fonda in early 1939. A novel about a family of dirt-poor dust bowl survivors, *The Grapes of Wrath*, was about to win the Pulitzer Prize for its author John Steinbeck. All of the film studios were bidding on this saga of the Joads, and Darryl F. Zanuck at Twentieth Century-Fox won. Zanuck turned over the script to his favorite screenwriter, Nunnally Johnson, and told Hank Fonda that he wanted him to play Tom Joad. Hank sent word through his agent, Hayward, that he would like nothing better, but when Zanuck sensed that Hank would do just about anything to play Tom, he proposed a seven-year contract, something that Hank had resolutely turned down again and again, as the price he would have to pay for the privilege. Hank was predictably furious, but gave in at the end. Of that decision he later said:

"I screamed. I fought Zanuck every foot of the way. I hated the son of a bitch. Because I fought him, I got out of some of them. I didn't get out of all of them. I did some of the most forgettable films of my career under Zanuck."

One of Fonda's most forgettable roles came up almost immediately when he played the part of Thomas Watson in *The Story of Alexander Graham Bell*, the title role going to a Zanuck favorite, Don Ameche. When his agent protested that this was no way to treat a major Fox star, Zanuck quickly agreed and cast him as *Young Mr. Lincoln*, a characterization so extraordinary that ever afterward Fonda's movements would often be described as "Lincolnesque." With John Ford directing, *Young Mr. Lincoln* was a critical and commercial hit everywhere and everyone was pleased.

In the wake of that success, the Fondas did two things: they bought the piece of land in Brentwood that they had coveted for nearly two years, and they set out on a belated honeymoon to South America. Leaving Lady Jane behind with her cheerful old nurse, Mary, and Pan with her nanny, they flew to Ecuador, where Frances found a postcard showing four squat, grim-faced Indian ladies and sent it off to a friend, writing that she had no fear of losing her better half. She complained of the filth and the food, which was, she said, "so lousy it's almost good!" She confided that she was pining for Lady Jane and Pan as well as good meals and a good bed. On their return in early June 1939, Frances found that she was once again pregnant.

Two American directors played prominent roles in shaping the destinies of the Fondas, father and daughter. The first of these was John Ford, an Irish-American from Portland, Maine, ten years Hank's senior, who had won his first Oscar directing *The Informer*, that dark-hued drama of strife in Northern Ireland made in 1935. The other, from a later generation of filmmakers, was an American Jew from Indiana, Sydney Pollack.

John Ford directed Henry Fonda in three major films, one after the other, and in 1939 they briefly became a significant partnership. Ford was aware that as an actor Fonda had an unerring instinct for what was natural and right. Following *Young Mr. Lincoln*, they made an impressive version of Walter D. Edmunds' *Drums Along the Mohawk*, a historical novel set in the days of the American Revolution in which much of the excitement comes from attacks on the colonists by Indians. Shot in Technicolor in locations at the peak of autumn (or at least giving that impression), the movie was interesting on one other count: it was set in the Mohawk Valley just below that part of upstate New York where the original, mostly Dutch-descended Fondas had settled in 1735, following a stay lasting two generations in what is now Albany.

Like John Ford, screenwriter Nunnally Johnson knew of no one in the movie business as instinctively natural before the camera as Henry Fonda. In the writing of *Jesse James*, he had tailored the part of Frank James so carefully to fit Fonda's talents that Fonda had got nearly all the critical attention, and it had led (much to Hank's dismay) to a sequel. During the writing of his adaptation of *The Grapes of Wrath*, Johnson once again had Fonda in the back of his mind throughout the scenes featuring the son, Tom Joad. He did not tinker with the Steinbeck characterization; he simply believed that Steinbeck must have had Henry in mind when he was writing the book. Carried over intact from the novel is Tom's farewell to his mother before he strikes out on his own; there has been violence against the Okies by Californians and Ma Joad is frightened.

"How'm I gonna know 'bout you? They might kill ya an' I wouldn't know . . ." Tom tells her:

> . . . a fella ain't got a soul of his own, but on'y a piece of a big one—an' then . . . Then it don' matter. Then I'll be all aroun' in the dark. I'll be ever'where—wherever you look. Wherever they's a fight so hungry people can eat, I'll be there. Wherever they's a cop beatin' up a guy, I'll be there . . . I'll be in the way kids laugh when they're hungry an' they know supper's ready. An' when our folks eat the stuff they raise an' live in the houses they build— why, I'll be there.

16

The conscience of the world was speaking once again, and this time it was heard by nearly everyone with any interest in movie-going. The war in Europe had pushed the plight of the Okies to a distant recess of the public consciousness, and now Henry Fonda was making people aware once more of that disaster.

So fine was Henry Fonda as Tom Joad that critics and audiences forgot for the moment that they were very familiar with this tall, laconic figure. The role was to become Hank's most unforgettable, contributing more than anything else to his elevation during the decades ahead to the status of film icon, and would awaken in his daughter Jane a fear of acting ("How can you compete with that?") that would take years to overcome.

The movie was released on January 25, 1940. Nearly a month later, on February 23, Frances gave birth to their second child, a boy, whom they named Peter.

3

"Little Petey," as his doting mother called him, was also born in New York City. "My lad is really adorable," Frances cabled a friend. The boy became his mother's favorite almost at once. She couldn't help herself, but it created problems for both children—for Peter because he was spoiled by his mother and for Jane because she was not. So Jane very early turned to her father for the love she so desperately needed, and when he sometimes failed her—not out of a lack of love so much as from the pressures of his position—she would do some mischief to call attention to herself. She later would say that she grew up in the shadow of a national monument.

The house the Fondas built at 900 North Tigertail Road in the Brentwood section of Los Angeles was patterned after a New England farmhouse. It had board-and-batten siding and dormer windows on the second floor, and was set atop a slight hill above the rest of their nine acres. There was a stable for horses, and two mares were bought almost at once, one of them being a burro for the children. Part of the land had a gentle slope which Hank had plowed for his vegetable garden, and there was a studio where he could paint. He had been drawing nearly all of his life and now he had discovered oils, watercolors and pastels and was improving all the time. It is evident from seeing Hank Fonda's talent for painting grow over the years that he worked very hard at this craft, which had become more than a hobby. His work exhibits the influence of Andrew Wyeth as well as some of his own melancholy. But in his acting, within a short time—less than a decade—he had perfected his talent and would remain forever splendid in nearly everything, while in his painting he would simply get better and better until he was thoroughly professional and his work began to sell—the difference between genius and talent.

Following Peter's birth, the Fondas remained East long enough to travel around New England picking up Early American antiques to fill the new house. Frances was given much advice on where to find things from Mrs. Electra Webb, a Vanderbilt and a Havemeyer who was one of the most important collectors of Americana in the country, and was at about that time establishing her own museum in which to show the hundreds of treasures she had acquired from quilts to cigar-store Indians. Frances had met her through Electra's son Watson, then a film editor at the Fox studio but a millionaire by inheritance who was building his own New England "farmhouse" no more than half a dozen blocks from the Fondas' estate.

On March 28, 1940, Frances wrote to Watson asking him to be "godpappy" to Peter and Jane. Apparently Hank had some qualms about the idea, perhaps because of Watson being a bachelor or even because of his being a Vanderbilt. He still had an actor's insecurity about his own position in society despite his growing wealth and that of Frances. Still, Hank personally asked Watson, who was delighted to be chosen. Josh Logan, too, was invited to be a godfather to the children and accepted, but only Watson attended the ceremony.

Jane was no longer an infant when she was swaddled in a christening dress for the church affair in April 1940. At two and a half, she was able to walk into the church herself, although for appearance's sake, Hank carried her. Harriet Peacock, Hank's sister from Nebraska, and her husband Jack attended, as well as the children's maternal grandmother, Sophie Seymour.

Euke Chapin remembers that Jane was very robust as a child: "She was plump, not fat, and she had beautiful

19

manners. And full of fun. Great child, just marvelous. Always swimming or doing something active."

Peter was slightly more delicate: when the childhood diseases struck, while Jane would recover quickly there were grave crises and much worry surrounding Peter.

Family gatherings were usually around the pool, and Hank attempted to teach Jane to swim when she was two years old. As long as he was holding her, she felt absolutely secure. A bond was forming between father and daughter that would affect to some degree all of their future relationships with others; it may have begun when it became evident to Hank that Frances unconsciously favored her Petey in nearly everything.

Before Jane was five she could ride the more tractable mare, and there were endless games of cowboys and Indians in which Peter was the loser. Social encounters, such as birthday parties at Joan Crawford's house for Christina, who was just Jane's age, only served to prove to Jane that she was "homely" and overweight as she looked about at Christina and the others done up in organdy and chiffon, with bows in their bleach-blond hair. She hated such affairs and couldn't wait to get home to the Fonda farm. And it didn't matter whether Peter was around or not; she was becoming more and more of a loner. Besides, Peter had a disconcerting habit of getting out of control while he was playing and running too hard and yelling too much, which always prompted their mother to bring him in the house to lie down.

So those unreal years passed. The Fondas, like so many others in the film world, were living a prosperous, fat, idyllic life quite in contrast to the rest of the world. Servants came and went in other homes; they tended to stay forever with the Fondas. Jane would remember growing up surrounded by them: "I can remember cooks and maids and gardeners and a series of nurses; they didn't call them 'nannies.' Some of them spoke French. I didn't know that anyone else grew up differently because all of my friends also were brought up in this way." The ones who spoke French were

20

invariably Pan's governesses, and the maids tended to be day help whom Frances rode fairly hard. But no matter; the Fondas lived with a great deal of style and comfort, and even their peers considered them rich.

There were frequent visits by relatives: Grandma Sophie Seymour, a large-boned woman with a strong profile and very dark hair, was Jane's favorite, along with gentle Grandpa Seymour; and there were her father's sisters, Aunt Jayne (Schoentgen) and Aunt Harriet (Peacock), and their spouses. The parade of family was traditional, but with the Fondas, perhaps because of that Italian strain in their Dutch ancestry (the surname Fonda is Italian) nearly five hundred years ago, blood counted for everything. Husbands and wives would come and go in Hank's life and later, to a lesser degree, in Jane's and Peter's, but the Fondas remained a tight circle and uncritical of each other except for a few years of rebelliousness when both children were trying to untie this knot, often in public and in print, but in the end with no success.

Robert Allen, an airline pilot who was a neighbor, remembers that screenwriter Laurence Stallings (*The Big Parade* and *What Price Glory*) was a frequent visitor and that Stallings, who ironically lost a leg while on leave in World War I, was teased "unmercifully" by little Jane. Her father probably allowed this to go on because he was totally at odds with Stallings' reactionary politics. If Allen's recollection is correct, it suggests that Jane's social encounters with adults were unpredictable. To Euke Chapin, she was "a wonderful little girl," and to Allen "an unmerciful tease."

There were many friends, close lifetime friends, surrounding her father. These, too, seemed as necessary to him as his family and remained a tight little band, allowing the Fonda wives to come and go as though swallowed up by the night. They included Johnny Swope, who in 1943 took as his bride the actress Dorothy McGuire; Jimmy and later Gloria Stewart (Stewart was a bachelor until 1949); Josh and Nedda Logan; Tyrone Power and his wife Annabella; the film editor at

21

Fox, Watson Webb in Hollywood and his mother Electra and sister Lila in the East; the Henry Hathaways; the Chapins; and, not least, the Leland Haywards and their children, Brooke, Bridget and Bill. Hank was like many major stars in that nearly all of his close friends were his peers, not underlings, grips, gaffers and other technicians; but unlike most he cherished his privacy, and the Fondas did not party a great deal, although Frances adored them. They passed on a great many invitations and finally their friends stopped asking them unless it was a really special occasion.

So Jane saw a great deal of her father. He was a presence but, like the weather, terribly unpredictable. She discovered a disturbing thing about him: silence. If he didn't want to talk about something, he would not answer. She would repeat her question or her comment and again encounter silence, sometimes accompanied by an ominous set of his prominent jaw. It was just as though Jane hadn't spoken; but she decided that she could live with that and became a little more careful about what she asked him.

Her mother had an answer to every question. She was, as a close friend observed, a woman who would rather be positively wrong about something than negatively right. Jane began to acquire the same outlook, since opinions were so dicey around her father. She also seemed to have inherited her mother's energy. Frances had no housekeeper and attempted to run the Brentwood farmhouse herself. "She could come down to my house in the morning," recalls Euke Chapin, "looking like a kitchen slavey and that night look like a queen." Frances accomplished so many things by following a strict regimen: in the mornings she straightened the house, got the children up and off to school, read the stock market reports in the paper, paid bills and balanced their checkbook, wrote friends and did her shopping; in the afternoons she prepared for dinner, usually at home, spent some time with the children, and before Hank's arrival home from the studio, bathed and changed into something fresh and probably on the pretty side rather

22

than the chic. If there were to be guests she was not above dressing Jane and Peter in similar outfits—Jane's blouse and skirt made of the same material as Peter's short pants and shirt.

The Christmas after Pearl Harbor, life at Tigertail Road hadn't changed very much. That Christmas Eve the Fondas had a small party, and around midnight Frances and Hank were photographed snuggled together on a sofa in front of the fireplace, both blissfully dozing. But, as with so many other people, the war altered things between them. Yet that period of the marriage from 1936 right up to Hank's departure for the U.S. Navy in 1943 was seven years crammed to the brim with great success, beautiful, healthy children and a delightful home base.

4

Jane was enrolled at the Brentwood Town and Country School during her grade-school years. Peter would follow her there later. Since the Brentwood private school, as run by a strict disciplinarian named Mrs. Cathryn Robberts Dye, was the antithesis of the progressive, libertarian schools to which so many film people sent their children, Frances felt that in Hank's absence the place would be good for her. Jane was allowed to wear blue jeans to school, as well as her plaid lumberjack shirt. With her two pigtails flying she would leap from the family car every morning at Twenty-six Street and San Vicente Boulevard to join her best friend, Sue-Sally Jones, similarly attired, at the school gate. Waiting for them there would be the school nurse, who made each student stick out his or her tongue and say "ah" on the way through.

There were other extraordinary rituals at Brentwood. After the pledge of allegiance the entire student body, comprising fewer than a hundred boys and girls, gathered in the schoolyard to face east and recite a "Salutation to the Dawn." Mr. Dye, the headmistress's husband, was a sort of superjanitor who would bang on an old artillery shell to signal a fire drill. After the children had eaten their lunches, brought from home, they were made to lie down on dusty cots for a "rest period" for a while and were read to from *Ivanhoe* and other uplifting works by Miss Stein or Miss Devey. Phyllis Devey was English and had brought with her to America a form of

24

punishment that was deemed suitable by Mrs. Dye: any serious act of mischief or of rule breaking would result in the child's being "sent to Coventry," which meant that no one could speak to him or her for a week. Jane quickly caught on to the rules, was scrupulous about not breaking any and was thought to be on the angelic side by most of her teachers. She was never sent to Coventry.

Nor was her closest and dearest friend, Sue-Sally Jones, a blond Valkyrie who became May Queen so often that the other girls never really thought they stood a chance of beating her. Sue-Sally was a budding Lady Godiva who was required as Queen to ride in on the school horse, an aging nag called Endicott who would die of old age while Jane was there. The girls' mutual love for horses had made them friends in the first place, so it is not surprising that both Jane and Sue-Sally were considered horse fanatics. Away from the school grounds in the forests of then partially wild Brentwood, they would ride naked, startling occasional birdwatchers and little boys playing cowboys and Indians.

Much was made of holidays at the Brentwood school, and every Thanksgiving there was a Pilgrim pageant which was followed by a donation of canned goods, lugged from home, for the poor. The student body sang at the ceremony's conclusion:

> We gather together
> to ask the Lord's blessing . . .

Nearly thirty years later, Jane recalled this hymn and sang a few snatches of it as the prostitute Bree Daniels in *Klute*, while lighting up a joint.

Before leaving for war duty Hank managed to complete a film version of Water Van Tilburg Clark's novel *The Ox-Bow Incident*, a dark and sardonic tale of vigilante justice in the frontier West in which innocent men are hanged by a posse. The picture was shot in late 1942 without studio head Darryl Zanuck's blessing. Zanuck thought the subject made the picture a loser no matter how well it was done, and he was proved right.

The picture had been a sacrifice for both its star and its director, William Wellman. Wellman was a vigorous, macho filmmaker with a reputation as large as John Ford's. He had made his debut in 1927 with the silent classic *Wings*, and it was his genius for capturing the excitement of flying that had enabled *The Ox-Bow Incident* to get studio backing. For the privilege of shooting what Zanuck knew was a lost cause, he had agreed to direct a picture designed to attract Air Force recruits called *Thunderbirds*. As cowboy Gil Carter, Fonda had a great deal of say in the production, but studio pressure forced them to make compromises once again and the actor felt beleaguered and helpless before the movie was completed.

What talk young Jane heard from her father and his friends at home about the movies was mostly critical. There was a great deal of anguish over "selling out," and the child was to learn her code of morality in a community where you had to "sell out" in order to survive. If there exists in the mature Jane Fonda a quality of sweet irony about nearly everything, it grew out of her own battles with the whoremongers who run the movie business, a slow awakening to the fact that what she was experiencing had all happened before to her father.

Jane saw very little of her father during the war years. He enlisted in the U.S. Navy in 1943, and was commissioned a lieutenant very soon afterward. Nearly all of his duty was spent in the Pacific area, usually at a forward headquarters in naval intelligence. When he got home on leave there were joyous reunions for a day or two, but overall the war seemed to deepen the profound sadness in the man. Although Jane and Peter did not yet know it, nothing would ever be the same again in the Fonda household. But there were still occasional moments of genuine tenderness: her mother wept in relief and surprise when a dozen red roses arrived on their wedding anniversary, arranged by Hank through his friend Watson Webb.

When the war ended and the family was reunited there was a semblance of the old Fonda unity. The Seymours had moved to California and lived nearby, and Grandma Sophie was in the house a great deal; if the marriage was in trouble, this was the only small sign that all was not well. Actually, the marriage seemed in no more trouble than many others; Frances did everything she possibly could to please Hank. Jane tried, too, and it must have hurt when she saw that she frequently failed.

Hank still had two pictures to do for Fox under his old contract, but turned down everything Zanuck offered until *My Darling Clementine* was ready and his old reliable John Ford was available. Zanuck saw at an early stage that this script was a certain winner; he had a very shrewd sense of what the public wanted. It was not the first time that the movies had exploited the legend of the Western frontier marshal Wyatt Earp, but with their version, Henry Fonda and Ford came close to achieving a classic almost on the level of *The Grapes of Wrath*. The completed film so pleased Zanuck that it became the studio's Christmas release in 1946, but despite rave reviews and huge box-office earnings nothing changed between studio head and star. Zanuck knew even before *My Darling Clementine* was finished that Fonda had come back from the war determined to get away from him, and when one more film was out of the way the following year—*Daisy Kenyon*, a potboiler starring a slightly faded Joan Crawford, Hank would celebrate his release from bondage.

While Hank was filming *My Darling Clementine* and Anatole Litvak's *The Long Night* (for RKO), a novel about wartime navy life aboard a small cargo vessel was published by a twenty-eight-year-old navy veteran, Thomas Heggen. It was a farcical version of life aboard that misbegotten ship the *Reluctant*, but grim and truthful, too, for Mister Roberts, the title character, dies at the end.

Hank's old friend Josh Logan read the book at one sitting, contacted Heggen at once, and within a few days was drawn into a collaboration with Heggen on the dramatization. The young novelist moved into the Logans' Connecticut farmhouse, and the two men spent several weeks writing almost around the clock until the final draft of the comedy was finished.

After the play was read to him by Logan and Heggen, agent Leland Hayward told them: "It's probably the greatest play that's ever been written in the history of the world!" Hank Fonda listened to it, too, although he was committed for several movies, and then told Logan, "I'm going to play it." With that simple affirmation, the Fondas' world changed totally and irrevocably. Hank began thinking of giving up the movies unless something exceptional came along; Hollywood and its petty wars drained him and he looked to New York and Broadway as his salvation. That summer he even sent Jane and Peter off to a summer camp on Lake Winnepesaukee in New Hampshire to give them a taste of the East while he was conferring in New York with Logan on the play.

Before Christmas 1947, *Mister Roberts* was on its way to Broadway, with Logan directing. There were only two problems in mounting it. One was Henry, the actor, who was such a perfectionist that there were frequent "tirades" against Logan, who later wrote:

> I cannot find it in my innards to object to Fonda's tirades. They come from a huge ego, certainly, but isn't that also what makes him a huge talent? He cares. It matters to him. He is not content to let well enough alone. "Well enough" to Fonda is a cardinal sin. It is a crime against his religion, the theater.

The other difficulty was the huge set, a re-creation of the ship itself, which filled the entire playing area. But it lumbered its way first to New Haven, where *Variety* complained about some of the filthy language, then to Philadelphia and Baltimore. It opened at the Alvin Theater in New York on February 19, 1948, the week of Petey's eighth birthday.

The New York *Times* said "Thank you, Mr. Heggen and Mr. Logan for a royal good time," and *Mister Roberts* became one of the most popular American plays of all time. The reviews were unanimous raves, and it was sold out for months in advance. That part and Tom Joad (in *The Grapes of Wrath*) would remain the two roles for which Henry Fonda would be forever remembered.

With a long run assured—it eventually ran for three years on Broadway before touring—Hank decided to leave California and settle in the East; he began looking about Greenwich, Connecticut, for a house. Frances was distressed: nearly all of her friends, especially Euke Chapin, who had a sympathetic ear, lived in California; her parents were there. Jane was almost as strongly against it. But Frances would not have dreamed of making an issue of her negative feelings; she was, in many ways, very old-fashioned, and deferred to Hank in nearly everything. That was the way she had been taught, and while she might say "Oh, no!" in the end she would concede and, in this case, start packing. During the week, Hank frequently stayed in the Webbs' large Park Avenue apartment. When Frances, the children and their small household staff were eventually settled in a rented Colonial house on a small gentleman's farm in Greenwich, he wrote Electra Webb a thank-you letter and said: "It's wonderful to have the family with me again. The children are soaking up the wonders of the East like dry sponges."

For Jane, there was only one saving aspect to the Big Move: the Haywards were already in the East and settled into an estate in Greenwich. They lived a mile or so away from the Fondas and the children attended the same school, the Greenwich Academy. Yet all had changed and Jane was no longer the "angelic" student who saved her rowdiness for horseback rides through the woods after school. One of her classmates at the academy recalls: "She was considered very much a rebel in a school that prided itself on a successful honor system, which most of us lived up to. Jane, however, enjoyed breaking rules, and tried to influence her few companions to do the same. She was . . . a sort of misfit. . . ."

Peter was still too young to rebel. When it happened with him, Jane's own small wars against the way things were would seem pale indeed by comparison.

PART II

Melancholy Justified

5

Nothing was the same after the move to Greenwich in 1949. In fact, things became radically different. Frances had suffered for months from what was finally diagnosed as a floating kidney, and finally decided to have it surgically corrected. She wrote a California friend in late May that after five weeks in the hospital, most of that time flat on her back, she could not recall ever having suffered so much. She said, "They just cut me in half!" She had a twelve-inch scar, but after two weeks at home she was gradually gaining back a little weight and strength. She thought that she was going to feel well again now that they had discovered the source of her trouble.

Jane and her best friend and classmate Brooke Hayward organized a pet show with proceeds to go to the Red Cross. They managed to find fifty entries, and they made Jane's father and Kenneth Wagg judges. Wagg was planning to marry Brooke's mother, Margaret Sullavan Hayward, since the Haywards had separated. Another Greenwich neighbor, Andrew Heiskell, a top man on *Time* magazine, also agreed to be a judge.

Peter and Jane's grades at the Greenwich Academy had greatly improved. Jane had moved into the seventh grade and Peter into the fifth. Pan was to graduate from the Garrison Forest School, a private high school, that June.

Frances described their Greenwich farmhouse as "really quite nice. There are twenty-three acres and two lakes, one for swimming. The kids are having a wonderful time." It was a large white house with black shutters and bright-red doors. They had moved in just before she went into the hospital.

Pan had fallen in love with her art instructor. On June 5, Jane and her mother joined Hank in Baltimore for the graduation ceremonies. Frances was still convalescing but she made a great effort to be gay. Plans were discussed for an early wedding for Pan and her fiancé, known as Bun Abry. They were to marry in late June, and Jane was asked to be flower girl. The couple planned to honeymoon in Europe, and Frances was asked, rather surprisingly, to go along. It is unclear just whose idea this was, but there was every evidence that the Fonda marriage was coming apart and Frances may have believed that her absence might somehow make things right again. If that was in her mind, it was a disastrous notion.

Hank, too, had fallen in love—with a young woman who had come backstage at the Alvin to meet him some weeks earlier. Her name was Susan Blanchard and she was Dorothy (Mrs. Oscar) Hammerstein's daughter by her first marriage. Even though Frances pretended to have no knowledge of the affair, some of her friends are sure that she did.

Frances caught a severe cold in Paris, alarming the newlyweds, but she recovered and continued her travels with her daughter and new son-in-law until July 29, when she sailed home on the *Queen Elizabeth*. She wrote Watson that "my better half will find me looking 100% better than when I left."

In the early autumn of 1949 Hank Fonda sat down with Frances and told her about Susan Blanchard; he said that he wanted a divorce because he wanted to marry Susan. The shock of Hank wanting to remarry was almost more than Frances could take so soon after her major surgery and convalescence, and she wrote a friend rather bitterly of that moment, suggesting that if Hank had waited a year instead of four months her nerves would have been in better shape for the news.

Since Hank went even further and told her that he had not been happy during their thirteen years of marriage, Frances reeled from the blow. After the conversation she felt sad for her children. She told her friend, "If it wasn't for them, you know where I'd tell him to go—I'd tell him to have his head examined." Frances told another friend that if she were only younger—she was forty-one—she certainly would get Hank back. She still possessed the old Seymour will and determination, but she knew that her age was against her and she was extremely sensitive about the twelve-inch scar on her body. Hank's comment about his unhappiness is difficult to accept as a stark and simple fact—*for thirteen years*. It requires some study and explanation, for the remark was to do psychological damage which Hank could not then have even dimly foreseen. Actors' outward moods are notoriously poor indicators of their true feelings. Marilyn Monroe joked on the last night of her life. Charlie Chaplin wrote of a life of unrelieved wretchedness and misery as a young boy in Lambeth and yet we know that he was elated by the sight of George Robey and other music-hall giants. He would stand outside the halls and often run alongside their carriages just to observe them. Is not this a kind of happiness—though, granted, beneath the gray umbrella of abysmal poverty and deprivation? What had happened to the Fondas was fairly typical of nearly all marriages. The one who was more in love had urged the other into a ceremony, and the one less in love, probably because he was so involved with himself (there is no shame in that), settled for contentment.

For Jane and Peter it was to be the grimmest Christmas within memory. Pan, pregnant after five months of marriage, lost her baby girl prematurely around the middle of December. Frances spent much of her time in Pan and Bun's New York apartment. Hank stayed in New York, but in another part of town, during Christmas week.

Frances could only lose herself by looking after Pan for so long: her elder daughter rallied quickly and Frances had to return to her own problem, to the end of her marriage, the end of her world. Rarely daunted by anything, now she was desperate. One day she decided that if she were mad, then Hank could not get a divorce. Euke Chapin remembers the months of enduring unpredictable episodes:

> I went through an awful experience there [in New York, where the Chapins had moved]. . . . She would drive in all the way from Connecticut. Sometimes she'd come in at two in the morning. Of course she had a key, and I'd hear her downstairs. She'd sleep on the sofa. And we'd talk and I'd say, "Frances, you're a beautiful woman. This is just a temporary thing with Hank. Don't pay that much attention to it."

But Frances seemed lost and far more concerned with clinging to what was left of her marriage than with anything else. Jane knew that something was wrong, but there was no one around to tell her.

Euke Chapin became a little desperate, too, and one day told Hank, "You know, Hank, I'm going to tell Susan everything I know about you that's unattractive," and he replied, "Go ahead. We're going to get married real soon." Now that he had made a clean breast of it to Frances, he felt relaxed and even eager to get on with his new life. It seems obvious that he was too happy in his relationship with Susan really to notice the depth of Frances's despair.

To understand the violence that was to come, one must look a little more deeply into the marriage itself. Within a dozen years—far less really since it had been going on a long time, Hank had slipped into a quiet placidity, almost ritually going through his duties as husband and companion. Sometime before Hank fell in love with Susan Blanchard, Frances shocked one of her closest friends by confiding that "Hank doesn't satisfy me sexually anymore." Frances was a passionate woman who was beginning to unravel when Hank's ardor, which she herself had fanned to a flame at the beginning, cooled.

*   *   *

On December 29, less than a week after Christmas and eight days after Jane's twelfth birthday, her mother announced through newspaper columnist Dorothy Kilgallen that she was going to sue for divorce. The front-page story read in part:

> It is understood Mrs. Fonda will take custody of the children without opposition from the actor, and also will be given an extremely large financial settlement. . . .
> Friends describe Mrs. Fonda as "terribly upset" over the prospect of parting from her husband, particularly since she believes Miss Blanchard is much too young for him. . . .

Miss Blanchard was described in the press as being a tall young woman with

> medium blond hair and a rather sardonic expression. She has had a variety of careers ranging from Broadway to 7th Avenue [the two are only a block apart] . . . appeared as a showgirl in "The Seven Lively Arts," took a fling at Hollywood, and worked for a while as an assistant to a 7th Avenue dress designer, in which capacity she made a trip to Paris. . . . paints a great deal—a hobby she shares with Fonda, who has done some extremely creditable pictures—and is an excellent mimic.

The description must have made Miss Blanchard cringe and Frances wonder just how her husband could be serious about throwing over everything worthwhile in his life.

Yet Frances knew that he had already rung down the curtain. Her friends, sensing her depression, tried to help. Euke Chapin recalls inviting her to meet some of her bachelor friends: "And I said, 'Let's go dancing,' and she would say, 'No, let's stay here,' and she was just lost." Later, Euke remembers Frances asking if she could sleep upstairs with her because she was very

37

upset. "And when I was sound asleep, I felt someone close and I opened my eyes and there was Frances just above me and looking at my neck. She said, 'I was curious about where our jugular vein is.'"

The months ahead were traumatic for the children. Peter became openly rebellious, and Jane may well have given up on her parents and settled for fending for herself. They had both decided by now that animals were a lot safer close companions, and their bruised sensibilities were nursed by a few horses and dogs. The depression in their mother had become too deep to penetrate. Their father was now banished from the scene except for infrequent visits.

In early February, Grandma Sophie, who had come East to see her daughter through this crisis, could no longer cope with Frances's anxiety. In the middle of the night the psychiatrist who had been treating her was called and he immediately arranged for her admission to Craig House Sanitorium in nearby Beacon, New York. If Euke Chapin was right and Frances wished to hold on to Hank through a mental breakdown, here was proof positive. But unfortunately it was no ruse, no melodramatic ploy to delay matters. Frances really had suffered a nervous breakdown. She was now down as far as she could go, but her doctor, her mother and others felt that there was every chance she could be restored to sanity and a new life. She was only forty-two, and she had a very strong will. Her comparative youth and her characteristic determination were all in her favor.

Hank was in some danger, too—of being pauperized by the divorce settlement. Frances had obtained the best divorce lawyer her money could buy, and her friend Euke was aghast at some of Frances's demands. "That isn't fair!" Euke told both of them, since the lawyer was a frequent visitor before Frances went into the hospital. "He has to have something. You're a very fair woman." And the lawyer glanced sharply at Euke and said, "Listen, Chapin, whose side are you on?" Looking back on the tragedy then building, it is easy enough to see Hank Fonda as a marrying man. He eventually had five wives spread over a period of nearly fifty years, not an incredible average. Once, when in the process of divorcing Susan, he asked Euke, "What's wrong with me?" Euke replied: "Hank, why do you keep marrying these girls? They're marrying you because you're Hank Fonda. You're very easy to love and you're a big star. And you want to sit home and paint, and they want to go out and show you off and you don't." He laughed at her wisdom, saying, "That's true!"

Craig House was a converted former estate, and the main house and other buildings were surrounded by rolling lawns and gardens. Frances arranged for her secretary to drive her there; she was still in control of that much of her life. It was all very voluntary, and it was in no sense a commitment. From what she told Euke, in the back of her distraught mind she doubtless felt that this act would put the brakes on everything. There would be no divorce because she knew that Hank was too nice a person to walk away from her now.

Frances was right—there would be no divorce and no marriage while she was recovering. Within about six weeks or so she seemed well enough to go out for a visit. What the doctors couldn't know was that it was Frances's *physical* appearance that she found abhorrent. She would stand in front of the mirror in Euke's presence when she was dressing and say, "Just look at me! No one will ever have me again." The sense of loss and faded beauty was so strong in her lament it nearly broke Euke's heart.

On one of Frances's visits home, her last, she was accompanied by her nurse, who had instructions to watch her at all times. It was a precaution that Frances's doctor felt necessary in severe depression cases. The nurse was talking with Grandma Seymour, Jane and Peter down in the living room. Frances, standing in the archway between the front hall and living room, suddenly ran upstairs, where she opened the top drawer of the dresser in the master bedroom, got something out of it and picked up a little Battersea-enamel box which

39

Euke had given her long ago. The nurse, who had come upstairs the moment she noticed that Frances was gone, saw her holding the Battersea box, smiled at her and suggested they rejoin the children downstairs.

On Friday, April 15, 1950, Frances was found dying in her bathroom at Craig House Sanitorium, her throat slashed with a two-inch razor blade. She had left a note on her nightstand warning Miss Amy Grey, her nurse, not to go into the bathroom. Miss Grey ran for help, summoned Dr. Bennett, the staff psychiatrist, and entered the bathroom to find Frances barely alive, with only a feeble pulse. But by the time Dr. Bennett arrived, she was beyond help, for she had lost too much blood. They found the Battersea box, in which she had concealed the blade, on the nightstand next to a letter to Dr. Bennett and one to her mother. "Very sorry," she wrote. "This is the best way out."

Grandma Sophie phoned Hank. He took the news hard although he forced himself that night to go on in *Mister Roberts*. Jane and Peter were told that their mother had had a fatal heart attack. Frances's body was taken to Hartsdale, site of a nearby mausoleum and cemetery, where it was cremated that afternoon. Jane, always less protected from the rigors of the world than Peter, may have guessed at the truth, although she seemed to accept Grandma Sophie's explanation. It is likely she perceived it from the moment she was told of her mother's death and its violence remained the most forbidding and troubling trauma of her life. Lovers could not discuss it, and even Jane would try eventually to fit it into a larger social context—mother as victim, not of her father but of the times.

Jane and Peter were left substantial trusts by their mother's will, enough to see them through life comfortably. Hank had been disinherited sometime between his announcement to her of his intentions regarding Susan and that last week of Frances's life. Pan, already wealthy through her father's estate, was now a very rich heiress indeed.

Hank tried not to feel guilty. Grandma Sophie understood her daughter well and never once criticized him, but Hank was ever on the defensive and they were either on his side or on Frances's. Euke Chapin passed the test and remained close to all the Fondas. Watson and all the other Webbs had been deemed too partial to Frances and were cut dead. When Euke took Jane and Peter up to the magnificent Shelburne Museum in Vermont to see Electra Webb's huge collection of Americana, Hank was outraged and warned her never to do such a thing again. Frances had done the unforgivable: by her suicide, she had blighted all of their lives. And yet strange and powerful forces were unleashed on that terrible morning in the spring of 1950 that might well have remained dormant—within Jane and certainly within Peter—had Frances Fonda recovered.

6

In 1950 Americans had not yet awakened from their dream of democratizing the globe. Bitter fighting was still going on in Korea to keep the North Koreans from turning the South, below the Yalu River, communist. At home there was considerable apathy about the war, and even more about whether the Marshall Plan* was working or not.

Jane was completing the eighth grade at the Greenwich Academy in December, when her father married Susan Blanchard. During their honeymoon, Peter, possibly in an adolescent rage over his father's action coming within eight months of their mother's death, shot and very nearly killed himself. He was spending the weekend with a friend, Tony Avery, at the R. H. Kress estate near Peekskill. While examining a shotgun, it went off, penetrating his liver. Peter later said, "I'm not sure if I was really trying to kill myself or not, but I do recall that after I shot myself, I didn't want to die—and I came very close to dying." A chauffeur rushed him to the Ossining Hospital, where his life was saved following surgery and three blood transfusions. In future accounts of the near-tragedy, Peter unfailingly dramatized

*The Marshall Plan, or the European Recovery Program, was an American undertaking supervised by General George C. Marshall, whereby countries shattered by the war could have their economies and industry put together again through American money and machinery. It was considered a great success.

the event, implying that it was probably not an accident. Although suicides among ten-year-old boys were a rarity in those days, perhaps it was not.

Hank and Susan flew back from the Virgin Islands. He was grimmer of face than usual and had little to say to Peter: the tiger's tail had flicked again. Yet it was at that early moment in their marriage that Susan revealed the spirit that had drawn Hank to her. She was able to make up for Hank's silence. She reassured Peter; there was a warm, living presence near at hand. And for Jane, too, Susan became an unusual kind of second mother. She was only twenty-one, which meant that she and Jane could do girlish things together, but she was a sophisticated adult, too, so she could discuss some of Jane's problems intelligently. One of Jane's frustrations was that she felt ungainly. She thought she was much too tall, taller than any of her friends, and she had a tentative way with strangers, as though she expected them to dismiss her from their lives for being awkward and far too tomboyish. Susan restyled her hair and helped her buy a whole new wardrobe. Within less than a year Susan had been able to turn on a light within Jane. In Susan Jane had what every girl hopes to have but seldom finds—a mother who is her best friend.

The nineteen-fifties have been described as a period of tranquillity in America. Overlooked by these chroniclers are the outrages, the execution of the Rosenbergs being the prime example, and the malaise that led to the beatnik movement. There was a semblance of peace in the world as Eisenhower quickly ended the stalemate in Korea and called it a draw, although he used other words. And there was a kind of peace within the Fonda family.

Hank had bought a town house on East Seventy-fourth Street in Manhattan and was limiting his acting to the stage and occasional television appearances. He would not return to the screen again until he repeated his stage role in the film version of *Mister Roberts* in early 1955, a project that ended his long friendship with John Ford, who was brought in as director at Hank's insistence but whose concepts for the movie treatment clashed with Hank's at nearly every turn and who finally resigned from the film.

Peter was dividing his time between his grandparents in Greenwich and New York. He had learned to play the trumpet—if he felt swallowed up by the big city at least people could hear him—and Susan encouraged his flair for arranging the fresh-cut flowers that were kept in the main rooms of the town house. In the summers he stayed with Aunt Harriet in Omaha. There was a kind of truce with his father; nearly thirty years later Hank was to tell a television interviewer:

It was only during the past year that I was able to say "I love you" to my son. Peter's forty years old, and I hadn't been able to say "I love you" to him. And he was the one who said it first. When I was talking to him on the phone, he said "I love you, Dad." He said it first and then it was easy. Now I can say it, and it's hard not to get emotional when I talk about this. But I can say it now.

Who knows how many warm emotions lay strangled beneath Hank Fonda's calm but forbidding exterior over the years?

In 1951, Jane enrolled as a freshman at the Emma Willard School in Troy, New York. It was a school that had been recommended as being the best possible preparation for Vassar, but it was six hours by train from New York. Still, Jane seemed relieved to have some distance between her and the pressures surrounding her father. She had worked very hard to suppress the memory of her mother and the manner of her death. Jane had her worst fears confirmed just a few months after the tragedy when she read about it in a movie magazine, and she blamed her father for that evasion, although the grandparents had concurred with it. At Emma Willard, she was on her own, or at least she was reliant upon those qualities that Susan had helped bring to light.

Unlike the situation during her first year at the Greenwich Academy, she was instantly liked and sought after. Her famous name did no harm, of course, but it had done her precious little good before.

Jane often skipped past Emma Willard in discussing her youth or she would say, "Girls' schools are ghastly. Women, even young women, should not be locked up together for long stretches." She preferred to talk about Paris and then the Actors Studio, but still she was to name her son Troy, which just happened to be the name of the upstate city in which the school was located. (Jane's later version of how her son was named would be that he was first named Troi, a favorite Vietnamese name, and it was then Americanized. She also preferred to have it known that her daughter Vanessa was *not* named after Vanessa Redgrave, a fellow activist and friend but almost always in a different political camp from Jane's.)

7

In the winter of 1955–56, everything seemed to come apart in the Fonda family. Hank's marriage to Susan had deteriorated to silences and complaints. Only the Peacocks in Nebraska seemed able to control Peter, so his summers with them were long pauses between eruptions. In his most recent assault on the establishment, he had gotten into a fight with one of the housemasters at his prep school in Connecticut. The young man had complained about Peter's being late for chapel and had accused him of being an atheist. Peter told him that he was closer to whatever God was than the housemaster could ever hope to be. "That upset him," as Peter remembers it, "enough to call my old man a son of a bitch. 'Anybody who's been married all those times . . . has gotta be a son of a bitch.' He had crossed me on a personal level, man, so I slugged him, knocked him out cold." Peter left the school and another was found for him in Massachusetts, where he discovered a new retreat in phenobarbital. Soon afterward he was "flipping out," and another student found him hiding in some bushes with his hair bleached by peroxide. The headmaster phoned Jane at Vassar since their father was in Europe on a new film. When Jane found him, she said, "Oh, wow, I think you're Holden Caulfield." She put him on a train to Omaha to stay year round with the Peacocks, his aunt Harriet seeing him through late adolescence and into his college years.

Jane had enrolled at Vassar to discover culture and

instead was awakened to the opposite sex. Her dates with the boys from nearby colleges began spilling over from the weekend into weeknight affairs, and her homework was something crammed in on the run or skipped altogether. On occasional visits to her old friend Brooke Hayward, she would admit to liking boys a lot. There was an intense rivalry between the girls: Brooke went out of her way to understate her attractions, to sustain a certain mystique about herself, which was easy to do since she followed her mother's (Margaret Sullavan's) quest for privacy and "normal" family life. Jane believed that Brooke had everything a girl might need for a great career as an actress—the looks, her mother's talent, and the great style of her father, superagent Leland Hayward. Jane kept a tight lid on her own ambitions for an acting career; she had extremely high standards even then, and decided that she didn't have what it would take to be the best, so she settled for being something of a party girl. Now that the boys, almost to a man, were interested, kiss the books goodbye!

Meanwhile, Hank was in Italy to play the role of Pierre in a gargantuan production of *War and Peace* being put together by Dino De Laurentiis and Carlo Ponti. The veteran director King Vidor was already in Rome when Hank arrived. Vidor had wanted Peter Ustinov for the role, but Ponti and De Laurentiis insisted upon Fonda, so Hank attempted to restructure his physique with padding to conform to Tolstoy's description in his novel. The Italian producers "went into shock," according to Hank, when they saw him in costume. "It seems that they didn't want a Pierre who looked like Pierre. One who looked like Rock Hudson is closer to what they had in mind." With costars Audrey Hepburn and Mel Ferrer, the film was in production for more than four months, costing in excess of $6 million, an extraordinary budget in those long-gone days of high-value dollars. Henry Fonda's Pierre and Audrey Hepburn's Natasha won approval from the critics almost universally.

47

Jane was about to leave for Vassar, and Susan Fonda left Hank somewhat reluctantly in Rome to fly back to New York to put daughter Amy* in school and help Jane pack her wardrobe for college. There was still a warm affection between Jane and her stepmother, a closeness that would survive the marriage.

That September weekend Barone Lorian Franchetti gave a dinner party for the *War and Peace* principals, all of whom, except Mel Ferrer, attended. In Ferrer's absence, Hank had brought Mrs. Ferrer, who was Audrey Hepburn. There, Hank met Lorian's sister Afdera, who was then twenty-three years old and already a young woman of considerable wit and exotic beauty. Lorian was slightly older and was known as Nanyuki. Her baronial estate at Cortina had formal gardens with much antique statuary. Their mother hated these scantily clad marble maidens and once proposed that they get rid of them by allowing guests to shoot at them. Ernest Hemingway, then much taken with Nanyuki, obliged her with an elephant gun.

Hemingway scholars believe that Nanyuki was the inspiration for the character of Renata, the nineteen-year-old girlfriend of the aging hero of Ernest Hemingway's *Across the River and into the Trees*. According to Hemingway's biographer Carlos Baker, Renata was a composite of Nanyuki and a close friend of hers, Adriana Ivancich. Afdera admired Hemingway and may have wished that she was older. Following the publication of the novel in 1950, Afdera began telling everyone that *she* had inspired Papa to create Renata. She also told a reporter for *Europeo* magazine that Papa was desperately in love with her and that she had visited him twice at his finca in Cuba and spent a month with him in Paris, where she had won millions of francs at Auteuil. When Hemingway read the account, he was said to have been hugely amused and wrote Adriana Ivancich that no one must scold Afdera "for her little-girl fantasies," adding that they were harmless, and "it was no sin to indulge

*Adopted by Henry and Susan on November 9, 1953.

48

them." While Lorian's relationship with the writer is documented, his closeness to Afdera requires further study. It was now six years later and Afdera was still seeking to give reality to her heroic-size longings to be memorable in some way, to become a part of contemporary doers of more significance than the "beautiful people" who surrounded her. Those longings had begun a long time ago as she was growing up. She had never really known her father, but he had been something of a national hero, an explorer who died when his plane exploded on its way to Addis Ababba in 1935. In Afdera's words:

They put the bomb under the seat. The plane had left Cairo. In those days, there were no jets. To go to Ethiopia, you had to take four different planes. There were thirteen on board. He crashed two minutes after takeoff. But the strange thing about his death is that he was very close to a medium who always predicted him everything. And when he had something important, he used to go to her for advice. She said, "Don't go, Raimundo. Don't go. I know you will go anyhow but there is a net closing around you and I don't think I'll ever see you again." A letter arrived three days after he was dead. It was a kind of will in case anything happened to him. . . . I just saw him three times in his life. . . . I had two sisters and a brother, but he wanted a second boy. One was named Simba, which means lion in Swahili, number one girl. Number two, Lorian, which is a big swamp in Ethiopia. And my brother, Nanook, Nanook of the North, because my father started exploring the polar north. And when I turned out to be a girl, he was so angry he called me after a volcano, Afdera, which was kind of making noises in Danakil [a desert in Ethiopia].

So the volcano from Italy who was always in some sort of gay eruption met the volcano from America, who seemed quiescent. The young woman not quite twenty-four whose father died in her infancy had finally met and impressed a famous man more than twice her age, but unlike Hemingway, he did not patronize her because of her fantasies. In fact, Hank knew little about them, and even when he was told, there were several of Afdera's friends who swore that the affair with Hemingway had really taken place. Besides, how reliable was the writer's word on such matters anyway? Afdera could not fail to note that Hank seemed at the peak of his physical and professional powers and not, like Papa, living on past glories.

Afdera did not consider herself a movie fan, but she had two great passions as an infrequent moviegoer. One was for Leslie Howard, "but he was *de-ad*," and she managed to make a two-syllable word out of his state of morbidity; the other was for Henry Fonda, who was very much alive and now charming her from across the table. As Afdera remembers it:

> I looked at Hank and he had a really distinctive beauty. When he was younger he was too beautiful to be good-looking in my eyes. But then [in 1955] he was a little weather-beaten but marvelous. Marvelous! And reserved and shy. It was fantastic, and I immediately had a crush. And I remember the first time I saw him, I decided . . . [She laughed.] He didn't know that. And then we met again, but at the time he was very much married.

Perhaps Afdera Franchetti did decide to marry Hank Fonda after that first meeting, but if so she managed to keep it from him for a very long time. In 1956, when the friendship turned serious as Hank was preparing to return to America, he decided to stay on in Italy and sort out his life. Most of her friends were in on the secret of their romance, but few of Hank's were.

Jane returned from Vassar that June to a virtually empty house on East Seventy-fourth Street. Susan, already aware of her rival Afdera, had not yet given up hope. She was alone with daughter Amy and the servants. More than anything else, the child doubtless prompted Susan to try to save their marriage. Adopted in infancy, Amy had enjoyed an affection from her father that was warmer and less reserved than that which he had bestowed upon Jane as a child. But when Hank finally came home it was to stop only briefly in the town house on his way to Cape Cod, where he was expecting his sister Harriet Peacock and her husband Jack to share a house with him that summer. The Peacocks adored Hank and apparently sensed that he was going through a difficult time.

And it was there on Cape Cod that Jane finally met the young woman, only five years older than herself, who would be her next stepmother. Afdera remembers that meeting, and thinking of Jane as

Magic, full of sun. A nice American. She was really *the* Vassar girl. Absolutely lovely, but with a special thing going for her. She hadn't developed yet. She had puppy fat and big ankles. But you saw those long limbs and beautiful hands already. And yet she didn't have bones really, just puppy fat. Still you knew that there was something there coming out that was very special. It was her direct way of talking and that look in her eyes, *and* looking like her father. She looks much more now [1980] than then. Peter for me was different. Peter couldn't have been sweeter in the beginning. He was very affectionate, but I didn't pick it up. . . . At the beginning, Jane liked me. She didn't know this or that. I was very friendly with them, you know. I was like a sister. But I wasn't motherly. I wasn't understanding, but I brought them a whole new world.

That summer Jane entered a dramatic workshop at the American Theatre Wing. She had a small role in Sheridan's *The School for Scandal*, and acquitted herself well enough to join her father at the Dennis Playhouse on Cape Cod a few weeks later in *The Male Animal*. But she got little encouragement from Hank, who rather quixotically wanted a "more normal" life for his children—as though they had ever known what *normal* life was. Apart from this, Jane felt crippled by a lack of technique beside Hank. Jane was uncertain about an acting career. Her huge ego, inherited from both sides of the family, demanded that the world should somehow know about Jane Fonda, but couldn't it be in a less public way? Appearing before a live audience was as frightening to her as it always had been to her father, but he could deal with it and she never would lose her fear altogether.

After much flying between New York and Italy, and Italy and California, Hank rebelled; for one thing, it was costing the devil. So during one of his flying visits to Italy, he proposed. He now had his divorce from Susan, who, according to Afdera, was bitter at first. The grounds for divorce, extreme mental cruelty, "had hurted him. And so this curtain came down to Susan. . . ." Afdera said that she forced Hank to see Susan because of Amy, and that relationship was kept on a civilized level.

It is time to make an attempt to take Hank Fonda down from the cross of inconstancy and fickle-heartedness. In every one of his marriages but his first—to actress Margaret Sullavan—he was the pursued, not the pursuer. He was married by them, not the other way around. Afdera insists that this was not the case with her, that Hank sent her mother letters, hoping that she might be more receptive to the idea of him as her son-in-law, but she is forgetting that she "knew" that she would marry him after first seeing him. Deservedly, she felt that she had every right to become Mrs. Fonda. Her pedigree was impeccable; her chic was not synthetic; and despite her occasional lapses in English grammar, she was a lively hostess who could put everyone at ease, even though he might be French (Afdera disliked all Frenchmen for some undisclosed reason). At fifty (although he told her he was forty-eight) Hank Fonda was at her feet and delighted to be there. Aging even more gracefully than Gary Cooper, he still retained a youthful wonder in those incredible blue eyes.

The Fonda life-style changed somewhat with Afdera's

advent. If the Fondas had lived baronially before, certain economies were practiced by Hank, who had been taught frugality as a boy. But now, as Afdera describes it, "Money poured out from everywhere, thrown out everywhere." Small wonder that Jane, already feeling guilty over their way of life, rebelled totally during the course of her father's fourth marriage, eschewing jewelry, high fashion and high living in general.

Afdera called her marriage on March 10, 1957, "an elopement." What she doubtless means is that her own family opposed the marriage. Her brother Nanook threatened to beat her up and said that Hank Fonda was "an actor who has had many wives." Sister Simba implored her to reconsider and her mother refused to have anything to do with it, nor would she even see her new son-in-law for more than two years. Only her sister Lorian, who had brought them together in the first place, thought the marriage a fine idea. Hank wanted the wedding to be as simple as possible, a family affair, and it was held in the Fondas' living room in Manhattan with both Jane and Peter present. Jane trained down on the Albany Line from Vassar, and as she was approaching the house on Seventy-fourth Street, the cabbie asked, "Did you know that Henry Fonda is getting married today?" Hank's brother-in-law, Jack Peacock, was best man. Harriet Peacock was a witness and, as a surprise, Hank had flown in as matron of honor Afdera's oldest friend, Maria Stella Sernas, who was then living in California with her husband Jacques. Peter gave Afdera away, and the entire ceremony had a cozy, improvisational feeling to it.

Then the newlyweds were off to Canada for an overnight honeymoon, since Hank had to be back on Tuesday for conferences on his New York-based movie, *Twelve Angry Men*, on which he was the producer. He was exhausted from sitting up the entire night before the wedding with Afdera, who was very uncertain about going ahead with it because of the age difference and on top of that was nursing a bad head cold. It was not the most romantic episode in Hank's life.

In April and May, the Fondas rented Billy Wilder's Malibu Beach house furnished, and Hank played the role of a bounty hunter in a Western, *The Tin Star*, for Paramount; his costar was the popular young leading man Anthony Perkins in the role of a naïve sheriff who learns much in Fonda's company. Perkins was ungainly and exceedingly thin, with a long neck and rather small head, as though he had been stretched out by a giant working in play dough, but he was idolized by teenage girls who must have thought he needed mothering.

In July the Fondas planned a long-delayed honeymoon, to begin at Pamplona in Spain. Both Jane and Peter were invited to join them, and they were each allowed to bring along a friend; Jane was to be accompanied by a Vassar classmate. On the eve of their departure Hank was asked by the producer Fred Coe and the author William Gibson to audition a talented young leading lady, Anne Bancroft, for Gibson's two-character play, *Two for the Seesaw*, in which Hank had tentatively agreed to appear. The reading was to be held at the Fondas' town house. The play was mainly concerned with the brief and hopeless affair between a girl from the Bronx named Gittel Mosca and a man who is no longer in love with his wife and is looking for a way out of a dead marriage. What became painfully clear during the reading was that Anne Bancroft was born for the part and that Hank had very few lines. Miss Bancroft would read and read and then Hank would interject a few lines. Gibson, embarrassed, promised to build up the man's role while Hank was away.

In Europe, first at Pamplona and then in Venice and at Cap Ferrat, where they settled in for a month or more, there were numerous *al fresco* dinners, often with Afdera's European friends. Someone took a picture of such a gathering and caught Jane standing some distance from the table where her father and new stepmother were dining; Jane seems to be studying Afdera with considerable detachment. During that vacation, Hank was not much interested in doing the usual touristy things. He only wanted to hang around the pool during the day holding hands with Afdera. At night, he liked to play word games, at which he was very good.

Count Rudi Crespi and his wife Consuelo were among the Fondas' international friends whom they had met frequently in Venice, in New York or at one of the European spas. Rudi Crespi recalls that during those European sojourns Jane attracted young men around her in much the way that Nicole had in Fitzgerald's *Tender Is the Night*, but she was far more naïve than Nicole. Among her admirers was young Count Giovanni Volpi, whose father founded the Venice Film Festival and endowed its coveted movie award, the Volpi. Jane and Giovanni had a number of dates together, but she seemed far more drawn to a handsome American actor, James Franciscus, whom she had met back in New York. And yet as Jim Franciscus moved closer inside the Fonda circle and his hopes with Jane soared, she deflated him by refusing to get serious. Afdera suggests "he was too nice and straightforward. She needed something more complicated." As for Volpi and the other Europeans, Jane was too intensely American even to take a real interest in their cultures. Her later critics might be surprised to learn that few American actresses have as much passion or patriotic fervor over things American than Jane Fonda. And yet she impressed many who were present with her exuberant sense of having a good time. It was not unusual for her to dance the night away at an Elsa Maxwell party on the roof of the Danieli Hotel in Venice, then with a bewitched ring of young men surrounding her, rush to the Lido beach for a swim at dawn, and come back to the hotel for a huge breakfast.

Back in New York, Jane's reservations about Afdera surfaced among her intimates; she was always coming up with a new "Afdera story," usually good for a laugh, and doubtless they had some basis in truth. On one occasion, when Count Rudi Crespi and Consuelo were staying at the Fondas' town house, they left at nine-thirty in the morning to visit some museums and do some shopping. Afdera intercepted them on the way out and told them not to come back until 6 P.M. because "tonight we are having the Duke and Duchess of Windsor for dinner, to which you are invited, and there will be much confusion in the house today getting ready." The Crespis said they understood, thinking that Afdera would be very busy arranging flowers around the house. Outside on East Seventy-fourth Street, they were bewildered to see a huge van in front of the house unloading elegant furniture, while the delivery men were bringing old furniture out of the house. That evening when they returned, they were amazed to find that all of the old furniture had been replaced by the best pieces from New York interior decorators. The dinner for the Windsors proceeded, the décor was much admired, and in the morning it was all whisked away again.

Afdera recalls, however, one brief period when she was very touched by Jane's innate kindness. During one of their frequent vacations abroad, the Fondas rented a villa on Cap Ferrat,

There were endless luncheons which I thought were very amusing. Jane was there watching like you'd watch a parade, and my mother suddenly got very ill . . . so I had to fly to Venice. And I was out of the house for five days, so there were five days of calm; nothing happened. When I came back, Jane said, "You know, the house was frightfully empty without you," which was very sweet.

8

Jane did not want to go back to Vassar when the Fondas were ready to return from Europe. Her college career was not taking her anywhere, and she felt impelled to flight. The Fondas' town house in Manhattan was becoming known for its cocktail parties; there were rarely fewer than two or three houseguests, many of them European. Afdera tried to befriend her, even to understand her, but when she took her aside and said, "Someday you will marry a banker and wear pearls at your throat and a little jeweled pin on your breast," all Jane could say was "Oh, God, no!" Her father was going straight into rehearsals for *Two for the Seesaw*, about which Jane had forebodings. She knew that her father's part needed work, and if the play wasn't ready when he got back, well, she didn't want to be around.

Before the family holiday was over, Jane had persuaded Hank to allow her to go on to Paris and enroll in a painting class in one of the French academies where Monet and Rousseau and other Impressionists whom her father admired so hugely had once studied or taught. Whatever disasters befell Hank Fonda, he always could retreat to his easel and find peace there. If Jane could learn to do that, then a year in Paris would be worthwhile.

France had suffered its humiliating retreat from Dien Bien Phu in Vietnam only three years earlier, in 1954. The United States was slowly but definitely blundering into the same folly in the same place. General Charles de Gaulle was about to become president of the Fifth Republic, coming out of retirement because of the Algerian crisis and the terrorist activities of the National Liberation Front (FLN), who demanded an independent Algerian state controlled by the Muslim majority. The Parisians had become wary of all revolutionaries and regarded de Gaulle as a kind of monarch by ballot box. Defensive about their threatened province in North Africa, and shifting to the right in nearly every way, Frenchmen were less welcoming than usual to free-spirited and free-spending Americans. The Paris in which Jane expected to be liberated at last from family ties was bristling with troops. Massive crackdowns on the FLN in Algeria were carried out by nearly half a million French and provincial troops, and many of them were brought back to Paris to recover between battles.

At the Académie Julian on the Left Bank where Jane attended classes, she seemed lost and out of place. She simply did not have her father's commitment to art and the rapid French rattled off by her instructors sailed right past her ears. But she felt she had to learn the language if she were to survive at all, so she began skipping classes to move about the city, eating in student cafés and taking in French films without subtitles. She fell in with other Americans of her generation, some of them on the staff of the *Paris Review*, a little magazine edited by George Plimpton, scion of an old New York family and future author of sports travesties in which Plimpton was the central, inept figure. The magazine specialized in profiles of celebrated living authors, pulled together from taped interviews. Jane ran errands and fell into the pleasant habit of hanging out at a sidewalk café with the other staff in the late afternoon. At nearly twenty, she had stretched out to five feet eight inches; her hair was blond that year; she was not yet thin or angular; was untaught in how to get on in the world but eager to learn; gifted, one sensed, but she could not tell you in what; droll; and totally dissatisfied with the humdrum. She suddenly became very popular with young male Americans and even an occasional

Frenchman. Her weaknesses at Vassar were surfacing again. Gossip columns back in New York went so far as to suggest she was "bed-hopping" and Hank became livid.

Hank did not need any more problems. Over the previous summer, playwright Gibson had extended the part of Jerry, the errant Midwestern husband, in *Two for the Seesaw* but he had done it in a way that Hank deemed unactable. Hank believed he was being asked to say things onstage that could only be expressed with conviction in a novel. Meanwhile Anne Bancroft, whose years of study under Lee Strasberg at the Actors Studio were now paying rich dividends, had moved into the vacuum left by Hank's tentativeness. She, in effect, took over the play.

Gibson, curious about Bancroft's human qualities onstage, visited the Actors Studio in the company of Hank's understudy, Kevin McCarthy (brother of novelist Mary McCarthy and a brilliant actor). In his *Seesaw Log*, Gibson wrote:

> . . . Lee Strasberg discoursed to two actors onstage, a tape recorder at his side, and a roomful behind him, on truth and human fullness in acting; I sat rapt. We went back to the actual theater as though from church to a gambling den. I came in on Hank again objecting to my man's "bad character," he had "an ungovernable temper" and was in other ways "nasty" and "ugly"; I was not bulletproof against this criticism, which lodged in the pit of my stomach next to my hunger for a view of the other qualities I believed I had written into the character.

A couple of weeks later Hank was objecting to Annie's rehearsal performance as "too emotional." It now became clear that two acting traditions were embattled on the rehearsal stage: the traditional and perhaps predictable technique of a master reactor now playing *à deux* with a blossoming acting *tour de force* from Bancroft, derived from the much newer and controversial so-called Method, created and sustained in theater and films by Lee Strasberg.

It is not easy to analyze the differences between the two schools; breaking down the approaches is too pat. But Fonda, perhaps the best film actor ever among the traditionalists, listens to the actor with whom he is playing, he reflects, he hesitates, and it is not all done with his body; we sense that he is thinking about what he says. When he is angry or amused, you are persuaded for the moment that these emotions are very real. Anne Bancroft, the Strasberg disciple, listens to Henry Fonda but she also listens to herself, to who she is and what she has felt and experienced in her private life. Or as Strasberg once told the author:

> It [the technique] makes it possible for an actor to reach the resources within himself, to stir his imagination, to stir his belief, and to stir his sense of the experience that has to pervade in various situations, and thus to be able to create them. Otherwise, he sometimes creates only the external aspects of it, which from the audience point of view is at times satisfactory enough, but it's not satisfactory either for the actress herself and it's also not satisfactory in the long run.

Gibson finally "beheaded" one of his main concepts in the play because of Hank's seeming intransigence and the total support of him by the director, Arthur Penn.

"I crossed a line," Gibson writes, "between two worlds of writing: henceforth material was to be shaped less by what I had to say than by what the audience would listen to." The play's producer, Fred Coe, was treading a delicate line between the needs of the playwright and those of his male star. Later he would produce Gibson's *The Miracle Worker*, once again starring Miss Bancroft.

When the play opened at the Booth Theatre in January, 1958, Hank was playing a part that satisfied neither himself nor the playwright. But it did please most of the New York critics, Brooks Atkinson writing in the

New York *Times* that "it is a finely wrought cameo. Thanks to Mr. Gibson's thoughtful writing and to the soft, shining acting by Mr. Fonda and Miss Bancroft, it has style, beauty, and a delightful point of view." A critic whom Hank admired more was Walter Kerr, who then reviewed for the New York *Herald Tribune*. Kerr wrote: "What he [Gibson] hasn't quite mastered at the moment—and this seriously involves the earnest and accomplished Mr. Fonda—is the business of sustaining a psychology, a troubled and uncertain state of mind, through all its possible dramatic complexities." Kerr confirmed for Hank all of his profound reservations about the play and the part. Gibson implies in his *Log* that he gutted the play of its psychology because of Hank's inability to project it.

Hank's contract was for six months and was renewable, of course, but he had no intention of staying for the run of the play. He hated every moment of his sold-out engagement and attempted to distract himself by appearing during the day in a movie, *Stage Struck*, being directed by Sidney Lumet in New York. The irony struck Hank at once, of course, that he was doing in the afternoon in the studio exactly what he was doing at night in the theater—playing second fiddle to a young actress, in this case Susan Strasberg. The irony was doubled by Miss Strasberg's stage and paternal origins. She was the daughter of Lee Strasberg, who had trained both Susan and Anne Bancroft. In *Stage Struck*, however, Susan seemed far less inclined to dominate the scene whenever she was playing with Hank; she seemed awed by him, so there was none of the bravado Method acting for him to contend with. While the script was an adaptation of the old Zoe Akins play *Morning Glory*, which had been Kate Hepburn's first major solo vehicle in its earlier film incarnation, its purpose was to help establish Susan as a popular screen star. It was not fresh enough to do this, and Susan Strasberg never did become a major movie personality. Most of her fans were New York theatergoers who were always waiting for her return to the stage.

When Jane flew back from Paris for a dressing down and a few questions from her father, such as "What are you going to do now?," she seemed very uncertain about her goals. Yet some of the mature Jane was beginning to surface. She wanted nothing less for herself than the best. Whatever she did, if she couldn't keep improving, she wanted to give it up. At this point in her life it involved a little trial and error. Now, for lack of any other firm goal, she enrolled at the Art Students League to continue her painting classes. There was no talk of going back to Vassar.

One day, Jane asked to be allowed to watch them shoot a scene between her father and Susan at the studio in Harlem. Afterward Jane was invited back to Susan's dressing room for coffee and a smoke; Jane had become a chain smoker by this time. The girls, who were nearly the same age—Susan was five months older— got on well together.

To Jane, Susan seemed dazzlingly successful. Since her success on the stage in *The Diary of Anne Frank* she had starred in two other major films, Joshua Logan's *Picnic*, playing Kim Novak's younger sister, and Vincente Minnelli's *The Cobweb*, which was about a mental institution and had been written by *Two for the Seesaw* author William Gibson. When she met Jane, Susan was trying to recover from an unhappy love affair with Richard Burton, who had played on Broadway with her in *Time Remembered* by Anouilh. This last detail interested Jane more than the others but Susan, understandably, could not bring herself to discuss it at any length. The girls had one other thing in common but it was not articulated: their fathers were both famous, remote and difficult. Lee Strasberg didn't even pretend to be a social animal, although some reports suggest that he is perfectly capable of being civilized and humane. He listens and he cares about the impression he is projecting. Jane's friendship with Susan would prove to be the first major wedge in prying open a window in her life so that her spirit might escape. Susan convinced her that she should consider becoming an actress. Apparently this was easy for Susan to do since in her own life she was only able to keep disaster at bay by working, usually on the screen.

In July of 1958, Hank was at last liberated from the torment of *Two for the Seesaw*, despite its still being sold out, and Robert Ryan took over on Broadway. Hank and Afdera celebrated the end of his six-month contract with a small party and then flew to California with Jane for the rest of the summer. There was no movie commitment awaiting him out there; he simply wanted to get away from New York, which seemed to be overrun with Gittel Moscas. They rented the furnished house of Linda Christian, awarded her in her divorce from Hank's old friend Tyrone Power, who was to die suddenly of a heart attack later that year while making a movie in Spain.

Oddly, Jane's talk of a career in films or on the stage was taken more seriously by her California friends than by almost anyone back in New York. In Manhattan, she had recently begun modeling ("because I like the money," she said), had befriended *Vogue* editor Alex Gottlieb, photographer Richard Avedon and others interested in the elegant way she looked in front of a fashion camera. And, of course, her father took her acting ambitions less seriously than anyone else she knew.

9

So Jane returned to the town in which she had grown up, but in the ten years she had been away much had happened to Hollywood. The big studios had been forced by various antitrust actions to get rid of their chains of theaters and block-booking, and as a consequence there were no stables of stars remaining at Metro, Fox, RKO, Warners, Universal, Paramount and Columbia. They were bringing new talent into each picture as it was packaged by the studios or—a new phenomenon—the big talent agencies; the talent was drawn from Broadway, off-Broadway and television.

Beatniks had taken over Venice, California, with their counter-culture (Zen Buddhism, pot parties, all-night poetry sessions in crash pads, i.e., homes or flats owned by other beatniks or by people friendly to them). "Beatnik" was said to have been derived from the beatitudes, according to the more religious among them; or from beat, as in "beat down" or "down and out," from the derelicts among them, and there were many. They outgrew the Venice colony and spread northward onto Sunset Boulevard in West Hollywood, along what was known as the Strip. Younger dropouts dominated there, lined up along the sidewalks late at night watching people (the straight world) go by. They were mostly not into poetry and were experimenting with heavier drugs. In a few years, their places along the curbstone would be taken by a less angry crowd of young men and women known as hippies. Jane made it a point always to drive along the Strip whenever she was in her car after dark. She studied them and they studied her, but it would be a long road with many changes before she could blend with them.

As was often the case in her life, Jane was taking the long way around to her career as an actress. She knew that she couldn't begin in Hollywood; she had to have stage experience first and that meant going back East. So she was quite idle in California, marking time and chafing at the paternal restraints that were imposed whenever she was under the same roof as her father.

It was during that long pause that she met Alexander "Sandy" Whitelaw, tall, twenty-eight and cosmopolitan, who from a distance resembled Hank Fonda more than a little. Sandy had a disarming casualness about everything; he was absolutely unflappable. He clung rather tenaciously to an American accent, something he had acquired at Harvard, sounding more nasal than was really necessary, but he had lived much of his life in Europe. His mother was an Englishwoman who had been interned as an enemy alien by the Germans during World War II, his father a Scottish career soldier with a private income. There was an air of mystery about him, despite his understated style. Few seemed to know whether he was American or not. He was multilingual, fluent in French, Italian, German, Spanish and, of course, English. Afdera had known Sandy in Venice when she was a child and he was two or three years older. She approved of him in a vague way but she didn't think his affair with Jane could develop into anything serious because Sandy was, like Jim Franciscus, "too straight" and "not complicated enough."

When Sandy was eighteen, he and his family were living in Venice, where the American superproducer David O. Selznick was shooting *A Farewell to Arms* with his wife Jennifer Jones and Rock Hudson. Sandy was a frequent tennis partner of Selznick's and soon became a production assistant. A good skier, Sandy often went from Venice to St. Moritz, and there he met the retired actress Norma Shearer, who was a seasonal resident of the resort along with her skiing-instructor husband, Marty Arrouge. So, as an intimate of Irving Thalberg's widow (Miss Shearer) and David O. Selznick, when Sandy first went to Hollywood he saw it from the very top.

Jane liked Sandy's placid exterior and his lack of braggadocio. There was no name-dropping around Sandy. He spoke of "Norma" and "David" and "Jennifer" as though they were Ethel and Joe and Gussie from San Diego. More important, he was a skillful lover with about a dozen years' experience. When they began dating nearly every night and Hank began to question her about her late hours, she simply moved out to her own flat in Santa Monica. Sandy believed he had fallen in love with Jane, which was a rather unusual experience for him, since he rarely allowed himself to get so enmeshed in an affair. But Jane was evasive; she refused to get serious. He began to wonder if he had a rival or if she was just not yet ready to compromise.

The affair with Sandy ended abruptly when Jane decided that she was seeing too much of him. As laconic as her father, Sandy brooded about his dismissal for several days, and then decided that he had to find out why she had dropped him. He knew that she kept a diary and perhaps in its pages might lie the answer. He felt that it might give some indication about the role he played in her life.

In the dead of night, Sandy entered Jane's ground-floor apartment through a bathroom window, went to her bureau, found the diary and fled with it. Jane feigned sleep, almost paralyzed with fear. She thought he had come to kill her. The diary was principally a glorified date book which Jane had only been keeping for about three weeks since her arrival in Hollywood. It included lists of all the people—gossip columnists and casting directors—she was hoping to meet in order to further her career, but she had also written that Sandy did not want to marry her and so she would have to stop seeing him. She seemed annoyed about this. Sandy never returned the diary and she never asked him for it back.

The Strasbergs—Lee and his drama-coach wife Paula Miller Strasberg—had come out to Hollywood with their children, Susan and John, to help Marilyn Monroe on a new picture, Billy Wilder's comedy *Some Like It Hot*. Marilyn was studying in Lee's classes whenever she was East even though her husband Arthur Miller felt that it made secret people in the most public art known to man. Lee and Paula Strasberg had become in effect Marilyn's surrogate parents, though there were limits then to what they could do to help keep her psyche intact, with Miller virtually abandoning his own career to do just that as her husband. The Strasbergs rented the old Fay Bainter house in Santa Monica, since many former Actors Studio students, now major stars, lived nearby at Malibu Beach. Jane and Sandy were frequent visitors; then, after Sandy was dropped, Jane alone. She and Susan had some serious discussions about the craft of acting, and when Lee decided to fly back to New York, leaving Marilyn in the capable hands of Paula, who was now a fixture on all Monroe films, Jane asked if she might come East and audition for Lee's classes. And so it was arranged.

PART-III

Jane and the Guru

10

The first time I did something in front of the class, Lee Strasberg for some reason stopped me and I don't know what he said but he was complimenting me and said he saw a tremendous amount of talent, which absolutely changed my life. Nobody had ever told me that I was ever good at anything.

When Jane was accepted as a student in Strasberg's classes, she realized that everyone considered her to be different. Henry Fonda was not just a great Hollywood superstar; he was among the best actors on Broadway. If royalty existed in America, and of course it did from a media point of view, Jane was a crown princess, there to prepare herself for the coronation and her reign. There was probably considerable resentment, too.

As for Strasberg himself, he was at that moment at his zenith as the leading influence in American theater and films. Brando and James Dean had come out of the Studio, and Geraldine Page, Shelley Winters, Eli Wallach, Anne Jackson, Paul Newman, Joanne Woodward, Karl Malden, Anne Bancroft and Carroll Baker. Already there in his classes or about to be were Dustin Hoffman, Robert de Niro, Faye Dunaway, Al Pacino and Sally Field. The Monroe connection kept his name almost constantly in the tabloid columns. Marilyn eventually would leave most of her estate and all of her personal effects to him.

Still, Henry Fonda had done very nicely without any

formal training and Josh Logan, while not yet ready to rap the Great Master of the Method, couldn't believe that Strasberg really had absorbed Stanislavsky's technique; in fact, Logan was to say that he himself was the only American ever really to study in Russia under Stanislavsky. Margaret Sullavan was an actress whom Josh Logan and many others would call "just the finest on the screen ever," who had reached that pinnacle without ever expressing any concern over or interest in "private moments" or "emotional memory."

Among Lee's advocates, however, and there were many, actress Estelle Parsons speaks for nearly everyone when she says, "Another like him won't show up for generations. Very seldom such an ability to teach shows up. He makes you discover yourself and your limitations. He has a deeper level of truth than anyone else."

Jane's limitations at the time, and she had a number, included the unsettling one of having difficulty discovering herself. She seemed to feel that if only she kept moving fast enough from one passionate enthusiasm to another, she never would catch up with her true identity. That race was begun soon after her mother's suicide. In that respect, she was very much like Marilyn Monroe. But in the immediate years ahead their trajectories would veer in sharply different directions: Marilyn would begin to disintegrate when she was forced to utilize her own inner resources, while Jane would begin articulating all of her inner conflicts, including her alienation from her father, hardening the shell about her psyche in the heat of public exposure. Only a certain restlessness, the incessant smoking and an all-too-ready sardonic laugh gave away her insecurities.

Although she was far from being self-supporting, Jane got a job while studying at the Studio. A friend from Hollywood, Warner LeRoy, son of the director Mervyn LeRoy, ran an off-Broadway theater called the York in the East Sixties. He was soon to expand nearby into the restaurant business with a singles hangout known as

Maxwell's Plum. Jane got a job in his office on the premises of the York Theatre. It paid for her classes (thirty-five dollars a week), but she remained at the family town house even though she was usually out all day and often into the night.

Jane always had a weakness for the most vulnerable people around her. Afdera would call it the "runt puppy" syndrome. This attribute had been in abeyance only when she was vying with other girls as the most popular girl on campus at Vassar or as the freest spirit in an uptight Paris. It was to be expected at the Studio that this trait would surface since the other students were in some awe of her name and family background. *She* had to approach *them*, and among the shyest was a boyishly handsome young actor and dancer named Timmy Everett. Timmy already had been on Broadway as the boy in William Inge's *The Dark at the Top of the Stairs*, and a few words from Jane to break the ice was all the encouragement Timmy needed. He proposed that they work up a scene together for their Strasberg class.

By this time, Jane had moved out of the family house once again, feeling that the atmosphere there was all wrong for her. With Afdera's continuing round of parties, she might become a dilettante actress but certainly not a serious one. An old girlfriend from Hollywood, Susan Stein, suggested that they share an apartment, and since Hank knew Susan's father, Jules, well, there was no parental objection. Jules Stein was the founder of the Music Corporation of America, the largest talent agency in show business and soon to absorb Universal Pictures. The girls shared an elegant duplex not far from from the Fonda town house but far enough to give Jane her independence.

Jane and Timmy worked up a scene from Dylan Thomas's *Adventures in the Skin Trade*. Very soon they fell in love and Timmy was around the duplex enough of the time to make it clear to Susan and to all of their friends that the relationship was serious. They made an interesting couple: she was physically far more striking, larger-boned and vibrant; he was slight, with fair hair, and obviously sensitive. On occasion he was taken home to the Fonda town house, where Hank was friendly and curious and Afdera polite but dismissive.

Among the directors working at the Actors Studio was one who stood a little apart from the others—Andreas Voutsinas. He had been brought to Strasberg's attention by the director Elia "Gadge" Kazan, who had seen promise in something he had done off-Broadway. In addition Voutsinas was a compatriot of Kazan's, having been born of Greek parents (in Khartoum, Sudan) and raised in Athens. He had a certain stiffness with others; he had no nickname, and was never "Andy," for instance, because he allowed very few people to get close to him. As a consequence many actors and others connected with the Studio thought he was impossibly arrogant. It also had something to do with the way he held his head, very high on his long neck, with his classically chiseled nose a little up in the air.

It was this alienation from others that first drew Jane to notice him—the "runt puppy" syndrome again, though this puppy was a favorite of Strasberg's. They were frequently seen in consultation together, and Andreas took Jane over to Eighth Avenue for coffee where both were extremely nervous and uncertain of each other. Chameleonlike, he took on the qualties of those he most respected, for good or ill. Strasberg, whose teaching techniques Andreas was soaking up like a sponge, was a difficult man on a social level: sometimes rude and cutting, and nearly always brutally frank. So Andreas was becoming. But very possibly Jane saw these attributes as defenses; underneath all of that was a warm, responsive and vulnerable human being. Jane had developed what Andreas was to call "X-ray vision" in maturity. She could "see through" everyone, and if they were phony, they were dead.

Andreas was real, and he seemed terribly alone. At first he tried to keep their friendship on a platonic level; he knew about Timmy Everett and he didn't want to interfere. His last relationship with a woman, the actress Anne Bancroft while she was still much involved with the Actors Studio, had been mutually terminated because it wasn't leading anywhere. But Annie had been generous enough to put him in touch with a psychiatrist, and he had entered analysis, something that Lee encouraged all of his pupils to do. That therapy lasted for a year and made him face up to a number of facts about himself, the chief one being that he was bisexual and doubtless always would be. It is perhaps worth mentioning that Andreas saw Jane almost at once as one of the great talents of her generation, something that, despite his declaration to Jane that changed her life, Lee Strasberg did not see as on the same level with that of Marlon Brando or Marilyn Monroe. Andreas not only saw it, but he would dedicate much of his own talent toward its perfection.

When Jane first saw Andreas at the Studio, she imagined from the faraway look in his eyes that he must have been a sailor once. He was five years older than Jane, the same age as her half-sister Pan, but unlike Pan born desperately poor. Around 1939 his father, Angelo, had finally managed to save about a million dollars as a spaghetti manufacturer in Ethiopia, but was banished from the country by the returning Emperor Haile Selassie, who accused him of collaboration with the Italians, and with all of that spaghetti in his warehouses he had no defense. The large family of five boys and one girl returned to Athens, where Angelo converted his million dollars into Greek stocks. Soon afterward World War II broke out and the Voutsinas family almost literally starved to death. "The stocks were under the bed giving us courage," Andreas recalls. At the end of the war in 1945 the Greek economy collapsed and the stocks were worthless.

Somehow the twenty-year-old Andreas managed to get to London, where, "at the Old Vic Theatre School, out of six hundred applicants, they accept twelve, one of them it's me!" From there he went on to Canada, to Stratford, Ontario, where he worked with James Mason in *Oedipus Rex*. And finally, on his way back to Greece, he stopped off in New York and met Kazan, who mentioned Strasberg's studio. At that time Andreas had never heard of the man or his school, but as with so many others, once he encountered Strasberg and his endless explication of humanity and drama, he realized that he knew nothing and felt that if there was something to be learned, it was with that "little man." Acting roles came along to sustain him while he studied, the most prominent being that of the Comforter Elifaz in Kazan's production of Archibald MacLeish's *J.B.*

So Jane's life had become suddenly very complex. She had a lover, Timmy, whom she would not hurt for anything, and an admirer in the wings, who would give her the world; at that moment she felt she needed both of them. She was falling more and more out of touch with her family. Hank had been swept into Afdera's world and seemed lost to her; it was a world in which he smiled a great deal and partied into the night and traveled to the Isles of Greece and beyond. On her infrequent visits home Jane would study the two of them together. Had she and her father moved poles apart through this last marriage or had they by some mystical force that neither of them understood moved perilously closer?

All egos need a certain amount of pampering. Actors' egos demand an extraordinary quantity, and successful actors surround themselves with a small army of sycophants, some on their payroll, some not. Hank Fonda made a considerable show of dismissing all of this as ridiculous. He liked to get his hands in the dirt and wear a baseball cap and be as simple as it is possible for a famous man to be. Nevertheless, at odd moments of stress his enormous ego would suddenly display itself and one knew that "plain ol' Hank" was a role he had learned to play so well that he thought it was truly himself.

In his perceptive book *The Italians*, Luigi Barzini touched upon this necessary "lubricant" to pleasant human relations. "[Flattery] is so common in Italy as to go practically unnoticed. One breathes it as one breathes the scent of violets in woods in the spring. . . . Everybody is constantly being vaguely praised by somebody else." Afdera had grown up with this attitude toward others. Not only did she reassure Hank that he was growing more gravely handsome with the years (which was largely true), that he was one of the most important actors in the world (she would be proved right in time), but she also convinced him that they were the most socially sought-after couple in New York, as indeed they were for a year or so. Her ceaseless compliments had so much truth in them that the marriage lasted far longer than any of those close to them, including Jane, thought possible.

11

If Jane seemed to have a direction in her professional life, she was moving close to chaos in her affairs away from the Studio. She had invited it, of course. Timmy was a young man of modest means, and she showered presents on him. She schooled him in upperclass manners and gave him a sense of style. Timmy taught her something, too—that there was nothing wrong with physical avowals of affection, and Jane became quite open in her need to touch or kiss Timmy wherever they were. She would retain this trait with other lovers throughout her life. Jane rather enjoyed having someone needing her so much and she told Andreas so. He said that he understood and tried to keep a lid on his own feelings for her, which was difficult.

Peter Fonda was now, in 1960, an undergraduate at the University of Nebraska and spending his weekends with the Peacocks in Omaha. Whenever he wrote to Jane or telephoned, he mentioned his growing interest in acting. He was a long way from the theater or any of the good acting schools, but if Jane received reluctant parental approval of her pursuit of an acting career, Peter had none at all. His record in adolescence had been blighted by trauma—much of it, in Hank's view, self-inflicted; life as an actor was unstable enough without coming into it burdened with hang-ups. Jane was able to reassure Peter by long distance and in person whenever he flew East.

Earlier that year, Peter had fallen in love with Bridget

Hayward, Brooke and Bill's younger sister, who bore a strong resemblance to her mother, Margaret Sullavan. Peter had hurried down to Topeka, Kansas, from the Peacocks' home in Nebraska when he learned that Bill Hayward was about to be married there. Also there were Bridget and Brooke, and their father, Leland, with his new bride, Pamela Digby Churchill, a very social lady who illuminated her rooms with pink light-bulbs. The groom, then in the Army, was in uniform. Margaret Sullavan Hayward Wagg had died of an overdose the previous New Year's Day but by that time she and Leland had long been divorced and she had remarried. Bridget had been in and out of institutions for nervous disorders and had finally been diagnosed an epileptic. Peter probably knew all of that family history and it may have heightened his interest in Bridget, although there was a fragility and beauty about her that would naturally have drawn Peter to her. After the ceremony, Peter slipped Bridget's white bridesmaid's gloves into his pocket and told her that he was in love with her. But Peter was to be denied any really close relationship with Bridget by the complications of her illness. At her own request she was sent to Switzerland to school for the next two years. On her own she was much abler to handle the seizures and tolerate them. Jane described Bridget as having

> a certain kind of brilliance, a crazy brilliance, erratic, difficult, neurotic, but still unique. I don't think society offers solutions to people like that, especially women. They were never provided with a constructive way of harnessing that kind of energy and brilliance. It turned inward and destroyed them.

Quite apart from her seizures, Peter and Bridget probably could not have made a relationship work. They were too much alike. Peter recalled the night he got the last tragic word:

I loved Bridget. I was at a Broadway play, *Tenderloin* I think, and I went home and my father said "Sit down and have a drink." He never even *talked* to me so I couldn't understand why he wanted me to have a drink, but I sat down and he kept saying, "Poor Leland, poor Leland!" Bridget's dead from an overdose of pills and I was falling thirteen floors to the ground and all he's saying is, "Poor Leland!"

Jane could view her last memory of Bridget more clinically. For Brooke's memoir of her family, she said:

And then we went to her apartment, which absolutely shocked me because it was so conventional. I had an enormous sadness when I was there with her, because it was as if somehow she'd sold out. I couldn't believe that Bridget collected antiques. She had become terribly concerned about porcelain or the right kind of glass; it was reflected in her apartment and the way she decorated it. Somewhere along the way, Bridget was trying to fit into a mold that had nothing to do with her. Her spirit had nowhere else to go.

The comment has as much to say about Jane as about Bridget. Jane had long ago given up trying to fit herself into a mold acceptable to her father.

No one will admit that there was collusion behind Jane's entry into films, but it is a fact that at a time when Hank Fonda was nudged out of his father role by Andreas Voutsinas, whom the elder Fonda now regarded as a Svengali and an androgynous one at that, Hank's great old friend Josh Logan put Jane under personal contract. In Logan's words: "I remember when I made that test of her for her very first film, which was *Tall Story*, she looked at herself terribly critically and she said that she had 'chipmunk cheeks stuffed with nuts,' but of course nobody else saw those chipmunk cheeks. . . ."

Logan also had placed a young actor named Warren Beatty under contract at the same time, and he wanted to pair him with Jane in *Tall Story*, which had been a moderate success on Broadway. Warner Bros., who was backing the venture, had never heard of Warren Beatty and wanted more of a name to play opposite Jane in her first film. Logan then sent the script to Anthony Perkins, who was the most popular juvenile in films; his latest picture, Stanley Kramer's *On the Beach*, was to open that December. Tony Perkins made no effort to be a sexual torpedo, and in fact was very low-key. He seemed just right in combination with Jane, and to everyone's relief he accepted the role.

Since this was all done with the blessing of Jane's father, Timmy Everett was much in evidence throughout all of these tests and negotiations, and Andreas remained far in the background. Jane knew without being told that Andreas would not be welcome around the *Tall Story* set in California, even as an off-camera coach. And that was not all that troubled Jane: she had heard that Logan, like her father, had no use whatever for Lee Strasberg. She hoped that her passion for acting would not be killed off in the process of making her a movie personality. Andreas remained in New York and continued with his work at the Actors Studio. The movie turned out to be of no consequence: the play on which it was based was a contrivance that had been dismissed as predictable corn by every Broadway critic when it had limped into New York eighteen months earlier. Josh Logan is a very warm, patient man whose genius lies in his lulling, persuasive voice and his sensitive, hypnotic, slightly protruding eyes. A few years earlier he had mesmerized Marilyn Monroe into performing at her peak as the befuddled and hopeless Cheri in *Bus Stop*. Looking back on his experience with Jane, Logan wishes that the part had been better even though he found her far more disciplined and better organized than Marilyn. "I will not say it was a dynamic start," Logan said, "because it wasn't a very good picture. But it was fun working with her."

Jane did not consider the experience very much fun. Just before she left for the coast, she had spent two weeks with Andreas touring in a new play by Jeremy

Kingston, *No Concern of Mine*, with Geoffrey Horne and Ben Piazza; they had performed at the Paper Mill Playhouse in New Jersey and the Westport Country Playhouse in Connecticut. Andreas had directed her for the first time—and to others he seemed to be digging at her mercilessly, trying to get down to the gut center of her emotional range. But Jane believed that she needed that then, and she was exhilarated when audiences responded to what Andreas had tapped. In Burbank, where *Tall Story* was shot, Josh Logan handled her with quiet humor and deference. She knew that what was being filmed was very bland stuff, and *Time* magazine agreed with her, saying:

> Nothing could possibly save this picture, not even the painfully personable Perkins doing his famous awkward act, not even a second-generation Fonda with a smile like her father's and legs like a chorus girl. The lines ("Beget—isn't that a sweet word for it?") are stupefyingly cute, the sight gags frantically unfunny, the climax about as exciting as a soggy sweat sock.

It wasn't really all that bad. It gives us a permanent record of an incredibly youthful Jane Fonda, looking like the ingenue she was supposed to be and with none of the strong character lines that would set her apart from everyone else in films less than a decade later.

Andreas thought Logan was exploiting Jane. She was being paid a small salary, a little less than a thousand dollars a month, but her wardrobe was being supplied by Logan's firm, as were all of her business expenses. When she was loaned out for a film, Logan's company would pocket her fee and continue with her usual salary, a routine followed by all movie firms with actors under contract. Through Andreas's constant prodding, by the time she was completing her fourth film, Tennessee Williams' *Period of Adjustment*, as Andreas recalls the details, a legal agreement had been reached between Logan and Jane whereby she would pay him $250,000 for her release from the contract, thus freeing her from long-term penury, as she saw it. The transaction seemed impossible to finance at the time, but Metro was willing to meet her stiff fee of $250,000 for starring in *Period of Adjustment*, making her financially secure again with this one picture. Occasionally in the years ahead, Jane would complain publicly about Logan's "squeezing" her. But the truth was that he did nothing but have the faith in her talent to launch her in a major way in show business.

When Jane returned from the coast, Timmy Everett was eased into the wings where Andreas had been waiting, and Andreas finally moved into the new East Fifty-fifth Street flat Jane had leased in a row of town houses known as the Rockefeller apartments. He was amused to find it half empty, and Jane living mostly out of suitcases. There were no decent chairs to sit on, no sofa, so he helped her furnish and decorate the place, with her money of course. Now that she was on her own, Jane was extremely cautious about where the money went, and although she would seem more than generous to numerous causes in which she believed in the years ahead, she would remain careful. She tried to account for every dime, but Andreas insisted that she purchase a few good pieces.

In all the ways that counted, then, Jane had placed herself in Andreas's hands. Her single attempt to bring him home for Hank and Afdera to get to know him better had turned into a ghastly experience for everyone. Hank seemed shocked by what he took to be Andreas's arrogance, and later he made some discreet inquiries into his background through his few Actors Studio connections. When he was informed that Andreas was close to Strasberg, Hank was not particularly pleased. Andreas believed that Hank had come to hate him, and he may be right. It seemed to disturb Hank deeply that his daughter would take Andreas as a lover, especially since he seemed determined to take over her life. Relations began to sour between Jane and her father, and, even unaccompanied, she began to visit him less frequently. Since Andreas was now advising Jane on her career and they were looking for a play they could do together on Broadway, there were few questions from Hank about her theater work. After these obligatory visits, she would return to the Fifty-fifth Street apartment emotionally bruised and flattened. Andreas had a marvelous sweetness in his nature and soon restored her spirits; he had stepped nimbly into the role of surrogate father, and even though there was a note of parody in the performance, they both knew that it stood for something she needed in her life.

While Josh Logan was still orchestrating Jane's career onstage and Andreas had begun doing the same off-stage, Logan tested her for the title role in his forthcoming stage musical version of Marcel Pagnol's movie trilogy, to be entitled *Fanny*. Jane knew she wasn't right for it and Logan had no great hopes, and it went badly.

Then without much ado Logan cast her in the central role of a melodrama written by Daniel Taradash, *There Was a Little Girl*. As Logan recalls the story, it was about "a young middle-class girl who is going to go out with her young lover and they are going to a motel, and on the way, the boy gets scared for moral reasons and begins to get drunk at a roadhouse, where they are seen by some young punks. . . ." The girl is taken out and raped, and, again in Logan's words: "There is the question that comes to her mind that people in her community believe that she asked for it. And because of the fact that she was planning that night to go to bed with this boy, she begins to wonder if she was indeed asking for it." The girl then begins to search all the seedy joints in the area for her attackers; she finally encounters them in a tiny taproom, where they reassure her, saying that she resisted every minute. She goes away despising the mores of the family and the entire establishment; eventually she gets into the sleeping car of a train where a young salesman picks her up and she goes to bed with him. As Logan puts it, "She does it now because she owns herself."

During rehearsals for the play and on the out-of-town tour, Logan first became aware of Andreas as a fixture in Jane's life. He did not ask what had become of young Timmy Everett. Relationships were constantly changing in the theater. The play opened on Broadway on February 29, 1960, and nearly every critic savaged it, although most had a kind word for Jane. Brooks Atkinson in the New York *Times* wrote: "Although Miss Fonda looks a great deal like her father, her acting style is her own. As the wretched heroine of an unsavory melodrama, she gives an alert, many-sided performance that is professionally mature and suggests that she has found a career that suits her." *There Was a Little Girl* closed in two weeks, and although Logan searched frantically for another vehicle for Jane to keep her career ascending, he admits that he didn't come up with a thing.

But scripts were now coming in for Jane to consider. Among them was one by Arthur Laurents, whose *Home of the Brave* had stirred up controversy some years earlier. The play was *Invitation to a March*, a comedy-fantasy dealing with the problem of individualism, of standing up against those forces that try to fashion people in one mold. A pretty young woman is so bored with what life has to offer that it literally puts her to sleep. Then a battle is fought by two mothers, one of whom would keep the daughter a pampered but somewhat comatose creature and the other who would give her a more vital life, if unpredictable and insecure. "People are afraid to fall on their faces," the author said. In Laurents, Jane was faced once again with a director hostile to Lee Strasberg's Method. Laurents remarked: "The Method school has been a blight. The only thing the actors excel in today is violence and grubbiness. . . . The theater should be a land of magic." Jane always managed to give directors what they wanted and Laurents found in her an intensely disciplined actress of surprising depth. Jane played a younger version of actress Celeste Holm's sleeping beauty with charm, grace and credibility. Besides Miss Holm, there were two other actresses in the

85

cast who were invariably critics' darlings: Madeleine Sherwood and Eileen Heckart. Miss Sherwood was still studying with Lee Strasberg and knew Jane from her classes.

Hank Fonda was hearing good things about his daughter as *Invitation to a March* rehearsals proceeded. He felt bad about their alienation so he telephoned and said that he would like to drop over to her East Fifty-fifth Street flat after his own play rehearsals on *Critic's Choice* for a visit; he had yet to see her apartment and he wanted to wish her well in the play. Andreas left the place about half an hour before Hank's expected arrival to see a movie that was on locally. Then the elder Fonda arrived and in a few minutes they were both relaxed and chatting furiously as though to catch up in one evening on all the thoughts that had gone unspoken. But suddenly at ten-thirty Jane stood up as calmly as she could and said, "You'll have to go now, Dad. Andreas will be coming back soon." Hank's eyes instantly convicted her of unworthiness as only his eyes could do; he slipped into his coat and went out the door. Andreas remembers that Jane later told him that Hank sank onto the curb outside, immobilized and in shock, unable to believe that his own daughter had asked him to leave in such a manner.

When the play opened to lukewarm notices with one or two raves on October 29, 1960, Jane was again singled out for special praise. Kenneth Tynan wrote in the *New Yorker*: "Jane Fonda can quiver like a tuning fork, and her neurotic outbursts are as shocking as the wanton, piecemeal destruction of a priceless harpsichord. What is more, she has extraordinary physical resources." The play ran for nearly four months.

After that, it now seemed time for the big move into the Actors Studio itself, which was something quite separate from Strasberg's private classes. It comprised an elite group of actors and directors, all of whom had auditioned before the entire Studio membership and either passed into its ranks or failed. Andreas proposed that Jane do a scene as the ill-fated John O'Hara heroine Gloria in *Butterfield 8*. She passed, and the assembled Studio triumvirate—Strasberg, Elia Kazan, and the producer Cheryl Crawford—seemed surprised and exhilarated by the size of her talent. Andreas, too, was congratulated for helping to bring it out.

PART IV

Late-Blooming Flower Child

12

The thing that really jolted the foundations of American society in the nineteen-sixties was youth's massive frontal attack on puritanism in all its aspects. It has never recovered; and it never will, despite the religious enclaves spread about the country in towns that are really fortresses against the great enemy—*permissiveness*. Those who profess to be Born Again are really the holdouts standing up to be counted, and those few who need someone to tell them how to behave, even if it has to be Jesus.

As early as 1961 Jane was speaking out for something that was not really new: free love (Victoria Woodhull had made it a plank in her presidential platform in the eighteen-seventies). By that time her father's marriage to Afdera was already foundering and they were about to separate. Jane began making pronouncements about marriage being "obsolete."

> I think people are not naturally monogamous animals. I think marriage is diametrically opposed to people's basic instincts, but unfortunately it is a social necessity. That's purely a hypothetical premise, and although I certainly have no interest in marriage at this time, it doesn't mean I would never engage in it in the right circumstances. The thing I object to is that everyone seems to expect a woman to get married. Why should this burden be placed on women? Why should a woman have to marry? I'm twenty-four years old and every one of my friends is married. I couldn't get married now if my life depended on it.

She also said: "If the institution of marriage were ever to be outlawed, now is the time in history for it to happen. I think it would solve three big social scourges: mistresses, illegitimate children and adultery."

In April, Jane was due back in Hollywood at Columbia Pictures for *Walk on the Wild Side*, an adaptation of the Nelson Algren novel to be directed by Edward Dmytryk, a man who like Elia Kazan had cooperated with the House Un-American Activities Committee in their investigation of communism in Hollywood but only after serving time in a federal prison.* It is unlikely that Jane knew very much about Dmytryk's political past since she was not yet politically awakened, but she did know that he had been inactive since a fairly disastrous remake of *The Blue Angel* in 1959. Jane was looking forward to a reunion with Barbara Stanwyck, who had played with her father in one of his favorite movies, Preston Sturges's *The Lady Eve*, back in 1941. As a toddler known as "Lady," Jane had come on the set and been jiggled on Miss Stanwyck's knee. The cast of *Walk on The Wild Side* also included Anne Baxter, Laurence Harvey and Capucine. Capucine was the girlfriend of the film's producer, Charlie Feldman, and was frequently in tears because of co-star Harvey's derogatory remarks about her talent. Harvey was the lover of Joan Cohn, widow of the legendary head of Columbia Pictures, Harry Cohn. Holding together this clutch of temperamental artists was a considerable achievement for Dmytryk, although tension was palpable. Jane and Andreas, who was with her constantly, steered clear of all this. No one got to know Andreas, and Jane was only a little more sociable. One of the major stars on the picture, Anne Baxter, recalls something of Jane's presence (or absence):

*Dmytryk found that he may have paid his debt to society, but Hollywood still shunned him. He bought back his career with an afternoon session of naming names for the committee.

Jane would closet herself with Andreas in her dressing room and stay there. For her he was a kind of electric security blanket. She was determined and avid. She had her own ideas. It was a very big cast and she wasn't about to be overwhelmed. She would do anything that Andreas asked her to do. Jane wanted to see that her contribution to the film impressed itself.

Miss Baxter was annoyed only once with Jane and that was when Jane misplaced her breast pads and "borrowed" Miss Baxter's bra. The star had flown in from her home in Australia six months pregnant and her breasts were larger than usual—and unlike Jane's, Anne Baxter's breasts were not small to begin with. Jane also soaked her tight-fitting dress in the region of her bottom with water to make it cling to her rear on camera. It was Miss Baxter's impression that Andreas really directed Jane in the picture, preparing her for each scene in her dressing room but never once appearing on the set. The star was impressed with what Jane and Andreas did with the part of Kitty Twist, although she felt Dmytryk might have been irritated by the situation. Jane's Kitty Twist starts out as a thief and ends up a prostitute. She describes the girl as being without "too many scruples. I love the part. I got a lot of humor into it. It's the little things that aren't in the script that make the role great." It is to Andreas's credit that Jane managed to overcome all of the trouble on the picture, including the paring down of Jane's role as producer Feldman strove to keep Capucine more prominent than any of the other women in the film, and finally the sudden firing of Dmytryk by Feldman over the director's interpretation of the Algren story. Blake Edwards was brought in to finish the picture. Yet none of this seemed to affect Jane and Andreas to the slightest degree. Their collaboration was the most stable and consistent thing on that Columbia sound stage, and their hard work was noticed upon the film's release. Jane's notices gave her movie career a decided boost. Paul V. Beckley in the New York *Herald Tribune* wrote:

Jane Fonda as a bouncy, wiggly, bratty little thief and prostitute, seems more like a Nelson Algren character than anyone else in the picture.

Almost unconsciously, Jane was beginning to develop antennae that would probe ahead of her as she chose movie vehicles. What this meant was that she would always seem just a little ahead with her stands on marriage and sex, on the role of women, on minorities, on war. Some would call it prescience, others an uncanny instinct for promoting herself and her films. Jane would say simply that she was a "slow starter" who was growing up. In any event, by late 1961 she was in Hollywood filming *The Chapman Report*, which was being directed by George Cukor from a novel by the best-selling author Irving Wallace. Its episodic story concerned a team of social scientists, much like the Kinsey team back in the late nineteen-forties, in this case surveying the sex habits of American women. Jane joined a cast that included Claire Bloom, Shelley Winters, Glynis Johns and Efrem Zimbalist, Jr.

The production, under Darryl F. Zanuck, former head of Twentieth Century-Fox, was being shot at the Warners studio under the immediate supervision of Zanuck's son Richard. It was plagued from the beginning by fears that it was too shocking for most audiences—in 1961 *everything* had not yet changed—and the screenwriters Wyatt Cooper and Don Mankiewicz were having to rewrite whole sections of the film while it was being shot. Even after it was finished, additional editing went on that prevented the movie from being released for nearly a year. The final result would be tepid fare indeed, prompting *Time* magazine to write:

Nothing to report . . . In the end, kindly Dr. Chapman explains that figures show that most U.S. wives are actually awfully good sorts, and the latest local sampling should not be taken too seriously. Neither should *The Chapman Report*.

But something exciting was happening to Jane as a performer. Andreas, a compelling personality in his own right, had finally convinced her of her own worth, of the depth of her talent. He was behind her constantly—in her apartment in the evenings as her coach, and at night in an entirely different role as her companion and lover. It is possible that she had put down marriage so strenuously because she was deeply involved with a man she would never marry.

George Cukor, who had so many other problems with the picture, was naturally pleased that Jane was always ready to deliver a polished performance in every scene. He recalled that first experience of directing her as a pleasant episode as far as Jane was concerned. "I don't mean to flatter myself," he said, "but I brought out something very fine in Jane in that film. She brought it out with me. It was already there."

Stanley Kauffmann, writing in *The New Republic* when *The Chapman Report* finally was released in October 1962, struck the first resounding note of appreciation:

> A new talent is rising—Jane Fonda. Her light is hardly under a bushel, but as far as adequate appreciation is concerned, she might as well be another Sandra Dee. I have now seen Miss Fonda in three films. In all of them she gives performances that are not only fundamentally different from one another but are conceived without acting cliché and executed with skill. Through them all can be heard, figuratively, the hum of that magnetism without which acting intelligence and technique are admirable but uncompelling. . . . In *The Chapman Report* . . . she plays a frigid young middleclass widow. The girl's pathological fear of sex, exacerbated by her hunger for love, is expressed in neurotic outbursts that cut to the emotional quick, with a truth too good for the material. . . .

Back in New York Hank and Afdera had separated, and he had set her up in her own Park Avenue apartment. He didn't want a divorce; he wanted her to "grow up." But that seemed unlikely. Later, Afdera would say:

I wish I had met him ten years later. Not even ten, but seven or eight. We would still be married. Or I wish I had had an unhappy marriage when I met him. Then I would really have appreciated him and would have been less spoiled, less self-centered and more of a wife. It's a pity that he was my first husband and not my second.

What had precipitated the breakup was an affair Afdera began with another man, an Englishman, with whom she flew to Mexico.

I flew to Mexico from Seventy-fourth Street. I was already in love with this man. . . . I was in tears, saying "What am I doing? What am I doing?" and Hank called me at six in the morning, saying "Will you change your mind?" And there was the man I was in love with just sitting, sitting, and I remember I took a huge cigarette lighter and I threw it in the sink and swore. There was a man, Hank, who was such a good man, maybe I am making a mistake. And there is the one I love. I was never *in* love with Hank.

Hank must have felt more betrayed by Afdera than by anyone else in his life. Before, it was he who had walked away. All of his friends sensed how wretched he felt about the breakup and they dropped Afdera completely, for all time. It did no good for Afdera to remind him of her own misgivings before the marriage; she had committed herself and now he was left stranded. Knowing that Jane was living with Andreas, whom Hank now frankly and outspokenly loathed, and that Peter was dropping out of college to try his wings as an actor away from Broadway, where his father might have been of some help, Hank felt more alone than ever before in his life.

"I'm still fighting being Henry Fonda's daughter," Jane said around this time. "I think I have to fight it a little more. . . . We simply come from different generations. The results [in acting] may not be different, but our processes are. When I try to explain my problems in acting to him, he just doesn't understand." And she said many other things critical of Hank; it was as though she needed to tell the world why they weren't in close touch.

It was at this time that Jane flirted with analysis. Everyone at the Actors Studio had gone in for it, and now she felt that she might even need it. Andreas was supportive but only because she turned to him for his opinion on practically everything and he had been taught by Strasberg that everyone had to undergo it if that was the only way they could look into themselves. Although later she was to say that she "learned a lot from analysis," she eventually gave it up. Apparently she was not yet ready to open that door on her mother's death, or she may have believed that it was securely bolted.

13

Scripts were still coming in, including Norman Krasna's sex comedy *Sunday in New York*, being prepared for the Broadway fall season. The role of Eileen Tyler seemed ideal for Jane, but after conferring with Andreas she turned it down. Jane told a reporter:

> Friends told me I was crazy to say "no." I could see why they wanted me for it, but I didn't feel it. It would no doubt have a long run and I am still so new in this business that if I have an experience of being stuck for a long time in something I don't enjoy, I might not want to act anymore.

Jane's comments, among her less brilliant, suggest that she and Andreas may have been searching among the plays proposed to her for a *succès d'estime* rather than a commercial hit. Once she had removed both Broadway and Andreas from her system in the years ahead she would develop an unerring instinct for what would be popular in a film. What Andreas did for her was raise her artistic sights, which never would be lowered very much.

Peter, too, had now pulled his act together and with no appreciable compromise. On October 6, he married Susan Brewer, the twenty-year-old daughter of Noah Dietrich, then chief aide to the billionaire recluse Howard Hughes. (Years later, at about the same time as

Susan's divorce from Peter, Dietrich's long memoir about Hughes would be read in manuscript by Clifford Irving, who would base his infamous Hughes "autobiography" on it, although Dietrich knew nothing of Irving's intention.) Susan was not an actress and all seemed to augur well for the success of the marriage. Afdera telephoned to ask if she might come to Peter's wedding, but was told, so she said later, that she might attend only if she returned to her own marriage. She was not present, and Andreas, too, stayed away, although he and Peter got along well enough. The Fondas were briefly reunited without any trace of tension in St. Bartholomew's Church in Manhattan, not far from the church where Hank had married Frances more than twenty-five years earlier. Later that same week, Peter opened in a principal role in the Broadway play *Blood, Sweat and Stanley Poole*, a comedy set in World War II not unlike *Mister Roberts* in its approach to the material but vastly inferior as a play. Peter managed to draw some encouraging reviews and even won an award from the New York Drama Critics Circle as the most promising young actor that year. The play survived only three weeks, but it was seen by one of America's foremost film directors, Robert Rossen, who three years later would offer Peter the second male lead in his movie *Lilith*, starring Jean Seberg.

Jane returned to California for additional work on *The Chapman Report*, from which the liberated views had been gutted. Andreas was waiting for her and they resumed their collaboration. On November 6, he was with her in her Wilshire Boulevard apartment in Westwood when heavy smoke began drifting southward from the canyons to the west and the hills to the north. The red glow in the sky above Bel Air, Brentwood and Beverly Hills could be seen for miles along the approaches to Los Angeles. Later that evening Jane learned that the Fondas' old farmhouse at 900 Tigertail Road, so lovingly built by her mother and father, had burned to the ground. So, too, did dozens of other mansions of the film colony.

99

The Great Fire of 1961 so distressed Jane that she couldn't wait to wind up her work in *The Chapman Report* and return to New York. Although she was already committed to do another Hollywood film, *Period of Adjustment*, in the early spring, she considered New York her home—a good three thousand miles from the ashes of her childhood. They spent Christmas and New Year's in Manhattan, back in the old East Fifty-fifth Street apartment. A great many actor friends drifted in and out of the place over the holidays—Rosemary Murphy, Ben Piazza and brother Peter with his new bride Susan.

Then, in March 1962, Jane and Andreas flew once more to Hollywood for the Tennessee Williams comedy. She was free of her contract with Logan, on which all of the necessary legal work had been done while she was back East. Knowing that all her future movie fees (less her agent's 10 percent) would be going to her, she felt flush enough to rent a small house. But despite the privacy Andreas could not live with her in Hollywood, not as the social code was constituted in 1962. It was still about as provincial as a small American town, not because the film star residents wanted it that way but because they were forced to be hypocritical in their off-screen lives. But Jane and Andreas remained a couple and were rarely apart.

Period of Adjustment is not a major Tennessee Williams work, but in its look at newlyweds it managed to take a number of good-natured swipes at the institution of marriage. When it opened on Broadway the previous year the critics had been disappointed that it was not on the same serious level as *The Rose Tattoo*, with which it was compared, since that had some comic moments. The play charts the parallel but very different courses of two marriages, one brand-new and the other nearly on the rocks. Jane Fonda and Jim Hutton were the just-marrieds, and Jane was warm, naïve and full of little quirks that brought her role to life. The original play's director, George Roy Hill, was brought to Hollywood to restage it for the screen, launching a film

100

career that was to reach its climax two years later with Nora Johnson's *The World of Henry Orient*, a major Peter Sellers film. Hill was soon made aware of Jane's reliance upon Andreas and was only grateful that she was always so dependable.

Hank had recovered now from his divorce but was angry and frustrated in his career. His agents had turned down the role of George in Edward Albee's *Who's Afraid of Virginia Woolf?* without ever letting him see the script, characterizing it as being "a loser about a couple fighting all the time." They had gotten him signed instead to do a movie called *Spencer's Mountain*, a project he hated from the first shot to the windup.

At the beginning of August Jane flew with Andreas to Paris. She was due at the end of that week in Athens, where she would join Peter Finch and Angela Lansbury, her costars in the film version of a novel, *In the Cool of the Day*. On a Sunday afternoon, as Andreas and Jane left a Paris movie house where they had seen Melina Mercouri and Anthony Perkins in *Phaedra*, they saw in the headlines that Marilyn Monroe had died—a suicide, the papers said. They were both stunned by the news; they hadn't realized that they felt so strongly about her. Andreas felt that the world had changed a little that Sunday, that nothing would be quite the same with Marilyn gone. Jane, of course, had known Marilyn as a fellow student of Strasberg's and as their friend. Andreas had seen her around the Strasbergs for years, but millions around the world who only knew Marilyn on the screen felt the loss almost as keenly. It was a body blow to the earth's inhabitants. No death had so affected the Western world since the passing of Franklin Roosevelt, although the assassination of President Kennedy the following year would provoke a similar response and set the tone for much of the violence in the nineteen-sixties that was to follow.

In the Cool of the Day was supposed to be a melodrama about a young woman and an older man who hope to pull their strained affair together among the ruins of

Athens. But the result was mildly disastrous—mildly because so few people ever saw the movie. It was missing so many important elements that were important for an understanding of it that you wondered if you had dozed through some essential part. John Houseman produced the film and was probably more active than anyone else in trying to salvage something—*anything*—from the chaotic footage shot on location in Greece. It is one of the few Jane Fonda films in which she seems at a loss in delineating a particular character. Andreas could not go with her as coach because he still had Greek citizenship and would have been conscripted by the Greek Army had he set foot in his homeland. Perhaps his presence there might have helped Jane, but it certainly could not have saved this picture. Peter Finch and his wife looked upon the production as a lark and enjoyed their holiday in Greece, but it was something that Jane could have done without.

Jane flew back to New York, where Andreas met her at the airport. She told him that she had just made her first bona fide flop movie. He assured her that no one would remember it in five years, and the fact was that the film very nearly did not come out at all. It remained for three months in the editing rooms at Metro, where all hands were called upon to try to make of it a movie that was fit to release.

PART V

Anatomy of a Failure

14

It was still in Jane's mind that she had to conquer Broadway as well as Hollywood. Doubtless it was part of her fierce sense of competition with her father. Over the summer she had committed herself to a Broadway comedy, *The Fun Couple*.

Something like four out of five new plays fail in New York. Jane had already declared herself on the kind of thing she was seeking on the stage—"something interesting" that would not run too long—and such plays are rather easily come by. Prestigious flops are always floating around—plays with sixty in the cast not written by Lawrence and Lee (*Inherit the Wind*, etc.), two-character plays in the wake of *Two for the Seesaw* and *The Fourposter* about a pair of very commonplace people, "thrillers" in which much of the predictable action is mercifully concealed by a stage direction for "darkness," and comedies written without a shred of adroitness or wit. Such scripts sometimes find backers, often related to the author or, more often still, luckless speculators taken in by backers' auditions at which the prospective stars read "brightly" with a pizzazz that turns clichés into what might pass for wisdom or perception.

Jane and Andreas convinced themselves that *The Fun Couple* was "offbeat," something that would get mixed reviews but raves for Jane and, they now decided, for Andreas as well. He had done so well for her throughout the filming of *Walk on the Wild Side* and *Period of Adjustment* that they both felt he deserved wider recognition. Jules Dassin had managed very well directing his wife Melina Mercouri, Andreas's compatriot, in *Never on Sunday*, a major hit comedy about a prostitute that seemed to be running forever wherever it was shown. Jane and Andreas saw no reason why they couldn't become an equally formidable team.

The Fun Couple concerned a very young and inexperienced woman and a youth apparently just out of a strictly policed Bible college, who meet in Tijuana, fall in love and marry, all within about four hours. They apparently marry out of an imbecilic notion that if they want to go to bed together they must be man and wife. It was a point that Jane had been attacking in the press for a good two years, but the play fell pitifully short of having any comprehensible story. Probably Jane thought it made a good deal of sense after being immersed for five weeks in the implausibilities of *In the Cool of the Day*.

The comedy had been written by a dentist and another gentleman (John Haase and Neil Jansen) and it was, in its own gauche way, an attack on the establishment. In the hands of a really funny man, say S. J. Perelman, it might have come off, but its premise is not one that Perelman would have considered worth anyone's evening. It was a half-humorous idea in search of some wit. The irony was that it seemed cut from the same pattern as *Sunday in New York*, except that the latter had been crafted by an expert hand at such matters, Krasna, who always managed to cover over with bright dialogue his lack of genuine wit. The major difference was, it seemed, that the producers of *Sunday in New York* had already hired their director. The producer of *The Fun Couple* was willing to accede to Jane's request that Andreas should direct. It was not the imperious demand of a temperamental young star; it seemed to make sense. Andreas was able to get the best out of Jane; he had really guided her through two motion pictures. Not least, his credentials at the Actors Studio were the very best. The production began.

The Fun Couple was certainly not Jane and Andreas.

During rehearsals, his head was thrown back on his extravagantly long neck like a lion tamer's. She carried an oversized stuffed tiger everywhere she went—they were as inseparable as Jane and Andreas. His dark Slavic eyes were piercing as he shouted at Jane: "*Stop! Let's do it over again,*" or "*I'm getting angry again.*" Jane was submissive and deferential. "*That's it!*" he would shout sometimes. "*That's what I want.*" Andreas left few decisions to others; he even chose Jane's wardrobe.

When the strain began to show and Jane seemed at a loss, Andreas was more affectionate in her dressing room and back at her apartment. They kissed a great deal, oblivious to others at such moments, and once he gave her a coiled-snake bracelet, pointing out that "its eyes are golden." Jane looked upon anything that came from Andreas as close to perfect.

Jane's movie, *Period of Adjustment*, was on at a Broadway theater at the time. It was a street where the name Fonda usually meant success. They were both hoping that after the play opened the name of Andreas Voutsinas would be a name to reckon with, too. It was a do-or-die thing. They were committed to *The Fun Couple*; there was no backing down, and it would either be another step upward in New York for Jane, if it were a success, or a slight step backward if it failed. For Andreas, failure would mean an enormous loss. It might be next to impossible to get another such plum if the play did not click. If it succeeded, then he and Jane might go on for years together. "I want," Andreas told her in his tortured English, "when you go on the stage that there is one single human being in the audience—*me*—that cares as much about you as if I was up there on that stage."

But little could counter Jane's nervousness, and it would have been the same if Kazan himself had been directing her. It showed constantly: she chewed gum, and relieved some of the tension by talking into the sound cameras of a television crew from Drew Associates/ Time-Life Productions who were doing a documentary called *Jane* about her current Broadway experience. Jane spoke of Marilyn and "the enormous thing that went on around her . . . and then she may have felt ugly, and she felt scared." About herself, she told film documentarian Hope Ryden:

> In the beginning there was resentment. I mean, "She got the part because she's her father's daughter." The consequence was that with the guilt that I had, I worked terribly hard. Everybody else would go to two hours of acting class a week. I'd go to six. You know, singing and dancing. I overdid the whole thing. I became twice as beatnik as everybody else. It was necessary for me to be able to feel "That's right, I'm Henry's daughter, but I've worked just as hard as all of you, if not harder."

Her relationship with Miss Ryden went on for more than six weeks, and they were together during their waking hours almost constantly. The formula was Miss Ryden's idea and her approach was cinéma vérité. She had just completed a similar hour-long study of the pianist Susan Starr, which Jane had seen. Miss Ryden's camera crew and, much of the time, her coproducer, Don Pennebaker, would track Jane and Andreas from their apartment to the theater or rehearsal stage. One of the camera's favorite haunts would be Jane's dressing room on the road and backstage at New York's Lyceum, where they would be very briefly. Jane made an ideal subject for such a probing view. She seemed unconscious of the camera's presence, which accounts for part of her genius as a film actress. There were no moments when she hid her face from the camera, whether she was weeping or making faces at herself. She even undressed and changed in front of the camera.

Backstage, when they opened in Wilmington, Jane seemed like a zombie, numb perhaps. She took a swig of brandy and said she was ready. But it was obvious at once that the show was in trouble. Jane's first line to her groom, "You're a nice man," was delivered to considerable applause as she stepped onstage. Then she was required to ask, "How long have I known you?" And her leading man, Bradford Dillman, tells her, "Four hours and twenty-seven minutes." A big laugh from the audience and the thought in the company's mind, "Maybe this is going to work." But then the laughter stopped; the hush in the audience deepened—death for a comedy. Only Dyan Cannon's raucous singing brought the crowd to life again, most of them a little desperate by now for something, anything, for their five dollars a seat. Everyone was asked to help save the play, even the crew of the television company. Jane and Brad Dillman tried to slap some life into their stillborn farce by simplifying their dialogue. "I just want to say one word—*yes!*" They cut everything they could, and before they arrived at the last town of their tryout tour, Philadelphia, Jane had written the synopsis "of a possible play." Between acts in Wilmington, Andreas came back to tell Jane and the others, "Everything worked." But early the next morning, Jane read the local reviews aloud: " '*Fun Couple* Suffers from Lack of Surgery. If failing to appreciate the shenanigans onstage is a sign of growing old, we aged ten years last night.' "

The producer told Andreas, "The last night [of the Wilmington run] when the performance is over, we're going to have that first act rewritten. And you and I are going to work nonstop."

The world came perilously close to nuclear war that week, but so cloistered is the theatrical community, especially in the throes of a new production, that the fears of the nonprofessional world outside failed to penetrate. Jane saw the headlines, "Russian Missile Sites in Cuba," but was too preoccupied with trying to stop her run of bad luck to comment on it. On only one evening, when President Kennedy was "nose to nose" with Khrushchev and had ordered the Russians to remove the missiles "or suffer the consequences," which of course would be suffered by everyone, did Jane and Andreas feel a little of what the outside world was going through.

But then, blessed relief, the Russians complied, and *The Fun Couple* moved on to Philadelphia.

Feeling close to both Jane and Andreas, Lee Strasberg came down with his daughter Susan and wife Paula to watch the last performance in Philadelphia before their Broadway opening. Never at a loss for words, he told them, "The material needs to be used for a play, not a sketch. The audience doesn't want to forgive mistakes at that particular moment [where the comedy died]. The things that are done, you've all done." They were rather chilling words, but at least they didn't pin all the blame on Andreas. Jane tried not to feel devastated by what was happening. Her father could have told her that he had gone through the same thing countless times, but most of his mistakes had been in summer stock or somewhere other than Broadway. In the back of her mind she knew this, but she was sometimes too willing a victim of circumstance: she had really asked for this sort of thing. She was already a star, having to mature on Broadway and in Hollywood in full view of everyone. She tried to seem calmer than everyone else, for she had her father's composure under fire, but she leaned more than ever on Andreas for emotional support. Yet some panic already was appearing in Andreas's eyes. He lost his temper more frequently and dressed down the crew more often than usual. In midproduction, when everything was going to pieces, he tried to convince himself that there would be a miracle, that in the end all would be well.

There was no thaw between Jane and her father before *The Fun Couple* opened. Backstage at the Lyceum Theatre in New York on opening night, October 26, 1962, Jane received flowers from Peter signed "from your admiring brother" but nothing, not even a telegram, from Hank. Hank's separation from Afdera was moving into the divorce courts. He had waited for nearly a year for her to come to her senses, but she hadn't. Jane was profoundly hurt by the silence but she had more urgent matters to worry about. She blocked out some of her fear by making horrible faces at herself

110

in the mirror, pulling her ample mouth into an idiot's grimace with her fingers.

When Andreas looked into the dressing room to wish her well, she noticed that he was as pale as death and said, "You're nervous!" He answered with a laugh like the fusillade from a machine gun. She countered with an old Bette Davis line, "What a dump!" It was gallows chatter. But then she smoothed out her feelings and said, "I was nervous before. Now I'm not."

When the curtain rose and Jane finally appeared, she got a bigger hand (possibly for past achievements and for her famous name) than she ever had on the road. But as the play continued, a number of people walked out, including the playwright Edward Albee. Jane spotted one or two of them as they moved toward the back, not seeming to care whether they were seen or not. Andreas came back between the acts to declare to Jane, "You were marvelous!" but his eyes already looked desperate. Dyan Cannon ducked in to say of Jane's performance so far, "Did you hear the laughs she got?" Dyan was almost convincing, but Jane, bewildered now by the audience's reaction, said, "I don't think they dug it." Being in a show that is sinking right in front of hundreds of spectators is a little like going down in a ship before a crowd gathered to watch the tragedy from a nearby pier. They can't help you, not even by throwing you a line. You have to pretend you're not in a death agony and smile and wink on cue and utter the playwright's banal lines as though they were Shaw's or Wilde's wittiest.

The ritual producers' party was held at Sardi's after the opening, and when Jane came in on Andreas's arm, there was a minute or two of applause from everyone in the theatrical restaurant. Jane made an exaggerated little nod of the head as though she had just bowed in a smash and was the talk of New York. Andreas's face said everything: hooded eyes half closed as though to shut out the sight of the party; head up and nosrils flaring. Jane declined to wait for the reviews, and everyone of course understood.

111

Walter Kerr of the New York *Herald Tribune*, whom Jane considered to be the wisest newspaper critic in town and whom she respected the most (she still clung to many of her father's opinions), wrote: "I find it impossible to believe that *The Fun Couple* ever went out of town. If they'd gone out of town, they'd have closed it." Jane was reading this as Andreas joined her, and she looked up, stunned. When the documentary crew asked Kerr to expand on his comment for their cameras, he said, "If you asked me for a list of the five worst plays of all time, *The Fun Couple* would be on it."

In her dressing room the next night, Jane wept. The Shubert management, having digested the reviews and the box-office take of $140 for future performances, was throwing them out of the theater, so their producer was closing the show that night. In the postmortem afterward, Jane said, "Having been through an experience like this, should the same kind of script appear, I wouldn't do it. The script [play] has to be there." Andreas admitted that he went too deeply into the characters "and I get fascinated by the character. . . . I would have done the same thing today. I don't know any other way."

Clinging to Andreas now was surely an act of defiance on Jane's part. He had been almost mortally hurt by this failure, but Jane felt profound loyalty; she knew, too, that he respected her talent and her humanity. Possibly he even saw in her a future Bernhardt. After the ignominy of not being sent another script to direct on Broadway, Andreas saw several arriving every day for Jane, for both stage and screen. She was going up, up, up, and nothing could hurt her or stop her, neither *In the Cool of the Day* nor *The Fun Couple*. Andreas was not surprised by the durability of her stardom and he adjusted to all of that even though some of his old swagger disappeared for a time. He became a background person in Jane's life, and they continued to live together and he continued to coach her in everything she did. If Jane had second thoughts about Andreas, no one around them ever heard them articulated. The one

112

thing that runs through all of this chronicle is that Jane Fonda is basically a *nice* person. If she befriends you, you will doubtless remain her friend; she is considered by everyone who knows her as "quite a dame." But lovers are always vulnerable, and because Andreas was more than a friend, that relationship could change.

In February Jane was cast as Madeline Arnold in the Actors Studio production of Eugene O'Neill's *Strange Interlude*. The company of stars in that revival was overwhelming: Geraldine Page as Nina Leeds, Betty Field, Pat Hingle, William Prince, Franchot Tone, Ben Gazzara and, in the role of the young boy, a former dancer named Richard Thomas, whom Jane and Andreas had recommended to the director José Quintero. Thomas would go on to stardom in television as John-Boy in *The Waltons*, which became one of the most popular family-oriented series despite its being set in the heart of the Great Depression, and in a much-praised television production of Stephen Crane's *The Red Badge of Courage*.

Strange Interlude won the Pulitzer Prize for O'Neill in 1928, mainly for its daring in presenting its characters' innermost thoughts through supposedly unheard monologues that preface much of the dialogue. It was called "stream-of-consciousness" drama, although it was not quite as deep and inchoate as that would suggest; rather it revealed the honest feelings and thoughts of the character in counterpoint to the direct dialogue delivered to the face of another character, which was usually hypocritical. One of the least hypocritical of the characters is nineteen-year-old Madeline Arnold, who is engaged to handsome, athletic Gordon Evans, the son and love child of strong but cantankerous Nina Leeds, who plans to sabotage the forthcoming marriage by revealing to Gordon who his real father was. This four-hour drama has nine acts, and Madeline doesn't appear until the eighth. Madeline is described by O'Neill as pretty . . . with dark hair and eyes. Her skin is deeply tanned, her figure tall and athletic. . . . Her personality is direct and frank. She gives the impression of a person who always knows exactly what she is after and generally gets it, but is also generous and a good loser, a good sport who is popular with her own sex as well as sought after by men.

In its description of Jane it was eerily prophetic back in 1927, when it was written. The dialogue, too, as well as the "stream-of-consciousness" reflections were all in Jane's idiom. It was unfortunate that the play had to be given on a limited-run basis because it was top-heavy with stars, all of whom, including Jane, had commitments looming ahead.

Jane was with Andreas when word of the shooting of President John F. Kennedy was announced. They felt the same chill that they had experienced coming out of that movie house in Paris when they saw the headlines about Marilyn Monroe. With Kennedy's death later that day, November 22, 1963, Jane, like so many millions of others, grieved and felt ashamed for her country. Andreas, who rarely watched television, sat in front of the set watching that strange chapter in history played out, including the shooting of Oswald. Like most Europeans, he believed that it was all a complicated conspiracy from the very beginning. Jane was less skeptical then, but she was inclined to agree.

In late 1963, all three Fondas were starring in films—Jane in the movie version of *Sunday in New York*, Hank in Franklin Schaffner's production of Gore Vidal's *The Best Man*, and Peter had begun preproduction work on Robert Rossen's study of schizophrenia, *Lilith*, which was mostly to be shot in the East. One weekend they were reunited in New York on an East Side street where Jane was shooting a scene from her movie. In a publicity photo taken of them together between movie setups, Hank's eyes, a mirror to his feelings despite his stolidity, look upon his two movie-star progeny with considerable wonder and even surprise.

Lilith's star, Jean Seberg,* and Jane were almost exactly the same age and came to prominence at about the same time. There the comparison ends, for Jane was totally oblivious to the camera and seemed completely natural in front of it, while Miss Seberg, defensively it would appear, distanced herself from the eye of the camera—not physically but emotionally. She was at her best only in films where the attitude or point of view of the filmmaker is stronger than the story, as in her first French film, *Breathless*, which she did for Jean-Luc Godard in 1959. The Godard film, about a Bogartlike petty gangster (played by Jean-Paul Belmondo), made Seberg a heroine of the French New Wave, which had swept Godard, François Truffaut, Claude Chabrol, Alain Resnais and Roger Vadim to international success. Older French directors such as René Clément attempted to become a part of it, and often succeeded. Among the New Wave's technical contributions to the language of film were, first, the extensive use of the hand-held camera, of which Godard was to become so fond, giving the viewer a slight seasickness until stabilizers were invented some years later; second, the freeze frame, which was introduced with chilling success at the end of Truffaut's *The 400 Blows*, when the young boy runs toward the water, away from all the hurt of the world, sees that great liquid barricade and turns to face the camera in anguish; third, grainy film quality, giving scenes a look of immediacy and reality as though shot by a newsreel camera; and fourth, digressive sequences, freeing the filmmaker from telling a story in the old straightforward style, which was anathema to someone like Alain Resnais.

*Like Jane, Jean Seberg was subjected to prolonged harassment by the FBI because of her involvement with liberal causes. Stories were planted by the FBI that she was made pregnant by a member of the Black Panthers. The stillborn baby was white.

Vadim was the least intellectual of them all, and he used the techniques of the New Wave to display his latest protégée in a drama of sinful intrigue. Unlike those of the others, his films are in the mainstream of commercial international cinema. He would become more interested in staging the love scene than in showing us the psyche of his principal characters; two of his films, however, would qualify as New Wave classics: *Les Liaisons Dangereuses* (1961)* and *The Game Is Over*, with Jane Fonda in 1967.

Considerable effort was made in Hollywood to adapt the New Wave style to the big studios' product, but it always failed because the French methods were antithetical to the big-studio way of doing things. Jane, unlike Seberg, was bright and scintillating onscreen but impressed few offscreen as being an original thinker. Seberg, who was married for a number of years to the novelist Romain Gary,† held her own in the company of filmmakers, writers and philosophers, and was probably too intellectual to be a fine actress. Some months after Jane received her second Academy Award, Jean Seberg committed suicide in Paris.

Jane's relationship with Andreas was now in serious trouble: conversations about the future were strained and usually avoided altogether. While she had become an international star, Andreas was merely her drama coach and traveling companion. He sensed that a showdown was looming ahead, but he had no idea when it might come. Her new movie, *Joy House* (*Ni Saints, Ni Soufs*) was

---

**Les Liaisons Dangereuses* was not only a prime example of Roger Vadim's talent but also a historic scandal in literary and film circles. There was such public outrage at Vadim's proposal to update (set in 1960) one of France's most celebrated erotic classics, a long trial was instigated by the *Société des gens de lettres*. François Mitterrand, now President of France, represented Vadim and won for him and for others who followed the right to revamp a classic on the screen.

†Romain Gary failed to recover from the shock of his ex-wife's suicide and killed himself sixteen months after her death.

to be made by René Clément, the veteran French director whose *The Damned* (1948), *Forbidden Games* (1952), and *Gervaise* (1957) had made him a master of the French screen nearly on a level with René Clair. *Joy House* was meant to be a thriller, but something happened to the script on its way to the screen very similar to what happened to *In the Cool of the Day:* all meaning was drained out of it.

Jane's costar was Alain Delon, who had risen to prominence two years earlier with *Rocco and His Brothers*. Delon had become a gossip-sheet favorite because of his occasional involvement with the French underworld; he was far too beautiful to be called handsome, and yet many women melted at the sight of him. Off camera, Delon had a huge reputation as a Lothario. Jane was usually drawn to men with perfect features—Timmy and Andreas come to mind, despite their slight builds—and now here she was cast opposite a man who was simply gorgeous. During the film Delon and Jane began a flirtation that Andreas observed. When the friendship seemed to be growing closer, a long and impassioned dispute between Delon and his girlfriend, actress Romy Schneider, followed. Before the production was over, Andreas and Jane had their own confrontation. The argument made him physically ill; he told her that he no longer could continue as her coach, and he flew back to New York.

PART VI

Enter Vadim

15

With Andreas gone Jane was free, freer than she had been since before she met Timmy. The break had been clean; she thought the wounds would heal. Yet it was a very unnatural state for her, and she needed a man in her life.

The director Roger Vadim was preparing a new film production of Arthur Schnitzler's *La Ronde*. This would be at least its third film incarnation, and the producers, the brothers Robert and Raymond Hakim, wanted Jane for the role of the unfaithful young woman. Jane had first met Vadim during her year in Paris in 1957. "It was at Maxim's," she recalled. "At the time he was with his wife Annette Stroyberg." He had had no more luck with women than had Jane's father. Following his divorce from Stroyberg, he had lived with the lovely Catherine Deneuve, billed by her television sponsor, Chanel, as the "most beautiful woman in the world." Vadim had children by both women, although none by his first wife, Brigitte Bardot.

Vadim was born in Paris in 1928 of White Russian parents, Igor and Marie-Antoinette Plemiannikov. As a small boy, he saw his father, fatally stricken with heart failure at the dinner table, fall facedown into a bowl of soup. As a man, he saw a horse crash through the windshield of his car, nearly killing his cameraman, while the horse limped away. In films, he had something of a scandalous reputation; offscreen, no man could be more charming. Far from being a beautiful man like Delon, his features were on the rough side, and except for his speech and dress he could pass easily for a coal miner or a French peasant. His voice was his most attractive asset, with a wide range of emotions and timbres, and his speech was that of a thinking man, far more serious than his movies would suggest. Vadim had tried to get Jane a year or so earlier for a film, *Angélique, Marquise des Anges*, but she had asked her agents to cable a refusal. Vadim writes that he is convinced she did this because

> Jane believed in my reputation as a cynical debauch-ee, an ogre lusting after virgin flesh, a diabolical magician who, unlike the alchemists, transformed precious metal into lead, roses into thorns.

But now Jane agreed to meet with him at the home of her agent in France, Olga Horstig. She went out of great curiosity. From a commercial point of view, Vadim was the boldest of the younger filmmakers. In 1957 he had been embattled for months with cen-sors over *And God Created Woman*, starring his wife of the time, Brigitte Bardot. He was one of the first to use nudity as something unremarkable, but of course he knew that it was quite remarkable and would bring in millions to the box office. He was more of a showman than a director of significance, although he came close to the latter with *The Game Is Over* (1966), his version of Zola's *La Curée* (literal French translation "The Quarry"). Of that meeting, Vadim writes:

> For the second time in my life, I was to be the victim of that strange disease, love at first sight. . . . From the very first symptom—three to ten seconds after direct contamination—you know you are lost. Some people become absolute fools, others outstand-ingly brilliant. Blind optimism alternates with irra-tional anxiety, without any transition. . . . In most cases, your sexual powers melt away without warn-ing at the most inopportune moment.

Jane was not altogether reassured, although she was pleasantly surprised to find that he was a civilized man who could be charming. She telephoned him before going to bed that night to say that she would accept the role in *La Ronde*.

After several days and evenings of sparring and avoidance on the set of Jane's movie, where they were winding up the luckless *Joy House*, she approached him in quite a different way:

> Someone had told Jane that I was there. The door opened, and Jane, out of breath, wearing a raincoat that she had not taken the time to button, ran into the room and stopped short, embarrassed at making her love so obvious, and then walked toward us. Her chest was heaving, her hair—just arranged by the studio stylist—had gotten wet and messed up in the courtyard, her skin was flushed under her makeup. She was beautiful and sensitive and vulnerable and divine. That evening we returned from Epinay to Paris together so that we would not have to leave each other.

Vadim writes up the scene much like a screenplay, describing emotions, movements and costumes. And in a very profound way he was to become the scenarist of Jane's life drama for the next half dozen years.

Vadim had done the same with three other women, all eventually screen actresses. Bardot was a girl when they met, much under the control of her parents; he waited until she was eighteen and then charmed the family into consenting to their marriage. By his shrewd exploitation of her sexuality, he was to help make her the symbol of the dawning age of sexual liberation. Then he had married Annette Stroyberg, who was not an actress but who, he insists, demanded to be starred in the movie *Les Liaisons Dangereuses*. Finally, just before he met Jane, he had broken with the beautiful Catherine Deneuve, or she had broken with him.

Jane, still unformed as a screen actress, could fit neatly into the role of sex goddess with the master molder of such images not only in love with her but anxious to share her with the world.

It is doubtless an unconscious thing with Vadim, but most of his affairs and marriages had to culminate in nearly total exposure of the beloved, both literally and figuratively, to the masses. In France, Vadim was enormously popular and highly successful. Jane may have felt uncomfortable at first with his circle of friends, but she trusted success.

16

Jane spent the winter of 1963–64 in Paris, filming Vadim's *La Ronde* and *The Love Cage*, and leased an elegant flat on the rue Séguier. Vadim moved in. Throughout their relationship, which would last over six years, Vadim tended to live in places provided by Jane. It was a pattern that had begun with Timmy and then Andreas and continued after the Vadim marriage fell apart—with her second husband, Tom Hayden.

The extent of Jane's modesty was ventilated in the French press for days while she was shooting *La Ronde*. Was she nude or wasn't she? "I am supposedly nude in bed," Jane said, "but I wear a bra and panties. There were ninety-five people on the set and I'd be embarrassed even though it would be what the role called for. I simply didn't do the role in the nude. I never did and never will do a completely nude scene." Later, Jane revised her code of dress, or undress, on the screen and appeared nude in a number of films, when nearly all actresses were doing their bedroom scenes that way. Vadim was able to reform her notions of propriety during their years together.

La Ronde was not a great success. Jane played the role of the married woman, which Danielle Darrieux had made her own permanently when an earlier film version of the Schnitzler play was produced. The Vadim film was eventually promoted in America as *The Circle of Love*, and a huge billboard showed Jane nude with her bottom as prominent as her face. She sued to have it removed from the DeMille Theatre building, but before the case was settled she had married Vadim so the matter was allowed to die.

There was a sober side to Vadim, who sometimes experienced the

> phenomenon of disembodiment. . . . From the age of thirteen, I have occasionally experienced an odd feeling of being in two places at once. For a short time, I had "double sight." It was in Paris in 1945 that I "saw" myself for the first time. . . . I woke up one morning with a feeling of extreme heaviness. . . . With great difficulty I managed to sit up on the edge of my bed. . . . I had been sleeping without pajamas. It was then that I very clearly "saw" the back of my neck and my back.

All of this led Vadim to look upon psychic occurrences with less skepticism than the average person, but it did not make him religious; he considered himself an "enlightened agnostic."

With Jane Vadim tried, successfully for a time, to live two disparate lives. With his backers and some other film people, including most of his friends, he was still rakishly the bold sexual pioneer, but with Jane he was mostly serious and pliant. He was a genius at anticipating a woman's moods, but then he had lived among women nearly all of his life. They shared a great passion for art, and spent much of their free time in museums. Jane began collecting religious triptychs, and since she was now acquiring possessions she decided that she needed a permanent place to house them; so for the first time in her adult life she looked for a home base. There was an old ruined farmhouse at Marchefroy, twenty-five miles outside Paris near St. Ouen, that seemed just right. She bought it and a great deal of her ready cash began flowing into its restoration; within about six months she was able to move in. "It's wonderful," she said, enchanted as much with the status of homeownership as with the old farmhouse itself, which she described as "kind of an ochre color outside." But she denied that Vadim was to be her live-in companion. "The only roommate I'm going to have is an otter. I'm not going to settle down for a long time."

It would seem that the farmhouse was also intended to create some breathing space around Jane to keep her from getting too involved with Vadim; it provided a retreat for her. He would come for days at a time and then be sent back to Paris, where he still lived in their apartment in the rue Séguier. It is likely that the first to begin speaking of marriage as a *desirable* thing was Vadim, who may have been afraid that he would lose her otherwise. One can appreciate her indecision. In the years ahead, when Jane began speaking out for women's liberation, she often said that she knew from her own experience what men expected of women. She knew by then that Vadim was a master exploiter of her sex; he seemed to have a patent on it. But he had taken that first big step toward liberating the screen. That nearly redeemed him, and of course it made him as famous in France as Jane. He had become one of the few directors who were celebrities of interest to the scandal press and the paparazzi. He was also compromised by commercialism: the bankers behind his films were no visionaries, so the women in his movies were tied to the past, when not to the bed.

At St. Ouen, Jane was her own woman. It was for Vadim to decide if she was being merely willful, as Bardot had become, or a woman fighting to retain her own identity. Vadim had to be far more pliable with Jane than with any of the previous women in his life. As an unmarried lover, his position in Jane's life was tenuous at best; he didn't seem to like all the freedom she gave him. Possibly both Vadim and his friend Christian Marquand spoke privately with Jane about his unhappiness, or it could have been Bardot, who was so often dashing out to St. Ouen for an afternoon or even overnight. Bardot and Jane got on well together, although Brigitte had that insecurity about her appearance ("I'm not pretty today") which Jane had been able to throw off years

127

earlier. There were also visits by his daughter Nathalie (from the marriage to Stroyberg), whose affection Jane succeeded in winning.

In August, President Johnson persuaded the American Congress to pass the Tonkin Gulf Resolution, following the attack on two United States destroyers by North Vietnamese torpedo boats. It would later be documented that the President had sanctioned a long period of secret bombing on North Vietnam and the torpedo boat attack had been provoked by heavy North Vietnamese losses. What would happen in the wake of the Tonkin Gulf Resolution would be a legitimizing of the war and a major land offensive involving finally more than half a million American troops. There would be saturation bombing of Hanoi and other cities, total defoliation of arable land areas, and the near-destruction of the entire countryside. Yet in the end the war was still lost. There was some conversation about it in Jane's living room and much criticism of America, but Jane was slow in awakening to the critical nature of the war. Like most Americans abroad, she was quick to defend her homeland.

There were two friends of Vadim's who seemed to understand Jane better than the others, a couple called the Vaillands. Roger Vailland was a screenwriter and a member of the French Communist Party. Vadim writes of Vailland:

> An analytical person, he used his sharp intellect and elegant language as the springboard to emotional abandon. Vailland loved coldly with great warmth. He would plunge into the untidy world of adventure, but he took with him an ordered universe that obeyed his own rules. He had codified all the elements of passion in order to enjoy it without losing control.

Vadim loved to speak in paradoxes, a trait that is evident here. Among Vadim's free-swinging friends Vailland was apparently a sobering force who remained calm amid bedlam, and Jane must have valued his friendship highly, while he lived. His wife, and very soon his widow, Elizabeth Vailland, became Jane's closest friend. The Vaillands were the first bridge that Jane had to cross to become a committed person involved with social injustice.

Vadim's closest male friend was the actor Christian Marquand, who had married Tina Aumont, daughter of the actor Jean-Pierre Aumont. While Jane joined Vadim's circle in smoking pot and apparently got some satisfaction from it, some of them were into harder drugs. Since the drug culture was already far advanced in America and had swept her own brother into its foggy midst, Jane tried not to be unnerved by its presence in her company, and she could always light up a joint to be congenial. In Hollywood, Peter was experimenting with LSD and other hallucinogens. He lived a hippie-style existence with Susan and their two children up in the Hollywood hills; frequently in trouble in the past, now he seemed to have smoothed everything out with chemicals. It was the greatest of ironies that Jane, who thought she had matured and had life fully in control, was echoing in France in her bohemian set—purely by chance and certainly not by choice—the coda of the nineteen-sixties, "Drugs will save the world." Occasionally, she would put her foot down, and Christian's brother, Serge, who seemed more involved with the new culture than anyone, would get quite annoyed.

Jane wanted a break from all this, and she proposed a visit to Vadim's native land, Russia; having grown up during the cold war, Jane wanted to see what this great enemy of capitalist society was really like. They flew from Le Bourget in an Ilyushin turbojet. They were there on the last day of April 1964, when the Muscovites were preparing for their great May Day celebration. At midnight an extraordinary roar and rumble made them run to their hotel balcony to look out. Hundreds of Russian tanks and armored trucks were rolling by, gathering for the huge parade in the morning. The noise was deafening, and Jane turned pale, threw herself on the bed, and buried her head in her arms. Vadim said, "The idea of war had hit her as a reality." But after all that display of might, the next day people from all over the Soviet Union paraded in brightly colored costumes; there were musicians and dancers; fathers carrying children; pretty girls smiling at the crowd. "It looks like a hippie holiday," Jane told Vadim, smiling broadly herself now. During that visit she learned that movie houses were crowded at ten in the morning (Russians *did* have leisure time!). Finally, as she got to know the Russian people better, she realized that she had been lied to back home about the Soviet Union. It may have been the first small step toward her political awakening.

At the end of August, Jane and Vadim were with other film people at their favorite playground, St. Tropez, which Vadim took partial credit for making popular with his colleagues. Life there was far more relaxed than in any American beach community, including the Hamptons. Here the drug culture moved from private living rooms onto the beach, and inhibitions could be socially disastrous. Jane and Vadim had come to a decision there, however, that seemed most extraordinary. After more than a year of talking against it, both parties had decided that they must get married. Or, as is more likely, Vadim finally sold Jane on the idea. Hank was contacted and seemed to be in favor of it, and Jane told the press that she and Vadim would be married on September 20 if her father was able to get to Europe in time for the ceremony. Hank was then completing a thankless role in a dreadful war epic. *The Battle of the Bulge* (1965), which was being shot in Cinerama, a three-camera process meant to give the illusion of three dimensions. He did not get to France for a September wedding, and by that time Jane was already back in America, unmarried, shooting a new movie.

17

In the summer of 1964 Jane was considering a role in a very dubious venture. *Cat Ballou*, a Western by Roy Chanslor, had been around for some time, but until Harold Hecht decided to produce it no one had had the courage to tackle this parody of dime novels. A Western satire is a rare thing, and a successful one had not been seen in years. Even new directors fought shy of the project, including Sydney Pollack, who had come to Hollywood from television that year; but Pollack recommended a television colleague of his, Elliot Silverstein. Silverstein is a soft-spoken, attractive Bostonian who looks and even at times acts like a meticulous and rather fussy professor. (He has a master's degree from Yale.) Appearances deceive: behind the mask of an academic is that rare bird in Hollywood, a man of genuine wit, which combined with an equally deceptive droll manner allowed Silverstein, the unknown quantity at Columbia Pictures, to take extraordinary risks.

Jane, too, was ready for a departure or at least a break from the sexy romps that were creating an image quite different from the one she had planned. She thought that the script by Walter Newman and Frank Pierson was marvelous, and after a chat with Silverstein she felt that they could bring it all off. Silverstein was initially struck by Jane's intelligence, but he had some misgivings about her Actors Studio background. While he had seen some of her films and was aware of her capabilities, he was to say:

131

Well, I have to tell you that that background was one of my first concerns. While devoted to a naturalistic style of acting, the Actors Studio training had often resulted in a self-conscious, subjective, neurotic actor—always "playing in terms of himself." Sometimes that becomes difficult for a director to deal with in a comedy where much of the performance depends on objective timing and rhythm. But I decided that in a comedy which intends to go "off the wall," there should be *a center core of credibility*. There must be something the audience can recognize and hang on to, and Katherine Ballou's mission (to avenge her father's death with the help of her ragtag gang), however silly it might seem, might make some use of the training in the naturalistic school [Jane's training with Strasberg]. If I could help her keep her performance light but *realistic*, the other characters around Cat Ballou could bubble, effervesce or even fall on their faces, but the center would remain credible.

Lee Marvin, the growling, squint-eyed baddie of a dozen Westerns as well as the second lead in many other miscellaneous films, was given the dual roles of Kid Shelleen and the silver-nosed villain, Jim Strawn. The casting was an actor's dream. As Shelleen, Marvin would play a comic drunk through much of the film, a washed-up gunfighter who can't hit the broad side of a barn; when Shelleen is brought in to protect her father the poor man is shot and killed almost within spitting distance of him.

Much of the film was to be shot in Colorado and at the Columbia ranch. Vadim accompanied Jane to the location and they made a colorful pair. As one in the company remembers it: "There was the Frenchman in horn-rimmed glasses reading *Mad* magazine, all by himself, sitting on a camp chair on the mountainside. They weren't standoffish. They joked around with everyone. He's a friendly guy." Between takes Jane and Vadim chatted in French. She seemed totally absorbed in him and obviously very much in love.

Silverstein recalled that after the production, back in

Hollywood, Jane, Vadim and he went to dinner at Chasen's, and the subject of marriage came up, as it seemed to do frequently around Jane:

Vadim said he thought it was an unnecessary burden to put upon a relationship and she agreed with him. Vadim said, "If we were to get married, that would change everything." I think I was a little envious of him because I was a little excited by her. . . . I asked her once [to go out] and that's how I found out that she was involved with Vadim.

No one involved with the film had any notion that they were making a big commercial success. On the contrary, the producer and the director were constantly being reminded by the front office at Columbia of the risks they were taking. These reminders often took the form of minor carping; Lee Marvin's fingernails, the editors said, were too clean. The major fear, and it was one shared by the whole *Cat Ballou* company, was that Marvin's performance was too far out to be acceptable. Silverstein comments:

Lee Marvin's character was a walk out to the edge of space. All of the actors and I had to try and find a style of presentation into which the hyperbole of the Kid Shelleen character would fit believably.

Jane, Mickey Callan and Dwayne Hickman commit the train robbery, then jump off the train and roll in the dirt. Well, we did this by having stuntmen jump off the train and then have the principals roll into the shot. I made them do the shot half a dozen times. When we were up to the fifth or sixth take, Jane went through the action exactly as required and not once did she say, "This is ridiculous."

Often the producer would be whispering in my ear, a kind of Roy Cohn syndrome* on his part. He maintained that the first seven takes were wonderful,

---

* Roy Cohn was counsel to Senator Joe McCarthy's subcommittee during McCarthy's infamous witch-hunt. Cohn was frequently seen whispering in McCarthy's ear and vice versa.

that the company was a half day behind schedule and I would lose my job if I didn't print the next take. I then asked Lee to play the part for sympathy, not comedy—to make me feel for him and his helplessness. Take eight provided the basis for the performance that won him his Oscar.

Silverstein was much impressed by Jane's lack of vanity. When other actresses came on the set there was always an extra eyelash to be fixed, but while Jane, "a stunningly beautiful woman," may have cared very much how she looked before the cameras rolled, "she never took the time away from the production."

There was in Jane, too, the same fiercely protected private self that her father had. When Silverstein intruded upon something she had worked out and seemed about to change it, a little invisible gate would come down that warned, "That you don't touch." This happened a few times to the director because, as he recalls:

> You'd only know what might provoke that when you got there. But if it hadn't been for that great integrity, evident throughout her performance, I don't think that the film would have provided the opportunity that it did for everyone else. I think she deserves now what she's got. She's worked hard in the vineyards.

Jane also would try something in a scene and then stop, saying, "No. I don't believe that." In these instances, she turned out to be right far more often than not.

The role of Kid Shelleen in particular changed Lee Marvin's professional life completely; no longer was he the first actor considered for a macho badman. *Cat Ballou* made him a superstar commanding a fee as large as any leading man in films this side of Marlon Brando. Marvin moved from this comedy into one of the several top male roles in *Ship of Fools* (1965), a film more prestigious than good. And, not least, Marvin won an Academy Award for *Cat Ballou*. Whether he was aware of it or not, Marvin won that award because of Jane. As Silverstein puts it:

> He played off a foundation that she supplied. She was a workhorse. It's hard to supply the means by which others have all the fun. . . . She had to hold it all together, which she did without any question. As we look back on it now, it was another story of a woman against the male world, I suppose.

The essential story was the old one of saving the ranch from the malevolent forces surrounding it, except that this time the rescuer was not a stalwart young cowboy but a young woman, Katherine Ballou. When she arrives, she sees that her father's ranch is in a state of siege by the baddies, including a black-hatted, black-suited hired gun named Jim Strawn (also played by Marvin) whose fair-sized nose was bitten off in a fight and has been replaced by a silver one.

Cat hired her own gunfighter, Kid Shelleen, whom she has never seen but who has done considerable terrorizing of his own in the past. She sends Shelleen an advance payment of fifty dollars, but she feels all is lost when he is dumped from a stage-coach near her father's property dead drunk. Before the Kid has much of a chance to do more than hoist a few fifths of booze, Cat's father is murdered in cold blood by Strawn.

Cat, in a rage and half crazed by grief, takes out after Strawn, and shortly Kid Shelleen follows, along with the rest of her father's hands. They trace Strawn into Wolf City, where they find he is in league with the sheriff. First she tells them in womanly outrage, "You won't make me cry," but then, shoulders squared as any leader's should be, she declares: "You tell Wolf City I'm going to make Sherman's march to the sea look like a bird walk!"

Thrown off her land by the sheriff's deputies, Cat and her gang become outlaws. They hold a conference to decide just which crime might do the most harm to

135

the Wolf City establishment. The men propose that they rustle fifty head of cattle, but Cat vetoes that. She wants to rob a train. Once aboard their train, all seems very uncertain until Kid Shelleen in a sort of hiccough of his old toughness persuades the baggage-car man to remember the safe combination. Their haul is enormous—thousands of dollars.

Now all Wolf City is in full cry after them on the way to their hideout. The Kid is ready to stick it out to the end, but Cat says in the voice of a frightened young girl, "I don't want to die!" She does herself up as an elegant call girl named Trixie and calls on Sir Harry Percival, the real owner of Wolf City, in his private railway car. After she gets him excited, she pulls a gun on him and orders him to sign a confession that he hired gunman Jim Strawn, who has just been killed in a high noon shootout by Kid Shelleen (who acknowledges that they were brothers). Sir Harry struggles with her for the gun and is killed by accident.

Cat is jailed for the murder of Sir Harry and sentenced to be hanged. The sheriff complains: "You took the bread out of half of the mouths of Wolf City by killing Sir Harry." A phony pastor arrives to lead her to the gallows through a jeering mob; he is in league with others to save her and off she rides or, as "The Ballad of Cat Ballou," a refrain sung at intervals throughout the movie, expresses it:

> So Cat rode into history—
> That's how her legend grew.

The film utilizes the ballad as a sort of jukebox Greek chorus, and we see the singers on the scene, Nat "King" Cole and Stubby Kaye. They also had Lady Liberty with her torch, the logo of Columbia Pictures, turn into a two-gun fast-shooting cowgirl at the beginning.

Cat Ballou became Jane's first great success, with *Time* magazine once again perceiving just what she contributed to the film:

In a performance that nails down her reputation as a girl worth singing about, Actress Fonda does every preposterous thing demanded of her with a giddy sincerity that is at once beguiling, poignant and hilarious. Wearing widow's weeds over her six guns, she romps through one of the zaniest train robberies ever filmed, a throwback to Pearl White's perilous heyday.

The comedy was a trailblazer, proving that when all of the elements were right, a Western need not be serious. Silverstein was nominated by the Directors Guild as Best Director of the Year, and, as expected, he was inundated by a flood of all the funny Westerns that had been gathering dust on studio shelves over the years. He was never sure that Jane was aware of her crucial contribution to the film, "whether she realizes or acknowledges to herself that the straight line that she maintains through the picture not only held all of the elements together but provided a kind of stable base for all the other wild activities that were taking place."

18

Arthur Penn, who staged *Two for the Seesaw* with such delicacy and success, is best known in films for his elegiac direction of *Bonnie and Clyde* (1967) and the powerful drama by William Gibson of Helen Keller and Annie Sullivan, *The Miracle Worker* (1962). Like most directors, he has had his share of failures: his two most disastrous movies were *The Chase* (1966) and his muddled inexplicable *The Missouri Breaks* (1976); the films were exactly ten years apart and both starred Marlon Brando.

By far the better of these two fiascos was *The Chase*. Produced by Sam Spiegel, who in 1954 had supervised an earlier Brando success, *On the Waterfront*, it was meant to be a strong contemporary drama with social overtones. The latter were written into her screenplay by the playwright Lillian Hellman, working from a Horton Foote novel and play. The target of the movie was Texas provincialism and vigilantism.

The cast surrounding Jane was top-heavy with expensive stars—Robert Redford, Angie Dickinson, E. G. Marshall, James Fox, Miriam Hopkins, Janice Rule and Robert Duvall. The fees paid to these people made this picture worthy of the Spiegel imprimatur, since in combination they cost about as much as his 1957 spectacular *Bridge on the River Kwai*.

Once again Jane was playing a small-town and small-time girl of little virtue, the faithless wife of worthless Bubber Reeves (Robert Redford). Brando played the local sheriff, who stands up to the local vigilantes and yahoos who form a lynch mob to find Bubber, a prison escapee wrongfully accused of killing a man during his flight to freedom. Brando, stalwart to the end, is mercilessly beaten in his own jailhouse by the leading male citizens of the Texas town. Horton Foote's Broadway play had been worked into the fabric of the story along with his novel, and he must have felt that they had inflated his small gem of a drama into an overblown movie with a message. Compounding the failure, it has been directed in an obvious, derivative way; Bubber Reeves is brought to the jailhouse through a mob of mindless town folk, sterotypes all, to be gunned down on the steps by a local assassin whose sawed-off shotgun is concealed in his coat sleeve. He wears a felt hat in the style of the killer of Lee Harvey Oswald and the entire murder scene is so close to the Dallas courthouse killing as to be totally offensive. It was Hellman's worst screenplay since *The North Star* in 1943, which was intended as a tribute to America's great wartime ally, the Soviet Union. For Jane, it was a setback despite her fine performance. She was caught in the downward spiral of Brando's career—all of his films made in the nineteen-sixties were failures—which would not turn upward again until *Last Tango in Paris* in 1973. Still Jane played Anna Reeves as a real human being, something of a feat under the circumstances, and Jane and Brando had one scene together when both actors brought the movie to sudden life as Brando tries to persuade Jane to bring Bubber in, with the help of her lover, Jake Rogers, played by James Fox, town scion and, oddly, Bubber's best friend.

While Jane was shooting *The Chase*, Peter was caught in yet another trauma: the suicide in Tucson of his best friend from his college years in Omaha, Eugene "Stormy" McDonald, a Zenith Radio Company heir who was found shot to death with slashed wrists. There was an inquest during which a coroner's jury agreed that young McDonald had killed himself "in the presence of person or persons unknown." The incident shook Peter profoundly. He later said:

139

There's never a day that I don't think about my best friend putting a bullet in his head. There's hardly a day I don't think about my mother cutting her throat. There's hardly a day that I don't realize this girl [Bridget Hayward] whom I was in love with, and who was almost like my sister, took pills and did herself in. I have no sympathy anymore. Compassion. But no sympathy.

That summer also had been a trial period of complete togetherness for Jane and Vadim. She brought him to Malibu, where she had rented a small house—"an unexpected paradise," Vadim was to call it. He writes:

At that time she did not consider herself a traitor to feminism, and in spite of her career as an actress, she was in fact an extremely good homemaker. I never interfered, because I thought it was what she liked. And so she did, I believe, though a few years later she would refer with self-righteous indignation to her "housewife" period. I myself would have been very happy to live in a trailer, but this dream existence she created for me to live was even more agreeable, and I saw no reason to turn it down. Had I known, I would certainly have done something about it, as it was Jane I loved, much more than comfort and good cooking. I am still trying to find some indication that should have enabled me to guess the truth, but I honestly cannot find one.

At the house, Vadim was writing a screenplay for Jane to film when they returned to France that autumn. It was *The Game Is Over*, an adaptation of Zola's *La Curée*, and it would turn out surprisingly well.

In August they were both shaken by the explosion in the Los Angeles black ghetto known as Watts, which was burned and looted by its raging, frustrated inhabitants. It provoked an armed military attack against the beleaguered community: tanks rolled through the streets of Los Angeles, there was heavy gunfire and a shocking toll of dead and injured. Vadim drove into the middle of no-man's-land to rescue their black cook, Martha, as well as her children and some of her neighbor's. A member of the Malibu chapter of the John Birch Society telephoned the police to say that blacks were occupying the beach colony. Vadim said:

> The sheriff and his men burst into my house, revolvers drawn, in the best American detective-film tradition. After a lot of hard talking, I was allowed to keep the children with me until Watts returned to normal, on condition that I did not let them leave the house.

The Watts riots were only a part of a national outburst that destroyed sections of Newark, Detroit and eventually Washington, D.C. For reasons that had more to do with the sophistication and tolerance of New York City than with any sort of preparedness, the disturbances did not erupt in Harlem, the most famous black ghetto in the world. Jane was sickened and angered by what she saw on the television news, by the sound of gunfire she heard on her way home, and by Vadim's encounter with the local constabulary.

Jane married Roger Vadim in Las Vegas on August 14, 1965; they chartered a plane in Los Angeles and the wedding party flew over for the ceremony. The group was a revealing cross section of their different worlds: Jane brought along her brother Peter and his wife Susan, with Peter's closest friend, actor and director Dennis Hopper and his wife, Brooke Hayward, who had been Jane's childhood confidante; Jane's costar in *The Chase*, James Fox; actor Robert Walker, Jr., and his wife Ellie; her cousin, George Seymour; and her agent Dick Clayton. Hank Fonda was conspicuously absent, but he was deeply involved with rehearsals for his next Broadway play, *Generation*, which would open in early October. Vadim invited Christian Marquand, who was his best man, as well as Tina, Marquand's wife, the Italian journalist Oriana Fallaci and Vadim's mother, Mme. Marie-Antoinette Ardilouze, who was matron of honor.

The newlywed Vadims flew back to France to begin filming *La Curée*, which was being shot first on location in a small village in the South of France. Far more extensive a role than her restless wife in *La Ronde*, her Renée Saccard dominated the film, and Vadim had been given a large budget because of Jane's status. The camerawork by Claude Renoir was gorgeous, and the movie had a visual beauty quite unlike anything Vadim had done before. Now that he was concentrating on Jane in a film, Vadim made the discovery that "Jane thought she had no personality and was desperately trying to find her identity."

This is a shrewd analysis and seems to fit in with everything that Jane had said and done until then. What Vadim did not appear to realize was that *she didn't want to know who she was*. If this can be accepted as fact, the rest of what he found can be fully understood:

> In front of the camera she analyzed herself, shut herself away in introspection and looked for an intellectual justification for her every word, every movement, every smile. She was basically afraid of herself. This lack of self-esteem was her greatest weakness. She thought that through hard work she could "fabricate" a talent for herself, but refused to admit that she already had something unique, infinitely rarer and more precious than fortitude and willpower. . . . I knew that she was a born star and set about trying to give her confidence in her natural gifts.

Some of her contained rage was subsiding. Over the summer, back in Malibu, she had made an accommodation of sorts with her father. Hank and Vadim had met in the beach house and they got along well enough. She was no longer shy about appearing in the nude, and there would be several such scenes with her costar, Peter McEnery. She was now a married woman, so that particular conflict was behind her. As Renée, she would be playing yet another self-centered wife with adulterous urges—this time toward her stepson—but Vadim and his collaborators, Bernard Frechtman and Jean Cau, had managed to depict a true sensualist with enough sympathy to allow us to care about what she does.

At some point during each of her productions with Vadim, there would be an unpleasantness that may have been related to Vadim's commercialism, but in those days of their marriage Jane managed to find him blameless. On *La Ronde* there had been her bare-bottomed billboard, for which Vadim declared himself not responsible; now on *La Curée*, on a closed set during her nude scenes with McEnery, a photographer concealed himself above the camera setup and snapped dozens of pictures of the couple. *Playboy* magazine bought them and Jane, outraged, sued for twenty thousand dollars' damages. Finally, on *Barbarella*, Vadim asked Jane to appear nude behind the opening credits, which he assured her would cover her nudity, but when she first saw them she was visibly without a stitch.

Meanwhile the partnership with Vadim was working. Since Jane rarely relaxed, it was important that she live with or be married to someone involved in her work. She had not yet split herself in two—into the actress and the activist.

19

The black rage that scorched through America's cities in 1965 was the inevitable collision of two forces: the legislation known as the Civil Rights Act of 1964, pushed through Congress by President Lyndon Johnson, and those who had dominated American life for most of its history—the white American conservatives. The act seemed all-encompassing and put teeth into every piece of similar legislation passed earlier. Discrimination was outlawed in hotels, restaurants, theaters, public schools, buses, taxis and trains. People could be thrown into jail for breaking these laws and sometimes were.

It was not the first time that the federal government had attempted to force a change in public attitudes and behavior, but it was its strongest effort. Polarization took place immediately, with the blacks and their supporters at one end of the spectrum and the racists at the other. Until the Johnson bill only education had been policed by the government, enforcing the civil rights legislation passed during Eisenhower's administration. Now most Americans had to face the issue of civil rights, specifically black rights, head on. Black agitation and revolt were fomented by many and not by a handful of leaders, as had been the case in 1957 in Little Rock and in 1961 when Robert Kennedy as attorney general assured the blacks that he was their friend. By the mid-nineteen-sixties civil rights militants had moved North in the face of powerful and often invisible opposition. Despite all the legislated gains, Johnson's rights bill had not satisfied the blacks. Historically, legislation always trails pressures and demands.

Black pride surfaced, and Afro haircuts were much in vogue, worn both by blacks and by many whites. For a time banners were seen frequently above public gatherings, declaring: "Black is beautiful!" All of this agitation led the way for other oppressed groups to assert themselves—the gays, women's liberationists, the Indians, the Chicanos (Mexican-Americans), other Hispanics (mostly Puerto Ricans), and even the Italians, who felt that in many people's minds they were far too easily just lumped in with the Mafia.

In 1966 black militancy was given a name in Oakland, California, by twenty-four-year-old Huey P. Newton, a charismatic black man, the youngest of seven children, who until the founding with Bobby Seale of the Black Panthers was known only within his home community for his gift for oratory. Just after the party began its explosive history, Newton said:

> I think that before the Black Panther Party my life was very similar to that of most black people in the country. I'm from a lower-class, working-class family and I've suffered abuses of the power structure and I've responded as black people are responding now, so I see very little difference in my personality than any other black person living here in racist America.

Huey Newton seemed to have a becoming modesty. He also was well versed in revolutionary literature, especially Frantz Fanon's *The Wretched of the Earth*, the works of Chairman Mao Tse-tung, and Ché Guevara's *Guerrilla Warfare*. He believed in arming blacks for "self-defense" but he had no use at all for black militants who were out to "get whitey." In fact, the Black Panthers had been founded when Huey and Bobby Seale rejected this attitude, broke with an antiwhite group and created the

Panthers.* At the time Huey's path would not seem likely to cross that of Jane Fonda, but it did within a very short time.

In early autumn 1966 Jane arrived on location in Louisiana for the shooting of her next picture, *Hurry Sundown*, directed by Otto Preminger and based on a long novel about race relations in a small Southern town. The two black stars, Diahann Carroll and Robert Hooks, were immediately asked not to use the "white" swimming pool. When they ignored the request, Preminger was threatened with death and the local Ku Klux Klan "ordered" him to put the "niggers" in a run-down local hotel restricted to blacks. Jane and the rest of the cast told Preminger not to give into the Klan or they would stop work on the film. Preminger, who has been ahead of most other liberals in Hollywood in his abhorrence of any form of discrimination, did not have to be given an ultimatum. He proceeded with the production and hired special police to guard their motel and outdoor locations.

Vadim was especially concerned one day when he and Jane were walking in the street accompanied by a French photographer, Claude Azoulay. A little black boy ran up to her and gave her a flower, and Jane bent down and kissed him. "Then something very strange happened," writes Vadim: "People stopped and stared at us in silence. The atmosphere in the street, which only a moment before had been gay and full of life, became heavy and uncomfortable and vaguely threaten-

* Paradoxically among the Black Panthers' pronunciamentos was one demanding the immediate release of all black prisoners from every detention facility in America, calling these men victims of the white establishment. Among them were many confessed murderers, rapists and drug dealers whose release into society could only have aggravated the plight of the black American. This was one of several stands taken by the Panthers that eventually would turn Jane Fonda away from total commitment to the group, although she was always quick to point out that miniorities were victims of the system.

ing." Azoulay sensed the change in the atmosphere before either Vadim or Jane. "They don't seem to like you kissing blacks," he said. Jane laughed, still unconcerned, and told him, "Don't be silly. He's only a child." But an hour later the town sheriff walked onto the location nearby, intruding on a scene Preminger was shooting. The director began yelling at him in a fury, but the sheriff let him finish and then announced that he was ordering the whole film company out of the area for "their own safety." They were given half an hour to get out of town, and as they left two of their caravan's windshields were shattered by bullets.

Jane's role, Julie Ann Warren, was a thankless one. She is married to the dissolute, weak and alcoholic son (Michael Caine, an Englishman who made quite a convincing Southerner) of the richest man in town. Jane and Vadim's Malibu neighbor John Philip Law played the idealistic farm boy who comes home from the Army to join forces with an old buddy of his—a black man—on a neighboring farm. They are both sharecroppers, but their venture winds up disastrously because of the perfervid racism rampant in the community.

It was an unhappy episode for Jane quite apart from the local Klansmen. Preminger has always been a "strong" director who pulls performances from his players by force, if necessary. Since Jane had become a "strong" actress, with concepts about her role and characterization fully worked out before she ever began a scene, there was almost constant tension between them. If that were not enough, Preminger made a strenuous effort, which Vadim could appreciate if no one else did, to make the male-female relationships in the film as torrid as possible. It is made abundantly clear that Caine is often too drunk to be successful in bed and in the most blatant, overstated piece of symbolism ever used in an American movie, Jane is required to blow a saxophone while attempting to stimulate her impotent husband. But Jane and Preminger never came to a showdown during the picture. Temperament was not a thing she would ever display on a movie set—at least not until A

Doll's House, which was much later. For his part, Vadim had told Preminger how much he was admired in France, which was absolutely true.

In August 1966 Peter was arrested with several of his friends for possession of marijuana, after the police had raided a house where he was staying. Peter's trial ended in a hung jury, but one of his friends was convicted. Peter claimed that he didn't know there was any marijuana on the premises, and the evidence wasn't strong enough against him to warrant a conviction. Hank had just come back to California to film one of his most engaging and durable movies, *Welcome to Hard Times*, and doubtless appreciated the irony in the title as he informed Peter that he didn't approve of everything he was doing but that he would back him all the way. The case was never retried.

By November 1966 American involvement in Vietnam had become a massive, all-out land and air war involving nearly half a million American troops. The usually invisible individual Vietcong soldier was known as "Charlie" by the Americans (collectively they were "gooks"), and he was despised for being largely unseen. Whenever a Vietcong soldier or suspect was seized, his chances of being neither tortured nor maimed were slim. Electrical torture, wiring the prisoner to batteries, was preferred, since it left no scars. For Americans who fell into Vietcong hands, there was less risk of physical torture since the Vietcong's intelligence about troop movements within their own country was naturally better than the U.S. forces. American pilots fared worst of all because they were seen as murderers by the North Vietnamese who had suffered more destruction from bombing than any other country in history. The airmen were usually heavily guarded en route to the "Hanoi Hilton," the huge prisoner-of-war camp on the edge of the North Vietnamese capital. Young Americans were beginning to agitate loudly against the war, charging that the United States was there illegally, that there was indiscriminate bombing of civilians, including hospitals and schools, and that the succession of governments the

United States was supporting in South Vietnam were all corrupt and only in power by grace of the American military presence. The protesters' average age slowly rose as millions of other Americans, many of them approaching middle age and a good many of them housewives, joined their ranks.

While there was some early agitation over the war in California and around Hollywood, notably within the folk music colony, whose most vociferous member was singer Joan Baez, Jane did not yet realize the scope of the outrages taking place in Indochina. She had another movie to make before she could return to France: her first Neil Simon comedy, *Barefoot in the Park*, was to be shot at the Paramount studios and on location in New York. Robert Redford, who appeared in the role of the fugitive in *The Chase*, had created the part of the young man in the Simon comedy on Broadway, and by bringing him back to costar with Jane, Paramount was giving him a major step up in his career. She was by now a very big star; among leading ladies, as bright as any in American films. The temporary eclipse of all women in films, which only one female star, Barbra Streisand, managed to resist, was still two years away. Redford and Jane were delightful together, and the film was a huge success.

While *Barefoot in the Park* was in its final stages, Hank Fonda married for the fifth time. He was then appearing in a play about the generation gap, *Generation*, a subject then much discussed in the press and around dining-room tables, and a matter about which Hank was as well informed as any parent anywhere. The new Mrs. Fonda, whom Hank had been courting for more than three years, would prove to be the most durable of all. The wedding itself was a harbinger of the quiet years ahead—a simple civil ceremony in Mineola, Long Island. The actor George Peppard and the actress Elizabeth Ashley were their witnesses. Jane, tied up on the coast with retakes on her movie, sent apologies for her absence and best wishes to the couple.

Shirlee Adams Fonda was a former airline stewardess

and, unlike any of the previous Mrs. Fondas, had a very even disposition, no social ambitions, no desire to be an actress and no visible insecurities. A beautiful woman with a very pale, almost translucent skin, trusting eyes that rarely narrowed in anger or suspicion, and dark hair, she looked younger than the middle thirties, which she said was her age. She had worked hard most of her life and she fitted in beautifully with Hank's agrarian notions about their free time. When Jane met her during the long period that Hank knew her before taking the big step of marrying again, they got on surprisingly well together, and all of Jane's past difficulties with Hank created a breach through which a warm friendship could grow rather than a barrier to it. This was especially helpful to Jane, since she would need all the family support she could muster in the immediate years ahead.

20

All of the acting Fondas had to find their particular niches in Hollywood—Henry as the strong, silent American with glory in his eyes; Jane as the bright, striking young woman who thinks sex is a marvelous joke, worth repeating. Now Peter was slowly easing his way into an archetype—the cool young American dropout who zips through his encounters on a motorcycle.

This image was first visible in *The Wild Angels* (1966), an exploitative-type movie made by American International to cash in on current interest in the antisocial biker gangs, known in California as Hell's Angels, but who already had been seen on the screen in 1953 in Marlon Brando's successful *The Wild One*. Director Roger Corman, who lately had brought an excess of sex into the horror-movie genre, presented a group of outlaw bikers indulging in gang rape and contempt for all nonbikers; their excesses reached their climax in a final orgy in a country church, which they had taken over, where sadistic sex, heavy pot smoking and doping out boggle the viewer's mind. When the film was shown at the Venice Film Festival, it caused considerable uproar, and a poster showing Peter in his leather biker's uniform became popular with teenagers around the world. Peter's success as the great American biker eventually would make him a millionaire. In 1967 Peter was clearly worth exploiting, and somehow Roger Corman and his producers conned the youngest Fonda into starring in a film designed to show just how stimulating and extraordinary psychedelic drugs can be. A college professor, Timothy Leary, had abandoned the campus to travel back and forth across America preaching the LSD gospel. Novelist Ken Kesey was rattling around the Southwestern United States in an old bus loaded with young "Merry Pranksters" who had painted it in psychedelic day-glo. On this prolonged acid trip they made a circus out of life, sometimes joined by Neil Casaday, a holdover beatnik and hero of Jack Kerouac's *On the Road*, who would burn himself out in his forties, as would Kerouac himself. It was a dangerous time to be a nonconformist because you could wind up with an overdose. Young people were tripping out everywhere on hallucinogens, the perils seen but not comprehended.

Corman's film script for *The Trip* had been written by an actor later to become a great star, Jack Nicholson. Since Nicholson had become a regular within Peter's Hollywood Hills antiestablishment crowd, he probably drew on personal observation for his screenplay. It was intended to take the viewer along on an LSD trip vicariously through Peter's eyes. A great deal of flesh is visible in the film—often that of Jane's old friend Susan Strasberg and, of course, Peter—sometimes grotesquely painted as the trippers play with colors. Corman made a major effort to make all of this significant, but its principal scene is taken almost intact from Peter's favorite movie, Fellini's *8½*, with a robed judge reviewing Peter's past sins and delinquencies while Peter revolves on a merry-go-round.

Despite the presence in the cast of his hippie pal Dennis Hopper, who knew as much about the scene as anyone in films, the reviews were savage. Yet Peter was proud of having made it, convinced that it eventually would be a major success with younger fans. He was counting on income from his percentage of the film to swing the purchase of a sixty-five-foot yacht, aboard which he planned to live with his wife, Susan, and their two children, Bridget and Justin.

Then Peter and Dennis Hopper withdrew from making films for others for a couple of years to start on the biggest biker film in history, although only Peter, Hopper and finally their scriptwriter, Terry Southern, knew what they were up to.

Jane and Vadim spent most of 1967 in France. He had several screen projects planned, but none of them worked out. Jane turned down everything that came in, including *Rosemary's Baby* and *Bonnie and Clyde*. Since she had seen so many failed marriages she thought she knew most of the pitfalls. Bardot, still a frequent guest at the farmhouse, had not made a movie since the fairly successful *Masculin/Feminine* in 1966 and seemed to have no desire to do so. She had become something of a recluse, keeping about a dozen stray dogs and cats in her home and appearing at animal benefits around France. But she still had an occasional fling with an attractive man.

When actor Warren Beatty, whom Jane had known since they were both under contract to Josh Logan, came to Paris, Jane decided that Bardot should meet him at St. Ouen, and she made elaborate plans to bring them together at a dinner she would prepare herself at the farmhouse. Her old boyfriend Sandy Whitelaw was also in Paris, working for United Artists; Jane asked him to drive Warren out to St. Ouen, and they would show him around before Bardot's arrival. What Jane did not know was that Bardot had met Warren soon after his arrival in France; in typical fashion he immediately attempted a conquest, and they had spent some time together.

When the men arrived, Vadim had been drinking heavily. Jane pretended not to notice and was the gracious hostess, proudly showing Warren the rooms that she had so lovingly restored, as well as the numerous paintings and antiques she had collected. Bardot arrived during the grand tour, and no one let on that she and Warren were by now old friends.

During dinner, Warren remarked that the dinner was

153

good, but—and now he looked mischievously at Bardot—he implied that he knew something that tasted better. Jane caught on at once and managed to suppress her sharp annoyance, but Vadim picked up Warren's comment and said that he understood exactly what he meant, adding, "In that, Jane is not quite in Brigitte's class." Sandy now saw that Jane's anger had changed into something terrible to behold. He turned to her and said, "This will all come out all right in the end." Jane flared up and told him to shut up. "I always thought you were a creep," she said. "Now I know it."

This view of the Vadim-Fonda marriage, supplied by Sandy, is one of the few glimpses we have into its troubled side. Togetherness wasn't enough for either of them, but still they tried. Vadim writes of those days with some nostalgia and a sense of loss:

> She showed the patience of a saint and had things removed or altered to suit my tastes. I felt that she was satisfying a deeply felt need, that she was an uprooted American planting roots for herself; in fact, she was playing the part of the ideal wife. She was showing less common sense than children who believe in the games they play but are not taken in by them; Jane took the game for reality. One day she would come to detest her role as mistress of the house. My mistake was not that I forced her to assume this role—on the whole I am against bourgeois marriage—but in not having realized that she was going against her own nature.

Vadim says that she planted trees around the place and he wondered aloud why she hadn't looked for a farmhouse that had trees in the first place. Because, she said, "I'd never find woods exactly like the one I want." She was the movie star's child recreating some dream of Arden in her head.

She had her mother's mania for lists of things to do every day; she looked after Vadim's daughter Nathalie, then seven years old, and his son Christian (by Catherine Deneuve) when he came to stay for a while. She forced herself to organize her time, her days, their life. It was not happiness, but it was a resting spot for Jane Fonda in the midst of a career that would draw on all of the energies she could muster.

21

Who reads adult comic books? Wicked children, of course, and grown-ups having trouble with their sex lives. By 1967, when Vadim and Jane decided to do a film version of *Barbarella*, a comic-strip heroine living in the year A.D. 40,000, an era of total sexual liberation was well advanced even though the film would seem quite tame and understated within a few years. The series had been available for several years in Europe and in the sixties in America, courtesy of the avant-garde *Evergreen Review*. Since the *Evergreen Review* was then intent on purveying new and pop culture to the intellectuals of America, the film *Barbarella* had at least three distinct audiences awaiting its release. The first group, the wicked children, would have to lie about their ages or pass themselves off as young adults, for *Barbarella* was to get a restricted rating: for mature adults only.

Dino DeLaurentiis, who had produced the epic *War and Peace* starring Hank, was to produce *Barbarella* for Paramount, which meant that the film would have a huge budget, much of which was to go for special effects since the genre of the film was science-fiction fantasy. As for Vadim, he was given a fairly free hand to make the movie as audacious as the comic strip itself. In this film, audiences could see the oddity and *raison d'être* of Jane's relationship with Vadim—commercial sex redeemed by Jane's innate class. Yet Vadim knows exactly what he is doing. He will be remembered principally for this film. He has a pop art sensibility shared by his designer, Marco Garbuglio.

Jane would be surrounded by an expensive cast including her handsome blond neighbor from Malibu, John Philip Law, as the Blind Angel; Ugo Tognazzi, who would have his first international hit in the down-to-earth but gay antics of *La Cage aux Folles* more than ten years later; Anita Pallenberg, David Hemmings, who had played the photographer in Antonioni's *Blow-Up* the previous year; Milo O'Shea; the mime Marcel Marceau; and Claude Dauphin. They all gathered in Rome in late summer to shoot the first scenes, and the Vadims leased a villa on the Via Appia Antica. In the autumn *Barbarella* would move to Paris for completion.

Jane played Barbarella much as she had Cat Ballou, with utter sincerity and innocence. As she had done in *Cat*, she held everything together by persuading you that she believed in what she was doing, whether she was doing a lesbian love scene with Pallenberg or engaging in a hair-raising, amorous ritual with Hemmings. Upon its release in 1968 Pauline Kael, writing in the *New Yorker*, best summed up Jane's appeal in the film:

> . . . And Jane Fonda having sex on wilted feathers and rough, scroungy furs of *Barbarella* is more charming and fresh and bouncy than ever—the American girl triumphing by her innocence over a lewd comic-strip world of the future. She's the only comedienne I can think of who is sexiest when she is funniest.

Relations between Jane and Vadim seemed good, although she was "outside" her part far more than on any previous film with him. Vadim said that she did not enjoy shooting the picture but had accepted the part because she was eager to make the film. He thought that she had been turned off by the character's lack of principles, her having to exploit her sexuality, and "her irrelevancy to the political and social realities of the day." Vadim, however, believed that *Barbarella* contained considerable satire on contemporary problems; yet other than suggesting that all sexual inhibitions are outmoded, it is difficult to see any reference in the film to either a political or a social reality. But it was characteristic of Vadim in interviews to elevate the themes of his pictures to something significant. Today, when everything Jane touches has to have some social relevance, she looks upon *Barbarella* with considerable distaste, seeing it for what it is, an archetypal sexist film.

Jane had become very fond of Vadim's eight-year-old daughter Nathalie. She was a lovely child, as curious and quick-witted as her father. She was frequently on the set and in Jane's dressing room during the final work on the movie in Paris, and Jane suddenly saw that she made a rather good mother; she had within her a surprisingly strong maternal instinct. As with most of her decisions and conclusions, she acted quickly on it: shortly after Christmas 1967 it was confirmed that she was pregnant.

When Jane turned thirty on December 21, 1967, she was terrified, not of getting older but because she had the mumps. She fell into a deep depression, certain—perhaps because of her lack of faith in the unreleased *Barbarella*—that she was through as an actress, that she would never work again, and she dared not think about the effect of her illness on her unborn child.

22

In 1967 dissenters were marching in American cities
against the war in Vietnam. Nearly a quarter of a
million poured into New York's Central Park in mid
April.* On the same day, an ad appeared in the Princeton
campus newspaper declaring that their students would
refuse to fight in Vietnam even if drafted. Martin Lu-
ther King, Jr, was urging his followers to merge civil
rights groups with peace movements. On the weekend
of October 21, between 50 and 100,000 protestors poured
into Washington for a rally sponsored by the National
Mobilization Committee to End the War in Vietnam, a
coalition of 150 organizations. At least 50,000 marched
on the Pentagon and thousands stormed the building,
some breaching the entrances. David Dellinger, Chairman
of the Mobe Committee, and novelist Norman Mailer
were arrested. The ~~Johnson~~ Nixon!!! administration was shaken
and was much concerned about repercussions abroad

* These peace marches culminated in a massive rally in
Washington in November, 1969, when more than half a million Americans moved into the area between the Lincoln
Memorial and the obelisk to sing folk songs, hymns and
anthems and the civil rights theme song, "We Shall Overcome," Calling the march "a mobilization against the war,"
few of the marchers were radicals; they were business and
professional people, members of the clergy, housewives beyond
number, blacks, gays, feminists and of course the ubiquitous
hippies. Their numbers and the *kind* of people they were
shocked the hawks in the capital and left the Nixon administration badly shaken.

Then in November Bertrand Russell opened the second session of his International War Crimes Tribunal in Sweden, whose avowed purpose was to compile a dossier of atrocities and criminal actions committed by the United States against the people of Vietnam. By this time, more than half a million Vietnamese civilians had been killed in the American war to "save" their country from communism. Russell was honorary president, the philosopher Jean-Paul Sartre executive president, and the historian Vladimir Dedijer the chairman and president of the sessions. Among the tribunal members were Gunther Anders, James Baldwin, Simone de Beauvoir, Stokely Carmichael, Dave Dellinger and Peter Weiss. Baldwin and Carmichael were black Americans; Dellinger was an American pacifist, a leader of the antiwar movement in the United States, and one of the Chicago Seven indicted the following year after the police-provoked riots at the Democratic National Convention, where heads were broken.

Appearing as eyewitnesses before the tribunal were journalists as well as simple peasants, mostly Vietnamese. Brought to Sweden at the tribunal's expense were schoolchildren and rice growers from Indochina who reported what they had seen. What they reported was shocking enough, but the picture emerging from all the testimony was one of a mighty nation, the United States, attempting through massive airpower, chemical warfare (some 100,000 tons of napalm had been used up to the end of 1967), and search-and-destroy missions to subdue an enemy, the mostly guerrilla forces of the National Liberation Front, known as the Vietcong; attempting through increased pressure, more bombs, more napalm, more steel pellets and more manpower to win a war which history clearly proved could never be won. The defendant, then, *in absentia*, was the United States Government, and the charge was that

. . . the air force of the United States has dropped in Vietnam, four million pounds of bombs daily. If it continues at this rate to the end of the year, the total will constitute a greater mass of explosives than it unloaded on the entire Pacific theatre during the whole of the Second World War. . . . In the South, the U.S. forces and their docile Saigon allies have herded eight million people, peasants and their families, into barbed wire encampments under the surveillance of the political police. Chemical poisons have been, and are being, used to defoliate and render barren tens of thousands of acres of farmland. . . . More than five hundred thousand Vietnamese men, women and children have perished under this onslaught.*

Jane followed the proceedings of the tribunal in growing horror and pain. She believed in her country, but this had shaken her belief in her government. She tried to come to some kind of terms with it, but the interests of Vadim's friends, except for the Vaillands, centered around the grosses of new films, acquiring glorious tans at St. Tropez, or the effects of some new trip-generating drug, and they found this expectant mother, Jane, "not the girl we used to know."

Although the Boat People of the future would establish that the "heroic" people of North Vietnam could be even more indifferent to human life and suffering than the Americans, liberals and peace-loving people everywhere followed the Russell tribunal closely. Lord Russell died in 1970 before the victorious North Vietnamese ruthlessly overran neighboring Cambodia, completing a pattern of destruction begun by the Americans years earlier.

Prominent on the tribunal was Parisian lawyer Leon Matarasso. He was president of the Juridical Commission and knew more than anyone else there about the details in the massive compilation and documentation of criminal acts—deaths through torture and mass starvation in the wake of napalm devastation. Matarasso had also been a lawyer at Nuremberg and saw the parallels as well as the differences.

* *The Autobiography of Bertrand Russell 1944-1967* (London: George Allen & Unwin, 1969).

In early 1968 Jane appeared at last in a film with her brother Peter, something she had thought quite unlikely as little as a year earlier. The movie was *Spirits of the Dead*, a three-part omnibus film of stories by Edgar Allan Poe. Federico Fellini directed one, Louis Malle and Roger Vadim the other two. Except for the Fellini episode, it was not very successful, and Vincent Canby in the New York *Times* found the Vadim episode absurd but "still quite fun," writing that "Vadim exhibits his wife . . . in various preposterous poses as a medieval woman who carries on a sort of love-hate relationship with a horse. This isn't as bad as it sounds because the horse is none other than Peter Fonda."

Peter enjoyed his working holiday with his sister, who was several months pregnant. Neither of them knew what to do about their father, who had now drifted so far away from them. Peter was at an advanced stage with preproduction plans for his martyred-hippie film, now known as *Easy Rider*, but the subject was of no interest to Hank. Indeed, communication between father and son had never been poorer. In an interview with Rex Reed published that February Peter had said: "I really dig my sister. Probably a great deal more than she digs me and she *digs* me. I dig my father, too. I have a great deal of compassion for him, too. I wish he could open his eyes and dig me."

Encouraged by the Vaillands, Jane had followed the Russell War Crimes Tribunal in the French press, while Hank went on a camp show tour to South Vietnam and came back a confirmed hawk. He said, ". . . every time there's a parade or peace rally in this country it will make the war that much longer, because this doesn't escape the attention of Ho Chi Minh." He insisted that he was "still a liberal," but his remarks might have been written by a propagandist at the Pentagon. Peter and Jane and their father were now at opposite poles on the war issue as well as much else.

When the draft was reinstated by President Johnson because of the rising number of casualties among the half million American troops in Vietnam, Peter was among those called up.

Peter's candor had made him a Hollywood eccentric, and many of his interviews were so heavily seasoned with scatological references as to be unpublishable. In the space of a few minutes at the induction station, he persuaded the Army doctors that they had blundered in calling him. Peter later said:

> I was standing in line when this doctor came over to examine me. I looked at him straight in the face and said, "If you touch my ass, I'll put my heel down your throat." As he started going down the line to each man, he said, "O.K., turn around, bend over. Spread 'em! . . ." But when he came to me, I guess he saw that heel in his throat and he passed me by.

The doctors turned him over to an army psychiatrist, whose questions so offended Peter that "I just walked right out of his office into the middle of the street—stark naked—and headed for my car. Then I realized, 'Oh, oh, you blew it.' I'd left the keys inside. I went back in. They gave me my clothes and let me go." Classified 1-Y, they periodically sent him postcards asking if his status had changed. "I just ripped it up and sent it to the President with a note that said, 'Stuff it up your ass.' " He kept doing the same thing with each postcard and they never called him back.

Peter was concerned about what man was doing to the earth. "We're cutting down all our forests and depositing oil into our oceans." His friends, directors Bob Rafaelson and Dennis Hopper and actor Jack Nicholson, were the advance guard of the nonconformist army of young people who would take over Hollywood filmmaking in the late sixties, removing movie production from the hands of the old, the tired and the studio-bound. His sister Jane would be one of the many beneficiaries of the New Hollywood they were creating.

*   *   *

Jane's first real taste of radical politics was during the students' uprising in Paris in May 1968. Probably inspired by student takeovers at Columbia, Harvard and elsewhere in America, the students seized control of all university facilities in the French capital, provoking strong police action that was so unpopular that the affair, lasting nearly a week, came close to toppling the government. Taking advantage of the general unrest, the Film Technicians Union was radicalized, prodded leftward not a little by speeches from Jane, who was finding that she could stir crowds with her occasionally shrill sincerity. She was exhilarated by the events surrounding the student insurrection and filled with revolutionary zeal. Afterward she was highly regarded by French communists and the Maoist director Jean-Luc Godard spoke to her about doing a film.

Jane's decided turn to the left ran into a temporary detour on September 28, 1968, when she gave birth to her first child, a daughter whom they named Vanessa, in honor of Vanessa Redgrave, despite Jane's later disclaimers about her daughter's name. Miss Redgrave had been leading antiwar marches against the American embassy in London and proving that an actress can become involved passionately in a cause. Motherhood quelled much of the restlessness in Jane, or so it seemed for a number of weeks. Vadim still wasn't persuaded that it was a permanent condition. He knew better than to expect Jane to settle into contented domesticity.

Vadim's world was circumscribed by his unique position in films: he had created a niche for himself with Bardot and, while he could do films as serious in intent as *The Game Is Over*, predictably any work in his hands would stress the sexual aspects. With Jane's peculiar foresight, she saw that moviegoers eventually would be bored by too much flesh, too much explicitness. She was a mother; that was a role that would not change. But she was also an actress, and that role *could* change if she did not get on with her career. She wanted to do more significant things; she wanted to connect her films with the real world and its problems; could she and Vadim coexist with such an ambition?

Meanwhile, in Hollywood something was happening at that moment that would answer this question for her, take the decision out of her hands and turn her career completely around, moving her in a direction away from Vadim. There would be nothing either of them could do about it.

In the mid-thirties Horace McCoy wrote a novel set in a dance marathon during the Great Depression entitled *They Shoot Horses, Don't They?* The book was well received in America and had a large sale in paperback, but during the fifties and sixties the book in translation in France had become a cult classic. Jean-Paul Sartre and Simone de Beauvoir had endorsed it and their followers had embraced it for humanizing existentialism. The heroine of *They Shoot Horses*, Gloria, enters a dance marathon simply to survive. She sees life as utterly hopeless, with everything rigged against her, including the cattle calls at Central Casting in Hollywood, where she can't even get registered. She believes in nothing, certainly not in God, which could only provoke a cynical laugh from her. As a series of misfortunes befall her, over none of which she has any control—and it is part of the progressive horror of the story that she is the innocent victim of everything that happens—we see some determination grow in her. And while we know what it is, we try not to think about it: the only thing still under her control is her choice of life or death. She has the freedom to kill herself.

The novel had been optioned by at least twenty different producers, including Charlie Chaplin. But every time a script was commissioned or discussed, the men with the money (in Chaplin's case, himself) decided against it because it was simply too depressing. It was unanimously felt that such a downer of a story would not make a commercially successful movie. Then a producer by the name of Martin Baum bought it for a new film company, Palomar, formed by the American Broadcasting Company to help fight a new and surprising threat to television's supremacy—old-fashioned theatrical movies. By the mid-nineteen-sixties, a great many people around the world were going out to the movies again. A few key directors had caught their attention— Ingmar Bergman, Federico Fellini, Akiro Kurosawa, John Huston—and ABC was the first of the big networks to get into the production of films for theatrical release. They had a screenplay of *They Shoot Horses*, by the veteran screenwriter James Poe, that was audacious and structurally sound. Baum and Poe felt that only Jane Fonda could play Gloria, the archetypal loser. Poe's script had been dispatched to St. Ouen and Jane, after quickly reading it and briefly discussing it with Vadim, cabled back that she liked it and would do it.

A sense of melancholy had seeped into the Vadims' marriage and the decision to do the film seemed to lift Jane's spirits. Everyone around her, Vadim especially, noticed that she was undergoing some quiet transformation. She didn't laugh as much as she used to. She was breast-feeding Vanessa and Vadim attributed the change to motherhood.

The Vadims flew to California in January 1969 and rented a house in the Malibu colony, where the atmosphere was subtly different from the beach climate of St. Tropez. No one tried to be chic or daring; everyone was rich or they wouldn't have been able to live there, so they adopted a casual counterculture. They all went barefoot; they wore jeans and sweatshirts. Everyone had a dog, which they would run on the beach. There were many cats, a number of them choosing beach decks as their permanent homes, where they could be seen sunning themselves along with their owners.

During their last stay there the Vadims had open house nearly all the time; now, invitations went out to just a handful. Slowly, but frighteningly, Jane was becoming the lost Gloria of the Depression. She had defused herself somehow; all of that staggering Fonda energy was drained out, and its place taken by an attitude of hopelessness. Screenwriter Poe, who had been asked to direct as well, thought the transformation marvelous. Jane's long luxuriant mane was cut to a thirties bob.

ABC Palomar had rented sound stage four at Warners' Burbank studios, where Poe had constructed a mock-up of one end of a dance hall. He also had written some scenes set under and around the auditorium, which they were shooting at Ocean Park pier in Santa Monica. There were, too, shots specified in the script which Jane questioned, illustrating a metaphor Poe had conceived to convey the dispassion of the audience for the down-on-their luck marathon dancers. He transformed the spectators into togaed Romans eating and drinking in the stands while being amused by the spectacle.

It was James Poe's first assignment as director, and he was having trouble handling the huge cast. Once again, Jane had Andreas in the background coaching her—their relationship now almost entirely professional with no chance of ever becoming intimate again—and she seemed to know exactly what she was doing. It bothered her to find someone like Poe who did not. The young actor whom Poe had chosen to play opposite Jane, Michael Sarrazin, was fairly new to movies and seemed incorrigibly shy and vulnerable; in fact, he had that kind of gangling grace that Hank Fonda had become famous for; he badly needed a strong hand, which he wasn't getting.

When they were about a quarter of the way into the shooting, the rug was pulled from under Poe: the Palomar people did not like his approach; the toga-clad Romans seemed pretentious and the whole thing threatened to become self-consciously arty in a way these commercially minded men thought very bad for business. Poe was fired, and production was shut down for over a month while a new director, Sydney Pollack, stepped in and attempted to put the film back on a commercial track again.

Pollack was not yet thirty-five, but had made a substantial reputation in television before coming to Hollywood to make *The Slender Thread* in 1966. He was a former actor and acting teacher at the Neighborhood

167

Playhouse in New York, where Sanford Meisner turned out nearly as many celebrated stars as Strasberg had at the Actors Studio. Meisner and Strasberg were rivals, but both were after the same thing: intense concentration and a way of getting at the truth of a character, of a given moment, concentrating on an action that would bring with it its own emotion.

Pollack scrapped the Poe script and brought in Robert "Red" Thompson to rewrite it. Pollack felt that Poe had overstated the metaphor. He also had blown the claustrophobic intensity of the movie by taking the moviegoer outside the dance hall. To borrow a title from existentialism's high priest Sartre, there could be no exit. He had the set designer and crew build a complete dance hall with adjacent dressing rooms and office so that the camera could make a 360-degree pan and show everything.

There was an exhilarating change in Jane on this production. She was like a colonel elevated to general on the field of battle. She was on top of everything: dialogue, costumes, background. It became increasingly clear to Andreas that she would not need anyone coaching her off-camera anymore. *They Shoot Horses* would mark the end of their relationship.* And this new Jane was not a Vadim protégée any longer; she was very much her own woman.

With only sixty-five pages of shooting script ready, Pollack began his version of *They Shoot Horses*. Among the veterans in the cast besides Gig Young, who played Rocky, the marathon master of ceremonies and promot-

---

* Jane's encounters with Andreas in the future would be most infrequent. He founded an acting school in Paris patterned after the Actors Studio and became most successful at it, with a substantial number of popular movie personalities coming to him for help. When Jane was asked sometime in the nineteen-seventies who might take over the Actors Studio in the event of Lee Strasberg's death or incapacity, she unhesitatingly said, "There is only one man who can and he lives in Paris."

er, were Susannah York and Red Buttons. Pollack added Bruce Dern, not yet a major star but already well known for playing heavies with schizoid tendencies, and Bonnie Bedelia, whom Pollack had admired in *The Gypsy Moths*. They were to play a desperate young couple hired for the marathon because the wife was expecting a baby—at any moment apparently. Pollack decided to shoot in continuity, strictly following the chronology of the script. This would achieve the effect of showing his actors and extras slowly coming apart physically under the strain of the marathon. In between setups and after hours, he screened old movies of the nineteen-thirties to envelop his cast in the despair of the Depression period. He even found one that was also set in a dance marathon of the times.

Jane had been studiously watching her progress in each film by viewing the daily rushes (the "dailies"), the hastily developed print of the last day's shooting. She had done this since very early in her film career, and had watched herself become more relaxed and secure with each new film. Now she was joined by all the other principals and many of the extras and crew as well. Pollack recalls:

It was the kind of picture, strangely enough, where there was something you hear about but seldom ever see. There was this enormous *esprit* that developed, some crazy identification with the roles they were playing. It became an ensemble piece where the people began to relate to others the way they were in the film. Every day, they would go to that same set in the same clothes and do the same things, and they really began to be pros at them. We would sometimes have days where there were seventy or eighty people watching the rushes. Every extra wanted to see them, particularly the derby. They were interested, fascinated. I was a little bit sadistic about it in the sense that because I liked all of them [the extras] so much and I had to choose three to be eliminated, I'd just let it play itself out. I said "The only way I'm going to be able to eliminate three of

these actors is for them to come in last in the derby."
So the last few minutes of that derby, they were really
struggling there.

Professionally Jane seemed to be on top of her role, yet
Pollack and others could tell from her mood, which
never seemed to lift itself out of the bottom she had
struck, that something was wrong with her marriage.
But she confided in no one in the production company,
and socialized with none of them. Susannah York said
later that she barely exchanged half a dozen words with
Jane off camera. But no one questioned this or thought
she was a snob, because it was assumed by everyone
that she was entitled to have Gloria's emotions offscreen, if that was the way she felt. Pollack saw the
role as

> . . . a fulcrum. It was the perfect thing for her to
> pour all of her own frustrations, her own disappoint-
> ments in life, and all of her aspirations to want to
> achieve something meaningful. . . . This was her
> chance really to make an indelible mark as a charac-
> ter that was fully done, fully executed, and she held
> nothing back. There was no vanity in the perfor-
> mance, no self-preservation. There was no hiding in
> it. She went all the way.

Vadim felt

> . . . She was living her part with almost morbid
> intensity. A tenuous shadow, an indefinable sense of
> drifting apart, as though some cold barrier was grow-
> ing between us, made me feel that I was living a
> waking nightmare. The sensation was so fleeting that
> by the time I left her, the worried feeling had be-
> come a memory, and I was always convinced that it
> was all an illusion. The erosion of love is a sordid,
> shabby, absurd thing. A shameful and useless sick-
> ness. It is not even a lost battle, it is a cancer that
> eats away body, soul and mind. No one ever com-
> pletely recovers from it.

170

THE FONDA FAMILY

1. Christening Day for both Fonda children, June 23, 1940. From left: Henry's sister, Harriet Peacock; Jane's half-sister Frances (Pan) de Villers Brokaw; Henry holding Jane; Frances holding Peter; Henry's sister Jayne Shotgoeun; and Jane's maternal grandmother Sophie Seymour. Godfather J. Watson Webb, Jr., took the picture.

2. Jane gives Peter a tender pat as their mother looks on. Pan's attention is elsewhere. Christening day, 1940.

3. Henry holding Jane at poolside, with Pan Brokaw, Prudence Peacock, and at right, Aunt Harriet, 1939.

4. Jane with her favorite nurse, Mary. Early 1939.

5. Jane's mother, Frances Seymour Fonda. Portrait by W. Seely.

6. Henry teaching Jane to swim when she was less than two years old. He is letting his hair grow for *Young Mr. Lincoln*. Early 1939.

7. Neighbor Tyrone Power seated on the front walk of the Fonda home with Pan Brokaw and Jane.

SUNDAY AT THE
FONDAS,
EARLY 1939

8. Jane examining a flower from the Fonda garden, 1939.

9. Jane plays with Pan next to Tyrone Power's Pontiac. Frances often dressed the children in identical outfits.

10. Henry letting Jane try his pipe. Frances' hand at left suggests the prank has gone far enough.

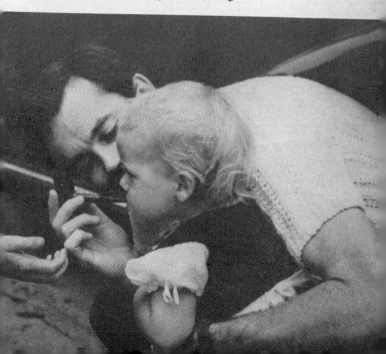

11. Christmas Eve, 1940, on Chadbourne Street at the Fondas'
rented home in Brentwood, California. Frances dozes on Henry's shoulder following a long and tiring flight from New
York.

12. Jane enjoying ice cream, 1941.

13. Peter and Jane play in the sandbox of their neighbors, the Fred MacMurrays, 1942.

14. Jane, 1942. Portrait by W. Seely.

15. A subdued Jane in 1942. She is attempting some painting.

JANE FONDA MATURES

16. 1959. (Culver)

17. 1967. (Culver)

18. 1979. (Photography by T. Bruce Tober)

19. Jane's first movie role, *Tall Story* (1960) with Tony Perkins. Veteran playwright and sometime actor Marc Connelly plays the professor in background. (Culver)

20. Jane with her companion in the early 1960s, Andreas Voutsinas, actor and director, at the Westport Country Playhouse in Connecticut, where he directed her, 1961.

21. Jane rolls her own during a wait between scenes, 1961. (Culver)

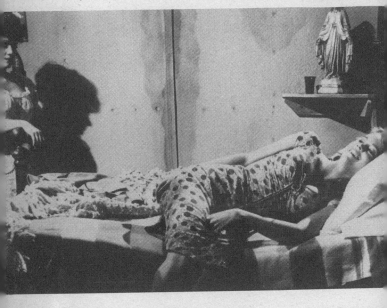

22. As Kitty Twist in Nelson Algren's *Walk on the Wild Side*
(1961). With Jane in this scene is Anne Baxter. (Culver)

23. *The Chapman Report* (1962) with Efrem Zimbalist, Jr., as a sex-study psychologist. (Culver)

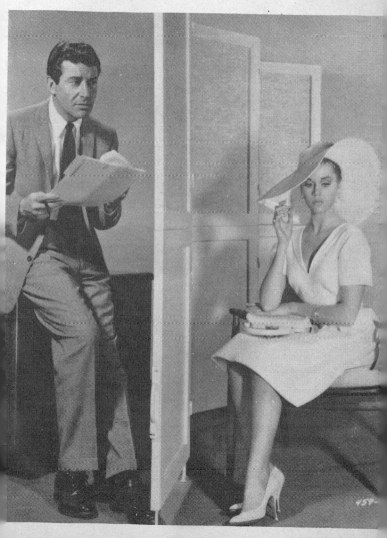

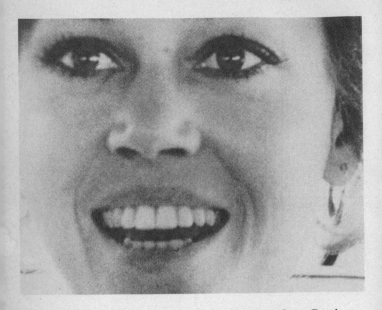

24. A close-up in the television documentary *Jane*, October 1962. (Courtesy Hope Ryden, a Drew Associated Production for Time-Life)

25. *Period of Adjustment*, Tennessee Williams' comedy, costarring Anthony Franciosa (1962). (Culver)

26. *Joy House* with leading man Alain Delon was directed by René Clement (1964). The movie marked the end of her close relationship with Andreas Voutsinas. (Culver)

27. Henry vists his daughter at the studio in 1965. (Culver)

28. *The Chase* (1966) was Jane's only film with Marlon Brando. They had one big scene together in the jailhouse. (Culver)

29. James Fox played her wealthy lover in *The Chase*. He becomes a close friend and later was drawn into the controversy-ridden Joe Losey production of *A Doll's House*. (Culver)

30. *The Game Is Over* (1967) was perhaps Jane's most beautiful picture. It was directed by her first husband, Roger Vadim. (Culver)

31. Otto Preminger directs Jane and Michael Caine, playing her weakling husband, in *Hurry Sundown* (1967) on location in Louisiana. The film company was forced out of town by racist vigilantes. (Culver)

32. Robert Redford joins Jane for the second time (he was her fugitive husband in *The Chase*) for the film version of a play Jane earlier had turned down on Broadway, *Barefoot in the Park* (1967). (Culver)

33. Jane's breakthrough performance as the doomed marathon dancer Gloria in *They Shoot Horses, Don't They?* (1969) was directed by Sydney Pollack. Here they confer on the set. She won an Oscar nomination for the role. (Author's collection)

34. Jane as *Barbarella* checks on stepdaughter Nathalie Vadim's progress with dinner as husband Roger Vadim attends to his. On the set of the film in Paris, December 1967. (Author's collection)

35. Henry and his fifth and last wife, Shirlee Adams, flank actress Phyllis Newman (*center*), 1979. (Wide World Photos)

36. Jane holding her son, Troy O'Donovan Garity Hayden, as Tom Hayden points something out to him, 1980. (Wide World Photos)

37. Jane and Tom Hayden at New York City press conference. 1973. (UPI)

38. Jane in handcuffs on way to hearing at Cleveland courthouse, November 1970. (© 1970 by the Cleveland Press)

39. *The China Syndrome* eerily anticipated a nuclear accident almost exactly like the Three Mile Island disaster in 1979. Jane played a TV newscaster while Jack Lemmon as a nuclear engineer tried frantically to bring a runaway nuclear reactor under control. Michael Douglas was the TV cameramen. (Culver)

40. *The Bluebird* (1974) was an extraordinary coproduction between the United States and the Soviet Union, the last gasp of détente. Among its many shortcomings was this costume of Jane's as Night. The photo is inscribed to her Russian interpreter in Leningrad, Alla Peigoulevskaya. (Courtesy Alla Peigoulevskaya)

41. After a long absence from the screen, Jane came back as part of this typical affluent American family so in debt they consider robbing a bank. In *Fun with Dick and Jane*, robbery saves their luxury homestead and becomes a way of survival. Jane's partner in crime was George Segal (1976). (Culver)

If one is to understand fully why it was in the years immediately ahead of Jane and following Hanoi that she never lost the enthusiastic support and backing of most filmmakers in Hollywood, despite a brief period in the early nineteen-seventies when it was difficult to find financing for her films, one must understand how significant her attitude toward acting was in creating that favorable climate. If Marilyn Monroe was famed for her tantrums, her moods and her unprofessionalism, and eventually fired because of them, Jane, who had studied under the same man as Marilyn had, Lee Strasberg, was in Pollack's words,

> . . . totally professional. . . . Her talent was functioning at its fullest, as it has been in all of her work, so that she's gotten better technically and she's understood and gotten more secure and more confident. And all that has done is allow her to concentrate better because she's less insecure as an actress. . . . There's nothing wrong with the Method, but there's a lot wrong with actors who abuse and misuse it, who will hold up production and be self-indulgent. That's not what the Method is about. It's about saving time, not wasting it. The Method is about doing your job better, not more self-indulgently. The Method is about a solid, secure and sure way of getting to the truth of a character or the truth of a given moment.

Jane had a no-nonsense approach to her roles, and she had begun to trust her directors totally. She would look for what Pollack called "the back story," the paths that brought the film character to the crisis dramatized on the screen, including family background, religion or lack of it, and previous miscalculations and triumphs. Jane would look for the right attitudes. Pollack recalls a particular instance when she looked for a hook to get to the emotion:

> There was a very tricky scene where she goes into Gig Young's office. Now my concept of that scene, a

scene that didn't exist until I came onto the film. . .
the idea is in the book because Rocky kind of makes
eyes at her there but I thought she had to denigrate
herself in a way, that she was so disappointed by
seeing Michael Sarrazin with Susannah York [having
sex in a janitor's storeroom adjacent to the ballroom]
that it was like saying to herself, "You idiot! You
should have known better than to start believing in
this Mr. Sunshine guy!" Finally he [Sarrazin] had
started to get through that hard cover of hers, and
she was beginning to really have affection for him
and right at the moment it was like somebody who
knows they're always going to get hurt, then they let
themselves go. And she started to let herself go and
then got hurt, and the only way to feel comfortable
again was to degrade herself. We had long discussions over how to play that scene and what the
attitude was and what to do. Should she undress,
should she not undress? Should she unbutton his
pants? How far should we go? One thing we knew
was it shouldn't be romantic. *Unromantic.* "Don't
touch me!" was all she said. It's the only dialogue.
The subtext was "I don't want this to be confused
with affection or lovemaking. That's not what it's
about. It's about me reminding myself of who I
am so I don't be such an ass anymore, and start to
believe Mr. Goody Two-Shoes over there who
sticks his face up to the sunlight and looks at the
positive side of life."

There is a handful of actors who never give a bad
performance. The film itself may be poor, even mediocre, but their performance is always interesting. Jane
had stepped into those select ranks with *They Shoot
Horses*, and she would remain there. Political attitudes
do not enter into such considerations. It is an area
where art transcends the personality and behavior of the
artist.

Jane moved into her trailer dressing room next to
stage four at Burbank. Even that early, Jane was carefully dividing her time, compartmentalizing herself. She

tried to see as much of her daughter as circumstances would allow, but little Vanessa Vadim must have learned very early that her mother was an actress, and actresses run on different timetables from other mothers. There would be a great deal of affection in their times together, much squeezing and hugging, as though to make up for the hours when they could not be together. There were moments when Jane must have risen out of the despair which had become her dominant mood. But when her key lines as Gloria were spoken on the screen— "The whole damn world's just like Central Casting. They've got it all rigged before we ever show up. . . . I'm going to get off this merry-go-round"—you had to feel a chill of truth. This was not just an actress speaking; it was a young woman who had reached a terminal point in her life.

Jane worked at an unconscious level of acting; it was visceral, shot through with intense feeling and yet coming out in performance as cut off from feeling; one of the walking dead. This was something she had worked out carefully with Andreas the night before, each defiant gesture, each deadly glance. Pollack saw her arrive fully prepared each and every day, ready for the cameras. It became his custom to film her scenes her way and then if they did not work, reshoot them following a conference at which she was her own fiercest critic.

By the strangest of ironies, while Jane was trying valiantly to cling to her role of mother and while the demands of her role as Gloria grew stronger and more compelling, the other strongest actor in the film, Gig Young, was divorcing his fourth wife, Elaine Garber Whitman Young, and within two years would file a most unusual "nonpaternity suit." He went into court to have put on public record that he was not the father of the child born during their marriage. "Nothing is easy," he would say. "It's a delicate subject. I hate to use the word gossamer, but there is a child involved, and I don't like to start something rolling that would be unkind in any way. It's a very sensitive, human thing

173

going on here." He asserted that he had had a vasectomy years earlier.*

Young was a brilliant actor who went on to win an Oscar as Rocky in the Best Supporting Actor category, but his private torments continued, and in 1978, he murdered his fifth wife and then shot himself.

The killing of Gloria in the last moments of *They Shoot Horses* caused the most controversy within the ABC film-unit hierarchy. Marty Baum came to Pollack and asked if there wasn't some way that she could be saved. "The kid's [Sarrazin] a bum shot. He grazes her scalp." The argument was that if Gloria were allowed to survive the movie, they could earn at least ten million dollars more than if she died. Pollack remembers the pressure and says:

> There's no way I would ever have done it, if for no other reason than that the book itself is a kind of miniclassic; the title of the book and whole point of the book is the killing. . . . I don't think it's true [that a happy ending would add ten million to the gross receipts]. When it came out, it was okay as a commercial picture, but it was much more a *succès d'estime*. It changed a lot of individual careers. Gig's. Mine. Jane's. Her career went in a completely different direction after that picture, and it gave me some sort of international reputation. It won lots and lots of awards. Not just Cannes, but in every festival there was. In Belgium, in Yugoslavia, in San Sebastian. . . . But finally it was too depressing a picture to be a big commercial hit. It made its money back but it didn't go into millions of dollars of profit or anything. By today's standards, it was a very modest financial success. Fifteen million in film rentals. So it made a little money.

*In 1972, a California Appeals Court declared that Gig Young was indeed the father of the child born nine years earlier to former wife Elaine.

174

And so both the management and Pollack were right. He kept his integrity as a filmmaker and they didn't lose anything by it.

In the Oscar derby for Best Actress, Jane was pitted against four other actresses, one of whom, Maggie Smith, had the advantage of being on screen as schoolmarm Miss Jean Brodie for two hours—nearly all of the time. Maggie Smith won the award, and there was some indignation among Jane's numerous supporters. What they failed to appreciate was that Jane's ensemble style in *They Shoot Horses* allowed her costar Gig Young to win his award and Susannah York to win an Oscar nomination as Best Supporting Actress. Jane learned from her father at an early age never to upstage anyone. The following December in New York, where there is considerable sophistication about such matters, Jane was voted Best Actress of the Year by the film critics. I can recall seeing the film and being nearly wiped out by her performance. It was almost too painful to view.

The wrap-up party on the film production of *They Shoot Horses* had some of the strong emotional tug of the last reunion of a closely knit family, the last picnic while Grandma is still on her feet. Seldom had a movie company worked so intimately together for so long under such rigorous circumstances. They didn't know whether to weep with regret or sigh with relief. The advance word on the film was that Jane's impact as Gloria was comparable to that of Bette Davis's Mildred all those years ago in *Of Human Bondage*. Scripts came in for Jane's consideration in ever increasing numbers, a few of them for immediate production, but Jane was too depleted even to consider plunging into something else.

PART VII

Saint Jane

"I reached the age of thirty-two and discovered I'd wasted thirty-two years of my life. I reached it because of the war, because of the kind of questions that the Vietnam struggle is forcing us to ask ourselves about who we are, what our country means and what we're doing."

23

In the spring of 1969 *Easy Rider* opened; for millions of older people it was like a gate swinging open on an unknown world. Throughout the nineteen-sixties the young had been in ferment throughout the Western world—whether they were hippies or bikers or Hari Krishnas, they were against the way things were. Major American cities contained youth ghettos like the East Village in Manhattan and Haight-Ashbury in San Francisco, where the dropouts lived communally and got fed and clothed in "free stores." With drugs or without, they were more interested in discovering the inside of themselves than they were in learning about the world. "What we're all about is chaos," one hippie said. "That's the way the world is and we relate to it that way." Fortunately, they were generally peaceful. There may have been black riots in that decade; there were peace agitators who clashed with the authorities and brought riot; but except among student groups there were few recorded *youth* riots. The young wanted peace; they wanted people to be nice and good and tolerant; they wanted to smile and have a good feeling about life.

Peter and his partner, Dennis Hopper, had lived through these years as part of the general chaotic searching. Jane had "matured" faster and moved with older people. Peter's Captain America is in its way as much of a movie milestone as Orson Welles's Charles Foster Kane. He was so right for the part that it was difficult to know where Peter Fonda left off and Captain America began. But one thing was certain. Peter knew that there was a big movie in the confrontation between older bigots and youthful dropouts. By the time their movie was being made, there was small need for expository dialogue from Peter about why he was the way he was such as the long, dead end exchanges between father and son in James Dean's *Rebel Without a Cause* (1955). His biker was mostly silent and we knew what he was thinking because we knew what had gone down in America before the film began between the young and the rest of the world, between fathers and sons. The one who seems to talk a lot is the dropout lawyer played by Jack Nicholson, who had written the screenplay for Peter's *The Trip*; he seems garrulous because there isn't much that needs to be said. What *Easy Rider* did for all of us was to make us realize that the land was still there inviolate, but that man had fucked everything up. Why belabor the obvious with dialogue? And we know too that these two bikers are going to be martyred once they breeze into redneck country. It is all worked out like a Passion Play and we know about Calvary before we get there.

After winning the Best First Film award at Cannes, *Easy Rider* was released around the world; there were long lines along Third Avenue in Manhattan, where it was showing. No film during the sixties had generated such excitement. The symbol of the era's alienated youth was now Peter Fonda. Hank must have been relieved to find that his own hippie son had turned out to be the most famous counterculturist ever; he was also going to be rich as Croesus. His movie, in which he owned a third interest, would earn nearly $25 million within a few years. Fonda the rebel, who always seemed to be out of step with everyone else, had struck it rich by hanging on to his nonconformity. Screenwriter Terry Southern, who had written the screenplays for *Dr. Strangelove* (1964), *The Loved One* (1965) and *Barbarella*, had helped director Dennis Hopper make it all work, but it had been Peter's vision and faith that had carried them through. Hopper had seemed thoroughly undisciplined in every direction before this film, and his control over *Easy Rider* was as much of a miracle as its worldwide success.

Jane was more surprised than anyone by the sudden elevation of her brother Peter to youth icon and film magnate. She had watched his movie evolve through its various stages and had given him constant reassurance, but there was no way she could have guessed that it was going to be a cult classic. Now Peter had come through and justified everything he had been doing *ahead* of her own breakthrough, *They Shoot Horses*.

She left Vanessa with Vadim and joined Peter in Hawaii, where he had taken his family for a vacation. They met there for the first time in their lives as peers, for Jane's career no longer put his in the shade. They had each done a film that would change their lives forever. The Fonda family had now become the most formidable family in show business since the three Barrymores were all stars. Hank was standing largely on his record of past successes, although keeping busy in such films as *The Boston Strangler* (1968), in which he played an arm of the law, and *Once Upon a Time in the West* (1969), a spaghetti Western shot by the Italian filmmaker Sergio Leone in Spain. They were not roles that would do much for Henry Fonda's status as a screen immortal, but it had become Hank's custom to accept any part that came along in this long twilight period of his career if the money was right and he was free. As restless as Jane, he couldn't face idleness. While Hank was becoming the busiest character actor in Hollywood—he made four films in 1968—Jane and Peter had become the hottest siblings in the movies.

Vadim was not above exploiting this, and he hoped to direct them both as brother and sister caught in an incestuous relationship in *Blue Guitar*, which Roman Polanski's partner, Gene Gutowski, hoped to produce. Jane seemed unconcerned about its moral implications; she and Peter had done much the same thing in *Spirits of the Dead*, although on a nobler plane (perhaps that was

181

what was wrong with it). If she had any objections to the story, she kept quiet about it, perhaps because Vadim was caught in a downward spiral. Possibly it had occurred to Jane that she might have to leave Vadim, and she didn't want to feel any guilt over his career. Peter seemed willing to think about it, but he later denied ever agreeing to appear in such a film.

From Honolulu Jane flew to New York, where she joined Vadim, Vanessa and Nathalie aboard the liner *France* for the journey back to Europe. Vadim recalls that as they said good-bye to the Statue of Liberty, "I had the feeling that I was saying good-bye to something forever. The five-day trip was my last clear memory of happiness between us. After that everything becomes confused." Andy Warhol had come to see them off and went about filling a bag with empty Coca-Cola bottles, since the French Coke bottles were embossed and rare. "He left with his heavy load, with much clinking, and radiantly happy."

Once back at the farm near St. Ouen Vadim seemed wholly caught up in *Blue Guitar*, since work was the only way he could cope with their troubled relationship. Although everything was far from certain, he pretended that his project was nearly pulled together and, at his invitation, the producer Gutowski came to the farm for lunch. Jane proposed that they contact the Irish novelist Edna O'Brien about doing the screenplay; this seemed agreeable to the two men, and they mapped out the other details. Jane was to get far more money than Peter; the men did not yet know the incredible grosses that would be racked up by *Easy Rider* before the year's end. But long before *Blue Guitar* could get off the ground, they found themselves quietly sidetracked by their prospective stars' popularity.

In July 1969 the first Americans landed on the moon, watched by the Vadims on the farmhouse television set. They were even more astonished to see little Vanessa take her first three steps just before an American astronaut took his "giant step for mankind." It was as though the child sensed that memorable walking was expected that day. Good feelings toward America ran high once again in France that week, and small crowds of Frenchmen gathered in front of television shops in Paris. It served for a few days to deflect some of the fierce bitterness over Vietnam.

Later that month Jane met a Frenchwoman at the barre of her dancing class who told her of the Indian mystics and of how they brought serenity to troubled people. This woman was leaving for India the following week and Jane made a spur-of-the-moment decision to go with her. "I've got to find myself in all this," she told Vadim. Feeling utterly helpless, he no longer protested. He stayed at the farm with Vanessa. In due course Vadim received "a long love letter from Nepal," and realized that it was all over. "She told me she loved me, that she would never allow life to separate us again. She needed me and wanted to be worthy of our happiness." But he saw through the good intentions. They were so shining with goodwill that "it sent a shiver" down his spine.

Just before leaving for India Jane discovered a novel by Hermann Hesse—*Steppenwolf*—which, she said, made her understand a great many things about herself and others. It is an extraordinary book for a young woman with nearly everything going for her to identify with. *Steppenwolf*, first published in Germany in 1927, is about a man, apparently a German, of late middle age who has begun to see that brutality and jaded appetites dominate everything around him and who recoils, when he becomes in reality or fantasy a wolf of the steppes who pounces on hapless hares and devours them. He meets a prostitute, who like him wishes to withdraw from the purposeless sensuality and sexuality surrounding her, but she sees her own death as her liberation. She is literate and entertaining and Harry (Steppenwolf) falls in love with her. For his folly, she insists that when the time comes he will kill her—as one last gift to her. (In this detail, the book resembles *They Shoot Horses, Don't They?*) During a carnival at one of the enormous

183

houses of pleasure in his city, he kills her with a knife while she is lying in a naked embrace with their friend Pablo, who is amoral and always smiling. Pablo accommodatingly pulls a fur rug over the dead woman, and the next moment the immortal Mozart enters the premises. There are other divertissements. Harry, it appears, is really seeking his soul. He also frequently sees himself fragmented. Someone asks him if he wants "instruction in the building up of the personality . . . to place a few dozen of your pieces at my disposal . . . the pieces into which you saw your so-called personality broken up."

Hesse himself wrote in the introduction to the 1961 edition of his book that:

> *Steppenwolf* is [among his books] the one that was more often and more violently misunderstood than any other, and frequently it is actually the affirmative and enthusiastic readers, rather than those who rejected the book, who have reacted to it oddly. Partly, but only partly, this may occur so frequently by reason of the fact that this book, written when I was fifty years old and dealing, as it does, with the problems of that age, often fell into the hands of very young readers.

Jane was thirty-two when she first read the book, but a self-confessed "late starter."

It seems to me that the key to an understanding of *Steppenwolf* is the suppressed rage and hostility in Harry for nearly all others, built up over years of witnessing small and large stupidities, cruelties and crude lusts. Certainly all of this was present in Jane and very possibly it continues to this day. It was the thing that bound her for so long to Andreas, for they had the same acute sensibility. They had both moved beyond caring what anyone thought of them, and knew that there were more important things at stake than the civilities. And, even more interestingly, both Jane and Harry are disciples; they line up behind a significant person or idea

184

and bone up on it—Harry, for instance, at fifty, learns the foxtrot for the love of Hermine, the girl he must kill.

The curtain was rung down swiftly on American hippies in mid-August 1969. Up until then they had been tolerated, if not accepted, by most city dwellers. A number of them were constantly high on drugs; nearly all of them were shaggy, many of them bathless for long periods, and their clothes, army green or denim blue, granny dresses for the girls, were as ripe as their bodies. They appeared to be a kind of ragged army and they certainly believed that they were on the front line of a never-ending battle with authority. But as the summer faded that last year of the sixties, a truce was in effect between straight people who took haircuts, bathed every day and wore clean suits and dresses, and the young unwashed of America. Their obvious sincerity in wanting peace, universal love and brotherhood and an end to the fierce competitiveness in American life had won them thousands of sympathizers in the cities, but they were shunned, jailed or prodded to move along in nearly all of the small towns of America, where Babbittry was just as strong in the sixties as it had been forty years earlier when Sinclair Lewis first indicted it.

When the actress Sharon Tate, Roman Polanski's wife, and four others were brutally slain in the Polanskis' rented estate on August 8, 1969, the police had no clue as to the killer or killers (they immediately decided there was more than one involved). But the killers had written the word "Pig"* on the front door in blood, and there was speculation that hippies might be involved.

Easy Rider was now in general release everywhere, but the Tate killings had altered the viewer's expectations.

* "Pig" was a denigrating term for policemen coined by the Black Panthers' founder Huey Newton, who explained; "The police . . . reacted in strange and unpredictable ways. In their fright, some of them became children, cursing and insulting us. We responded in kind, calling them swine and pigs, but never cursing. That could be cause for arrest."

No longer was the movie a parable of the young in rebellion, but a horror story. Far too many members of the audience identified with the rednecks. (Weren't the bikers drug dealers? Didn't they deserve whatever they got?)

The crime had been an obscenity committed by emotional cripples. The sixties had run too fast and too recklessly, and far too much had gone down without any protest. Haight-Ashbury had once seem a youth ghetto bursting with color and promise; now it was half deserted, with ragged acid heads sitting dazed on the sidewalk and curbstones. The sixties had careered into a stone wall, and those last victims who crashed were limping homeward or withdrawing into communes in the mountains or the desert for last-ditch stands. When the killers were caught more than three months later, they were described—Charles Manson and his "Family"— as hippies. There was some danger that most of the world would feel justified in condemning all hippies because of the atrocities committed by this false messiah of Haight-Ashbury. The hippie movement had freed America, and eventually the Western world, of its Calvinist hang-ups; it had made every thinking American reappraise his or her values and goals; through its basic identification with the earth and all the environment, it had turned ecology from a science into a standard of decency which many embraced.

While Manson's Family did give ammunition to the provincials and the rednecks, they changed few minds. A more conservative mood was upon the land and all that this tragedy did was write "*finis*" to a chapter that would soon have ended anyway.

Jane had known the Polanskis as close friends, as part of the international film community, and she and Vadim had entertained them often in their Malibu home. Her father was a client of another of the victims, men's hairdresser Jay Sebring, and Peter knew Sebring well. Hank had for a short time rented the guesthouse on the murder site. Both of the male Fondas attended Sebring's services at Forest Lawn.

Sharon Tate Polanski was a much less complicated woman than Jane; at the time of her murder she was about where Jane was when she married Vadim in her awareness of the social realities, but she was a strikingly beautiful woman with an innocent sexuality reminiscent of Marilyn Monroe. She was pregnant at the time of her death and Jane, who believed that she would have made a sensational mother, considered her death a terrible waste.

With Jane still in France, following her trip to India, Vadim had flown to California to close a deal to direct the film version of Gore Vidal's send-up of America's "sexual revolution," *Myra Breckenridge*. He lost out to a British director, who made a dismal affair of something that could have been incisive satire. He was back in Malibu with his daughter Nathalie when the Tate killings were discovered. The randomness of it frightened him, as did the murders that same weekend of a grocery tycoon and his wife, butchered in a similar fashion with the word "War" etched into the skin of the man's chest. It was all too close, and while Vadim could not see the parallels to their own situation when Charlie Manson was found hiding in a desert cabin, Jane must have. Manson's girls, all Haight-Ashbury runaways and drop-outs, were even more docile than Sharon Tate had been, but they all had been exploited by one man.

When Jane returned to California, she took a suite at the Beverly-Wilshire Hotel. She telephoned Vadim and said that they must talk; though Vadim knew it was all over, he drove in from Malibu and they sat in her hotel sitting room and talked about how best to end their marriage. It was a familiar scene to Vadim, to whom it had happened three times before. The image of a "destroyer of young womanhood" was quite unfair to the desolate man who left the Beverly-Wilshire to drive alone back to the beach.

24

Throughout most of her life Jane had allowed herself to be dominated by men, but now that was all behind her. The women's movement had begun rattling doors and windows a few years earlier and some of them had sprung open. Women were now running banks in a few places, publishing their own magazine, and finding mass-media voices in Betty Friedan, Gloria Steinem, Bella Abzug, Kate Millett and Germaine Greer. Finally Jane was in control of her own life. She was a mother, a screen star who was rich and internationally known; and she was also a daughter, but circumstances had made that fact less and less relevant. She was now as famous as her father; she was not in close touch with him; and even if her fame should happen to evaporate, which seemed quite unlikely, the trust left behind by Frances would still keep Jane economically independent of Hank Fonda.

It is extremely rare for a fine actress to be original in her thought. In this century, Mrs. Patrick Campbell comes to mind, but it is difficult to think of a single American example. Shirley MacLaine writes successful, witty books, and suggests that she is grand company, but scarcely brilliant. Jane was open and ready to do something significant; a fulcrum ready for the whole body of her frustrations to be swung to the light and given meaning and direction.

It is interesting to speculate about what might have happened to the life and career of Jane Fonda, had she at that moment turned for guidance to a woman, a feminist perhaps who would have been only too happy to have her join the coalition. But women weren't running the things that mattered to Jane. They were not yet in charge of a single movie studio—that would not come for nearly ten years; they were not key directors. Though *Ms.* magazine was much read and discussed among women, it had little weight as a major publishing force in America. The boldest publishing venture of the day was *Ramparts* magazine, published by a fractious young man named Warren Hinckle and staffed mostly by men with a sprinkling of young women in its lower echelons. Its target was the establishment, especially various branches of that principal bastion of the status quo, the U.S. Government. It was essential reading for most students, whether they agreed with it or not; it was the strongest voice that the disparate, angry movements of the nineteen-sixties could find.

Jane had been reading *Ramparts* ever since her political awakening in 1968. Now, in early 1970, she returned to America from weeks of sorting out her life within the tranquillity of the farmhouse at St. Ouen. She knew two things for certain: that fame was a dead end, and she had been frittering away her life among her illustrious peers for much too long; and that her visit to India had convinced her that the oppressed peoples of the world could not pull themselves up by themselves, but needed the help of more fortunate people like herself. Jane brought with her a copy of a recent *Ramparts* article describing the situation on Alcatraz Island in San Francisco Bay. Once the site of the most secure federal penitentiary in America, it had been closed as being outmoded and then in November 1969, "occupied" by tribes of American Indians fed up with the mismanagement of their lives and resources by the Bureau of Indian Affairs. A staff writer on *Ramparts*, Peter Collier, had visited Alcatraz and written an eyewitness account that had moved Jane profoundly; she wanted to meet Collier and she wanted to visit Alcatraz. She said that she "wanted to become involved in the movement for social change." As she became more and more radicalized, Jane's rhetoric would tend toward the didactic rather than the personal, and it became more and more difficult to find the real Jane Fonda underneath the stream of pronouncements. Collier writes of their first meeting:

> She showed up at the San Francisco Embarcadero on the appointed morning, materializing out of fog that seemed provided for the occasion by a Hollywood special-effects crew. She was wearing tight jeans and had a helmet of hair cut in a shag: It was the proper uniform, but she didn't seem quite comfortable in it. The features that struck me were the marvelous, toothy smile and eyes of tremendous depth. She said she was nervous about how she would be received, yet she radiated a kind of coiled energy and confidence in her ability to meet and master the new situation.

The situation on Alcatraz was still a stalemate, for the government chose not to storm the place. Local yachtsmen were keeping a steady supply of food, medicine and blankets flowing onto the island from the mainland and the Coast Guard was being deliberately ineffectual. Rallies were being held by wealthy friends of the Indians to raise funds to keep the occupation going. Collier recalls that Jane instinctively made for the center of the ruling Sioux Leaders. When Collier left her that evening, she was smoking marijuana with them and joking about the Bureau of Indian Affairs.

Jane's new militancy was not the usual Hollywood star excursion among the faceless oppressed. She had embarked on a journey no American actress of her stature had ever undertaken before. Without the inheritance of her mother's bottomless energy, she never could have managed to undertake so many rallies, so many causes, nor endured so many sleepless nights moving from one podium to another; and with all that, still continue appearing in films.

Following Collier's suggestion, Jane set off on a cross-country tour of Indian reservations, accompanied by her old friend from her first days with Vadim and now her traveling companion, Elizabeth Vailland. They drove in Jane's station wagon, first to Puget Sound, Washington, where they were caught in a melee between Indians and the military police at Fort Lawton, an Army Reserve post. The government contended that Jane and the others were trying to occupy the fort, much as the Indians had Alcatraz Island, for use as an Indian cultural center. It is certainly possible that their apparent success in taking over the former prison in San Francisco Bay might have led these militant Indians to embark upon a program of taking over little-used government facilities as token compensation for the theft of their land generations ago by the white man. Ellis Island in New York Harbor was doubtless on the list.

Although they were arrested, Jane and Elizabeth managed to get away without being jailed, and by the end of the following week they were in Denver, where, filled with junk food from the road, Jane announced at a press conference that she was going on a fast for a day and a half to protest against the Vietnam War. The gesture brought her spiritual and physiological relief. She casually and frequently tossed the words "genocide" and "exploitation" into her speeches. When closing letters to friends in her tall, slanted "lefty" script, she always wrote "Power to the People." It is difficult to assess her value to the Indian cause. She would breeze into a city or town or reservation, persuade everyone of her undying allegiance to their cause and then be gone, never to be seen again.

But there were several white men who volunteered to help steer her toward the right causes, the chief among them at the time being a lawyer called Mark Lane, a huge, bearded bear of a man who was known, along with New Orleans district attorney Jim Garrison, as the most prominent exponent of the conspiracy theory on the killing of President Kennedy. Lane had made the theory something of a full-time job, lecturing for a fee all across the country and promoting his book, *Rush to Judgment*, which refuted point by point the Warren Commission's Report on the assassination. There were in the book accounts of witnesses who had disappeared from the face of the earth; proof of a second gunman; and assertions of the complicity of government agencies in the murder. Lane met Jane and told her that he would be pleased to defend her if she got into any trouble, and in the months ahead her skirmishes with the authorities became so constant that Lane seemed to become a part of Jane's retinue.

Jane was a prize plum, ready for plucking by any resourceful militant. Mark Lane moved up to become her defender, and a leftist screenwriter named Fred Gardner, who was concentrating his antiwar protests on the soldier in uniform, became her mentor. She had a great deal to learn, but she was a very quick study once she was on her way. And there were others, some of whom she met socially in Hollywood: Donald and Shirley Sutherland (he was a Canadian actor who had graduated from horror films such as *Die, Die, My Darling*—to leading man status) and publicist Steve Jaffee, who earlier had done legwork researching the assassination theories of both Garrison and Lane.

When Jane returned to California, she discussed the role of a prostitute in a new film to be shot in New York. Meanwhile she found herself swept up by several militant groups, all interrelated.

The Black Panthers interested Jane as much as the Indians and, as time went on, far more so. The Indians never succeeded in relating to Jane, but the Panthers seemed to. Perhaps they were more exciting to her since they differed from the Indians on one significant point: the Panthers armed themselves against the enemy— authority, usually represented by the police.* In early

* Later, there was a prolonged shoot-out between Indians and the authorities in South Dakota, ending in a negotiated settlement.

December 1969, just before Jane's return from France, there had been a major shoot-out between the Los Angeles Police and the Panthers, resulting in several black fatalities and following a pattern initiated earlier that year to wipe out the Panther leadership. The Panther cofounder, Huey Newton, was in prison, convicted of involuntary manslaughter in the death of an Oakland policeman back in October 1967. Huey's ordeal had begun the night of October 27, 1967, when he was celebrating the end of three years of parole following a felony conviction in 1964. At four in the morning he was driving with a friend, Gene McKinney, from a party, headed for an all-night café. They didn't make it. Their Volkswagen—which really belonged to Huey's fiancée—was stopped by policeman John Frey, who recognized the car as a "known Black Panther vehicle" as well as Huey, whom Frey addressed as "the great, great Huey P. Newton." Frey radioed for assistance and patrolman Herbert Heanes arrived. Huey traditionally kept a small lawbook nearby for assistance in such circumstances or to aid other brothers who had been similarly stopped. He pointed to a passage in his lawbook and told Frey that he had no reasonable cause to arrest him. Frey allegedly then said, "You can take that book and stick it in your ass, nigger." The succeeding events are murky to this day. Within seconds, Huey was shot in the abdomen, policeman Frey lay dying of a bullet-wound, patrolman Heanes suffered multiple wounds, and Gene McKinney vanished. Huey's version in court of the confrontation was that the policemen, intent on killing him, shot each other.

"Free Huey" was still a constant slogan upon Jane's advent among the Panthers; it was shouted at rallies and was seen on bumper stickers everywhere. The Sutherlands were especially involved in the Panther rallies in Hollywood.

Fred Gardner, aiming at the individual soldier for conversion to his antiwar views, opened a series of "GI coffeehouses" near army bases around the country. These friendly retreats were funded by donations which often came in large sums from antiwar groups. Gardner, who had once been a Hollywood screenwriter and had contributed to the script of Antonioni's disappointing study of youthful alienation in America, *Zabriskie Point* (1970), called upon his actor friends to join him in developing a number of satirical sketches that would be booked into the various GI coffeehouses. The company of players called themselves the FTA troupe, which usually amused the soldiers since among the troops, FTA meant "Fuck the Army." If asked, Gardner, Jane and others used to say that the initials stood for "Free the Army." Peter Boyle, who had become established through one surprisingly successful, low-budget movie, *Joe*, joined the acting company, along with Donald Sutherland and comedian Dick Gregory. "Country Joe" McDonald, a folk rock singer, joined them early, although later he fell out bitterly with Jane and Sutherland and left. Gardner, too, eventually defected. Gardner contributed most of the ideas for the skits, and Jane improved on them with bits of business or dialogue. Other writers signed on to impale the military establishment were the cartoonist and playwright Jules Feiffer, the playwright Herb Gardner (no relation to Fred), Barbara Garson, Robin Menken and Roger Bowen. Two film-makers, Francine Parker and Nina Serrano, were the producers.

For the next eighteen months Jane was in constant motion, traveling from one Army base to another, from one college campus to the next, catching naps on planes or at airport motels. She lived on vitamins and the conviction that there was no time to lose; that the war in Vietnam was masterminded by criminally irresponsible men in the Pentagon and President Nixon. Jane aligned herself with every viable antiwar group in existence among students, within unions, church groups, show business, draft protesters and soldiers. She was in touch with teachers, lawyers, clergymen, North Vietnamese and those South Vietnamese who wanted a coalition and an end to the conflict, writers, folk singers and actors beyond number. Her fees—when she was paid—

went back into the movement or to keep the FTA shows moving. She often had trouble keeping herself presentable, getting a bath and finding some decent clothes, so she had stripped herself down to the barest essentials. She was a one-woman army on the move.

25

Film stars on the top plateau of stardom are forced to come to terms with coveys of fans who follow them around. Whenever she was in New York Marilyn Monroe was shadowed by a group known as the Monroe Six, who hung about the front of her apartment building, had an uncanny instinct for knowing wherever she was dining and were at the curbstone when she emerged. Marilyn treated these young people with remarkable kindness.

Jane was shadowed by an equally vigilant covey of groupies from mid-1970 on. They were not especially young and rather than courting her attention and favor they made every effort to stay out of her sight. They were members of the FBI, and for nearly three years they relentlessly pursued Jane from airport to airport, from house to house, from rally to rally. They paid hundreds of thousands of dollars to informants who "documented" her opinions, her friends and even her appearance. (The chances were good that if the informant noted what Jane was wearing, that party was another woman.) In 1975 it was revealed that Jane's long distance telephone calls and telegrams had been intercepted or monitored by the National Security Agency in 1970. Transcripts were then circulated to top government officials, including President Nixon and Henry Kissinger, who was then in charge of national security. Known by the code name "the Gamma Series," the surveillance was handled by special officers in the CIA, the FBI and the counterintelligence branch of the Defense Intelligence Agency. One government informant said at the time, "What Brezhnev and Jane Fonda said got about the same treatment."

Her government file grew to more than five hundred pages over the next couple of years. Most of it was stamped "Confidential" and placed in "Group 1," which excluded the document from automatic downgrading and declassification. Many of the papers were classified top secret with the notation that "No foreign dissemination—No dissemination abroad" was allowed. She was variously labeled "subversive" and "anarchist." A diligent search through this file fails to provide a clue as to why she was considered to be so dangerous. Her interest in the Black Panther Party never moved close to real involvement in their paramilitary skirmishes with the police; her anger at antiwar rallies scarcely made her an anarchist.

The FBI used "pretext calls" to Jane's home, hotel or agent's offices in attempting to obtain her traveling plans and whereabouts. The government investigators were not above clipping out daily newspaper stories about Jane and sending them to Washington as "confidential" material. One such item reads:

Page A-12 of the March 9, 1971, issue of the "Harald-Examiner" [sic], a daily Los Angeles newspaper, contained an article entitled "Jane Fonda Visits Jailed Angela Davis," which indicated FONDA visited with DAVIS on March 7, 1971.

Spelling in many of these government documents is atrocious, but the paragraph suggests that the FBI found such a meeting of interest: two of the world's most beautiful activists clasping hands in a jail cell. Miss Davis, who was black and an avowed communist discharged from the University of California because of her radical views, was later cleared of gun smuggling (to black prisoners involved in a shoot-out) and freed.

The government surveillance of Jane probably began

as a direct order from President Nixon, who had a paranoid hatred of her; and he no doubt expected that if the FBI and Secret Service agents and their informants dogged her long enough, "They would get the goods on her." In Nixon's eyes, Jane was the anti-American gone public. In 1973 when the Nixon administration was tottering amid wholesale revelations of chicanery and criminality, his "enemies list" prominently included Jane. Compiled into a list at his direction by aide Charles W. Colson, these enemies were meant to suffer prolonged harassment. The intention of this campaign against Jane and others was to discredit and hopefully to destroy them as political foes. Tax audits were suggested to the Internal Revenue Service, but that department was singularly uncooperative.

Nothing Nixon ever did deterred Jane in the slightest degree. Her activities must have appalled him: she was raising money and giving large sums of her own to help the Black Panther Party, which was radical, racist and anarchistic, as the government saw it. She was traveling back and forth across America speaking out against the war in Vietnam, urging students to resist the draft and soldiers in uniform to refuse to fight.

There were a few legal difficulties to nailing Jane. The Black Panther Party had not been outlawed, despite a number of incidents with the police. There was a rabid fear within the government that if the BPP were outlawed it would go underground and then could wage its guerrilla war against the white establishment with impunity, since the black ghettos would protect their brothers and sisters within the Panthers. And despite the Gulf of Tonkin Resolution, there had never been any congressional sanction of the war in Vietnam. The illegal nature of the massive American military presence in Vietnam was undoubtedly the strongest factor in saving Jane's career in the years after American withdrawal in defeat. By the time of this debacle, nearly every American of normal intelligence now saw the recent war as a tragic miscalculation. Those who had once branded her a traitor were forced to concede grudgingly that she was really a shrill prophet.

FBI director J. Edgar Hoover, a man not celebrated for his ethics, personally intervened in the "Jane Fonda matter" in June 1970. He dispatched a memorandum to the subversive activities chief in Los Angeles authorizing him to send a phony letter to a well-known Hollywood gossip columnist appearing in *Daily Variety* ensuring "that mailing cannot be traced to the Bureau" and fabricated the following:

> . . . Jane Fonda, noted film actress, would attend a Black Panther Party fund raising function on 6/13/70. The proposed letter states the writer attended the function and was searched upon entering, urged to contribute funds for jailed Panther leaders and to buy guns for "the coming revolution." Also, that Jane and one of the Panthers led a refrain "We will kill Richard Nixon, and any other M. . . . . F. . . . . who stands in our way." It can be expected that Fonda's involvement with the BPP cause could detract from her status with the general public if reported in a Hollywood "gossip" column.*

This is one of the few documented instances of a clear-cut frame-up of a citizen by a high-ranking government official.

The FTA shows continued. They were a great success as entertainment, diversion for the troops, but their main intention—of damaging the soldiers' will to fight—was blunted by the impact of Jane's personality on the GIs, who turned out in large numbers to see someone whom most of them considered to be an eccentric movie star on an antiwar kick. She was sexy and enthusiastic and they were rarely disappointed. Afterward, half a dozen of them would be called in by the security officer

* Extracted from "Hearings before the Senate Select Committee to Study Government Operations with Respect to Intelligence Activities" (the Church committee).

at the base, who had instructions from U. S. Army Intelligence to monitor her statements so that they could be forwarded to the Secret Service.

In fact, the earliest known date of an FBI report on Jane was May 8, 1970,* and it noted that a soldier by the name of George W. Darwin reported to the security officer at Fort Carson that he saw Jane at the Inscape Coffee House on the base on the evening of April 21.

> Darwin advised that most of her comments were to the effect that the war in Vietnam was wrong and that we should not have soldiers in Vietnam fighting the war. He stated that to the best of his recollection, she made a statement to the effect that soldiers should submit a Conscientious Objector form if ordered to go to Vietnam and in this way they could avoid serving in Vietnam. Darwin stated that to the best of his memory, she did not advocate that anyone go AWOL to avoid serving in Vietnam. He stated that she made some comment to the effect that going AWOL was one way of protesting the war in Vietnam, but he could not recall her urging anyone to protest in this manner.

Other soldiers interrogated at the same time were Gary Lee Simzak, who backed up Darwin's story, and John William Barnes, who had surprisingly contradictory impressions:

> Barnes stated to the best of his recollection, she stated that everyone [meaning the soldiers] should get together and refuse to go to Vietnam. She stated that if you are being ordered to go to Vietnam you should go AWOL.

A chaplain's assistant, Dan Greer, added that she told a group of about thirty GIs at the Inscape Coffee House

* It may have been no coincidence that it was the week of the student killings at Kent State University by National Guardsmen.

that the GIs and the poor were lackeys of the rich. Then Geer's boss, Chaplain James Goodner, asked Jane if she were wealthy. She told him: "Oh, you think I'm rich. I could be sitting on my ass in Beverly Hills enjoying myself, but I have to face myself in the morning." Greer added a touch of color to his recollections by telling the interrogator that she answered "all questions with the traditional raised right hand clenching her fist and stating 'right on'." The more conservative the informant, the more radical the portrait of Jane, which only proves how subjective all memory is and how unreliable much of an FBI dossier may be.

A Legal Clearing House was organized by Jane and others to give aid and counsel to protesting soldiers. A group of "50 to 100 GIs [at the Inscape Coffee House; the size of the crowd varies from account to account] heard Fonda state that she was going to make lawyers available to the GIs who are presently facing court-martial, so that GIs would be aware of their individual rights." The Legal Clearing House's first legal adviser was Jane's friend Mark Lane, and funds were raised, again some from Jane herself, to keep the legal service going. Ostensibly its purpose was to defend only those soldiers who refused to go to Vietnam or had gone AWOL because of a lack of faith in the war's justification. It was not a refuge for criminals or for insubordinates with chips on their shoulders.

Paralleling the tours of the FTA was a growing fraternity among soldiers who tended to be pacifists. The most prominent group on Army bases was the Bahai sect, who gave soldiers a moral and philosophical foundation for their refusal to fight; the FTA gave them an emotional divertissement toward the same end. Frequently, Jane would be accompanied around the Army bases by members of the Bahai group, in uniform, of course.

When Jane first sought out Peter Collier for help in making contact with the oppressed, she was leaving herself open to exploitation. Her closest friends and her family could see it, but she seemed blind to it. If anyone warned her, she gave them didactic explanations

201

drawn from those against whom she was warned. For a time she seemed to have been programmed by the Panther leaders and by the Indian militants. A few of her remarks were so foolish that when she came out of this stage, when she finally became aware of what they really were about, she would recant some of what she had said, admitting that it was both naïve and stupid. Not everyone took such advantage; neither Fred Gardner nor Peter Collier did, and it is much to their credit. But while the spell was on, Jane was a great prize on the radical circuit.

Her presence always guaranteed a crowd, her wealth might be tapped so that she could start the fund raisers waving a check, her own. The Black Panthers seemed to adore her*; the American Indians, it should be said, merely tolerated her and when Jane herself sensed that they considered her a bit of a nuisance and too diffuse in her involvements, she eased away from them.

During Jane's last trip to Paris she had visited a movie set where Jean-Luc Godard was filming. Now that she had fluent French and was well versed in radical jargon they could discuss the importance of films having something to say about society. A seed must have been planted there. From then on she spent a great deal of time pondering the issue of social relevance in movies. She thought Godard's approach was too austere; message films should be entertaining as well, but she did not challenge the great French filmmaker.

* It is important to point out that Black Panther founder Huey Newton, a canny leader, probably sensed that Jane was going to become increasingly important both as a public figure and as an actress. For that reason she had to be handled with great caution since there was every possibility that her own celebrity might eclipse the growing notoriety of the Panthers and thus limit their revolutionary capability. Limits may have been set on just how close to the Panther leadership Jane could move.

*   *   *

By mid-April Jane and Elizabeth Vailland were in Idaho to powwow with members of the Shoshone tribe. They had arranged to meet there LaNada Means Boyer,* an Indian woman who usually lived on the Fort Hall Reservation in northern Idaho but who had spent months in San Francisco rallying support for the Indians occupying Alcatraz, where Jane had first met her. Jane and Elizabeth were very tired from their long drive. They were travel-worn and needed rest. By contrast, Mrs. Boyer stepped off her plane in Pocatello that evening looking refreshed by her flight and prepared to confer all night. This they did, and Jane managed to draw on her usual reservoir of energy.

For at least two years, perhaps longer, going back to her awakening while with Vadim to the world's problems, she had seemed to be in a constant state of expectancy of something wonderful about to happen, or something dreadful. Among the militants Jane was seen as very naïve. She thought that all of the oppressed peoples in the nation should join forces against the establishment, and spoke of blacks aligning themselves with Indians. LaNada Boyer told her that a more urgent matter was to forge some sort of unity among the Indians themselves. Mrs. Boyer had come to the reservation to muster support for their brothers on Alcatraz, none of whom happened to be Shoshones. She was getting nowhere. After two or three days of conferring with Indian women and tribal chiefs, Jane realized that LaNada's cause was only stirring up hostility among the Shoshones, so she and Elizabeth moved on.

* Her brother was Indian activist Russell Means.

26

In June Jane was due in New York City for her new film. *Klute* was described as a psychological thriller concerning a neurotic call girl, Bree Daniels, and was to be directed by Alan Pakula, who had entered the movies as a producer. Pakula had begun directing in 1969 with *The Sterile Cuckoo* (a study of a young woman at college who believes she is an ugly duckling trying not to be a social misfit by having a meaningful affair), after supervising the filming of a number of serious and provocative pictures directed by Robert Mulligan—*Fear Strikes Out* (1957), about a baseball player's fear of failure; *To Kill a Mockingbird* (1963), an indictment of white man's justice in the South; and *Up the Down Staircase* (1967), a drama with comic overtones about the perils of teaching in a Manhattan high school.

Klute was no ordinary thriller. It was meant not only to terrify audiences but also to reveal to them the psyche of an intelligent prostitute, showing the split dividing a sensitive, educated, high-priced call girl at war with herself and her feelings. She allows herself to be exploited as part of a corrupt system (which Jane was eager to indict), but Bree Daniels really wants to leave the life and settle into a long-term affair or a marriage. The plot device holding the movie together is Bree's brush with a sadistic killer, who is a corporate kingpin and aware of her intelligence. Despite all her efforts to "control" her situation, to call the shots, Bree is reduced to helplessness when terrorized over the telephone by the killer. While making the film, Jane was to become aware of the women's revolution in a new way. She said:

> Well, my whole thought and thinking changed. . . . I began to realize that this particular revolution is not only their [women's] revolution, it's my revolution, too. I mean, if I don't fight it, nobody else is going to.
>
> Suddenly I could view my entire life in a totally social context. I was able to understand, for the first time, my mother; I was able to understand my sister, myself, my friends, the women I know. I was able to seek out women, not just because there weren't any men around to talk to, but because I really preferred to talk to women.

She befriended a number of prostitutes, telling them that with this picture they would be shown on the screen, perhaps for the first time ever, as something more than stereotyped floozies; they would be depicted as human beings. She had a hand in decorating her room on the set at Filmways Studio up on 113th Street in Harlem, where the picture was shot.

Pakula hired a twenty-three-year-old call girl as technical adviser, perhaps one of the girls Jane met during her research into the "back story" of the film. Pakula recalls that the girl was very helpful but often late, with bizarre excuses:

> I waited two hours for her once for a meeting a few days before we started shooting. She said, "I'm sorry, but I was looking for my contact lens on Sixth Avenue." I sat her down with Jane the night before we shot a scene in a hotel room [a real hotel room was used]. The girl said, "The first thing you do, no matter what, is get your money. You get it before, because you're not going to get as much afterward. The second thing you do is make sure the man thinks he is different. You need the money because you can't afford to take him for free, but he is different . . . and he really turns you on. You get

more money that way. . . . I've lost all respect for men because they all believe they're different, every one that comes along."

If most people learn by doing, actors often learn by watching others do. Jane plunged deeply into the netherworld of New York's call girls, and when we are given an intimate sequence of Bree Daniels turning a trick—a john from Chicago who believes he is into wild sex (which his Calvinist past dictates he should whisper to Bree)—she pretends great amusement and enthusiasm. "Oh, I like your mind!" she tells him, and almost in an aside, suggests they get the $100 out of the way (double the usual rate because of his "eccentric" tastes), so they can enjoy themselves without *that* on their minds.

Bree Daniels' apartment has some pretensions, but the style is cluttered, cramped chaos, especially in the bedroom area (it is an oversized studio apartment), where Bree spends most of her time. It has exposed bricks around the fireplace, an effect all intellectual bohemians sought and landlords quickly supplied from the early nineteen-fifties on; a reproduction of a drawing of President Kennedy, a plebeian touch that Jane picked up while studying the living quarters of the call girls she got to know; and a fake Tiffany lampshade. There is a bookcase crowded with paperbacks that look read. The total effect is oppressive, part of it from the set itself and much of it from the way it is filmed. It was so claustrophobic that one of the backers complained to Pakula about the look of the picture. Here was a movie shot in wide screen that made its audience feel trapped in a tunnel—precisely the reaction Pakula was seeking.

The investigator Klute, tracking the psychopathic killer, was being played by Donald Sutherland, already an old friend along the antiwar trail. During the film and for some months afterward, Sutherland and Jane became close; a relationship was begun.

Sutherland's Klute is a repressed, puritanical, fussy product of bourgeois America. He secretly condemns what Bree is doing while doing everything he can to track

206

down the killer and save her. Sutherland was to replay versions of this same character in a number of films, most disastrously in *The Day of the Locust*. Offscreen, he was anything but repressed. Jane did not take their relationship seriously, although she was grateful for Sutherland's support in the internal warfare that occasionally erupted among the FTA performers and staff. They were sometimes wrong in their positions, but at least they were wrong together.

Pakula establishes the mood and tempo of Manhattan perfectly, but it becomes another character in the film and not just the "big city" where prostitutes are expected to be. Bree lives in a seedy brownstone apartment house next door to a funeral parlor; at one point the killer uses the long cortege of hearse laden with coffin and flowers, and the limousines with family and other mourners, as a screen behind which he can stalk Bree as she leaves her building. A factory floor in the garment district, with newly made dresses hanging on acres of racks, becomes ground zero for Bree when the killer corners her there alone after hours.

Jane understands all the little corners of Bree's psyche. She is bright, sardonic, nervous and neurotic. When asked by her analyst why she stays in the trade, she tells her: "I know I'm good . . . you control it. You call the shots." To the private eye of Klute she confesses: "I'm afraid of the dark," and asks to sleep in his room, which has one small bed with a trundle beneath it, and no extra pillow. Klute gallantly surrenders his bed, but until now has not surrendered his will and has rather stonily turned aside her bantering passes. Now she slips in beside him as he sleeps and finally awakens his libido, afterward telling him with much affection that he was "a real tiger." Later, she admits to her analyst that Klute has gotten to her; she is not numb inside with him as she has been with all the others, and that distresses her.

Small details reveal that Jane missed nothing in putting together her Bree Daniels. When she is trapped in the dress factory and being forced by the killer to listen to his own tape recording (he goes around bugging his murders and acts of sadism so that he can play them back later for additional kicks) of the sexual torture and then the murder of her friend Arlen, Jane weeps real tears and mucus drips from her nose. During an audition for the title part in *Saint Joan* off-Broadway, aspiring actress Bree affects an Irish accent, which the casting director tells her is "interesting," but of course is impossible. This was at a time when the Irish actress Siobhan MacKenna was at the height of her success and had just played the role. Jane's Bree is up on everything, even to her own disadvantage.

Pakula recalls how Jane, off guard, contributed a little piece of business with the Thanksgiving hymn from Brentwood Town and Country School days:

> . . . when Bree Daniels sings that little hymn in her room . . . that was not planned by the way, it was Jane Fonda relaxing between takes. We had tried several things for that scene and I wasn't happy with any of them. They were reloading the camera, and she was sitting there smoking, off in her own world, and I suddenly heard her singing that hymn. I whirled around, and she looked at me and stopped. "Oh, God," she said, "you want me to use that!" "Yes," I said, "that's it, that's what we've been looking for." It's one of my favorite things in the film because it's the moment when you really feel her vulnerability.

Jane's evenings, after she had studied her scenes for the next day, were often spent with various Panther groups. In late July a Panther official named Thomas Jolly was to escort Jane to a rally and during the evening "whisper something sweet in her ear and tell her he needed some money." She was wearing her *Klute* shingled bob hairstyle and looked sensationally beautiful, but, so the government spy in their midst reported, there must have been a cultural or ethnic barrier to Jolly's appreciation of her, for he allegedly told a friend afterward that his mission revolted him "because she was so ugly." Jolly reportedly asked her for ten thousand dollars but he did not get it. Perhaps for once Jane sensed that she was being exploited, and gave him a substantially smaller sum.

That time in and around the shooting of *Klute* saw the last, frantic spasm of Panther activity for Jane. It coincided with growing public impatience with aggressive black activism in America that would lead within less than a decade to an astonishingly weakened black minority rendered nearly helpless by the wave of ultraconservatism sweeping the country. Jane did not become impatient with them; she began to find connections between the problems of the blacks and the Indians and the war in Vietnam.

"Free Huey" was still the group's battle cry, and in the middle of the summer Newton was freed on fifty thousand dollars' bail pending a new trial.* At earlier Panther meetings, Jane had been moved to say of Huey Newton that he was qualified to be president, and she further described him as the only man she had ever met who approached sainthood. She was at the time deep in her hyperbolic period, deep in the spell of radicalism. Later she would recant, but so skillfully that no one would notice. Few would ever see Jane leave a cause. But her enthusiasm for Huey was understandable and was shared by many. Huey was a remarkably even-tempered, thoughtful leader, concerned about his Panther brothers keeping within legal bounds, promoting a free lunch program for black ghetto children, and helping to provide bail money for blacks in trouble (as did Jane when asked) and in jail. If he had a blind spot, it was his belief that his leadership of the Black Panther Party ruled out any close emotional ties with others. He wrote: "We (the Black Panthers) have no romantic and fictional notions about getting married and living happily ever after behind a white picket fence. We choose to live together for a common purpose." Some of Huey's cool preoccupation seeped into Jane's attitude toward

* His conviction was eventually reversed by a higher court.

attachments, but to a lesser degree. It was a way of "handling" relationships, following chaotic childhoods in an impoverished ghetto in Huey's case, and a rich ghetto in Jane's.

The antiwar movement and student agitation against the war in particular were being closely followed by President Nixon, all of the armed forces, the Secret Service, the National Security Agency, the CIA, the attorney general, and FBI director Hoover. In a Secret Service report outlining the "highlights" of such activity, they were especially interested in the current movements of a priest called Philip Berrigan and Jane Fonda:

[She] spoke at the University of Florida, Gainesville, Florida, on January twenty-three last [1971]. Approximately six thousand individuals attended her speech for which she was paid twelve hundred fifty dollars from student government funds. Fonda criticized United States policies and called for support for the "Soldiers Winter Conference" [sic] which will be held in Detroit, Michigan, and will attempt to publicize "atrocities committed by United States soldiers."

On January twenty-four last, Fonda spoke at Florida State University, Tallahassee, Florida. Prior to her speech, a representative of the National Student Association discussed the "People's Peace Treaty" which the NSA is negotiating between students in North Vietnam and students in the United States. Fonda supported this treaty and urged everyone sign petitions to support it. She claimed United States soldiers in Vietnam no longer desire to fight.

The "white paper" went on to describe the vigils being held around the country in support of the Reverend Berrigan and the five nuns who were accused of plotting to kidnap the architect of Nixon's foreign policy, Henry Kissinger, who was also the man most responsible for the destruction of Cambodia through saturation bombing. Kissinger was, if anything, even more loathed along

210

the antiwar circuit than Nixon, possibly because he was deemed the cleverer man and thus capable of greater mischief in the world. This absurd kidnapping charge was eventually dismissed, but only after large sums of money had been spent on their defense.

Jane's performance in *Klute* was very much a carryover from that in *They Shoot Horses*, her last film, made two years earlier. They were both extremely strong scripts, masterfully directed and filmed. The supporting casts were absolutely right in every role. Interestingly, they both contained scenes of rather explicit, depersonalized sex. The film was to win many awards for Jane, including an Oscar, and there is a clue here to her endurance as a star and her step-by-step elevation to superstardom. These extraordinary performances were two years apart because Jane had other things to do. Her causes kept her from taking even enticing parts; *she was waiting for a great part*. If she had been a spendthrift or had not been born rich, she could not have afforded either to devote so much time to various movements or to wait so long. With one or two exceptions, all her films in the nineteen-seventies would be carefully chosen, and nearly all of them from 1975 on produced at least in part by her own company, I.P.C. (Indochina Peace Campaign) Productions.

27

The deaths of four students at Kent State University in Ohio were sobering to everyone, perhaps even to President Nixon, whose order to bomb Cambodia had triggered the vast unrest in the land. It would only be much later that everyone would learn that Cambodia had been bombed secretly for many months by American airpower.

Jane was thirty-two, but she looked and felt at least ten years younger. A little like Petula Clark, the darling of the straight world, a singing actress from England who had achieved immense popularity in America when past the bloom of youth with one extraordinary hit song, "Don't Sleep in the Subway," Jane was becoming her opposite number among the young counterculturists. Jane and her young partisans were going to redeem the country, purify what the older generation had sullied, stop the slaughter of the innocents. When some of them fell at Kent State, their resolve hardened.

That fall (1970), Jane went on a grueling speaking tour of college campuses. On November 2, she spoke at Fanshawe Community College in London, Ontario, and was to appear at two schools in North Carolina the following week. On her way into the United States by way of Cleveland International Airport shortly after midnight on November 3, she arrived at customs. She did not know that the Canadian Mounties, once so glamorized by Nelson Eddy in his musicals with Jeanette MacDonald, had put a "stop" on her for, as her

FBI document later stated, "possible smuggling of narcotics as she is an admitted user of marijuana and exponent of drugs." It was typical of the authorities to confuse Jane with her brother.

Jane was exhausted and slightly disheveled as she moved through the customs area. She was taken into an alcove for a search, while her luggage was seized, including her handbag. Customs inspector Lawrence Troiano asked her to sit down and wait while he called his superior. In Jane's suitcase they found her address book, which they confiscated and copied since it contained the names of Americans involved in antiwar activity, including the economist John Kenneth Galbraith, actors Tony Curtis, Donald Sutherland and George Segal, writers Norman Mailer and John Updike, comedians Dick Gregory and Tommy Smothers, and dozens of other activists from California to Massachusetts. They discovered 102 vials of "drugs" which were sent for examination; it did Jane no good to protest and say that they were vitamins, part of a regimen that made her, in her own words, "a health-food freak." Special Agent Edward Matuszak then approached them, and ignored Jane's request to be allowed to go to the lavatory.

The record becomes confused at this point, but it seems clear that the two customs men tried to prevent her from walking toward a women's lavatory. When one of the men grabbed her by the arm, Jane struck back. Patrolman Robert Piper was a few yards away, watching this, and immediately came forward. He later told the court that Jane kicked him in the left thigh, and said that she snarled at him to get the hell out of there. Jane was arrested and jailed, and spent the night in the Cleveland jailhouse, her eyes open to everything around her. She later said:

> I spent my time in jail on the floor of a cell with Barbara Kahn. She told me she was repeatedly beaten on the arms and legs by guards. She has the bruises to prove it. She is a political prisoner like thousands of political prisoners in this country. . . . I found it

[the jail] deplorable, criminal, violent. The inmates are assaulted physically as well as psychologically. They all told me to tell them what it's like when I get out. If this can happen to me, you can imagine what happens to less visible people who are trying to do something in this country.

The Barbara Kahn she spoke of was an activist, too, arrested for trying to disrupt a parade by the United Hard Hats of America, a group of ultraconservative construction workers.

Jane demanded a trail by jury and was free on bond in the custody of her lawyers, Mark Lane, who had flown to Cleveland as soon as he heard of the episode, and Irwin Barnett, from Cleveland. The experience was, overall, exhilarating to Jane. Always before, authorities had backed off when they saw who she was. Now someone, possibly the President of the United States himself, had been advised that she was crossing the border and might be picked up on a drug charge. Headlines screamed "Jane Fonda Arrested on Drug Charge" around the world, and Nixon must have been elated that he finally had her where he wanted her. One can imagine his chagrin when the report came back from the Cleveland police lab that the pills were all vitamins and Valium.

28

In February 1971, the Winter Soldier Investigation of atrocities in Vietnam was held in Detroit. A former Green Beret officer called Donald Duncan, who had visited the Fondas' family home in Bel Air at Jane's invitation, was chief moderator. Jane was not present, although she had helped finance it. There was nothing, no outrage, no slaughter, no mutilation, of which she had not already been informed.*

All of the Vietnam veterans who testified had been honorably discharged. They spoke, often in hushed voices halted at times by emotion, of Vietnamese hamlets set on fire where there were no Vietcong to be found and then machine-gunning the women and children as they fled the flames; of rape and violation and mutilation; of Vietcong prisoners thrown out of helicopters; of torture of prisoners.

Many of these veterans later repeated their stories to the Senate foreign relations committee. The horror was building and it would reinforce a feeling that had been growing everywhere in America since the trial of Lieutenant William Calley for the massacre of three hundred civilians in My Lai that American sensibilities in Indochina had been dulled; that our

* Even more significant than these atrocity stories to Jane in forging her critical antiwar views was her meeting with Ron Kovic, paralyzed by battle injury from the waist down, who told her, "I've lost my body, but I've gained my mind."

soldiers there were capable of barbarities as monstrous as this.

A documentary film was compiled of the investigation, *Winter Soldier*; perhaps the most graphic proof yet of the true horror of the American presence in Vietnam. In their halting, shamed voices, these soldiers articulated their own step-by-step dehumanization. They were able to kill with impunity because this elusive enemy was everywhere and nowhere. Who were they? *Where* were they? *Trust nobody!* Any handy Vietnamese could die or, in the argot of the day, "be wasted." No one in higher authority had given them a legitimate reason for their being there to kill, so a reason had to be found. The death of a buddy was reason enough; then revenge would be the justification. Finally they were dropped into an alien, nearly exotic, land that had been certified as hostile to Americans. So they were really involved in a large-scale pest-control operation. The sprayers of Agent Orange and other defoliants and the flamethrowers were fully prepared.

The film *Winter Soldier* ran into difficulty getting distributed. Perhaps out of fear of later blacklisting, none of the eighteen filmmakers who contributed to the film would agree to a credit, so it went out as an anonymously made documentary, too raw and shattering for any movie house to exhibit as a theatrical feature. Then it was offered to television, and all three major American networks turned it down, although later—about five years after the American withdrawal and the success of the movies *Coming Home* (made by Jane and her producers) and *The Deer Hunter*—the networks suddenly would "discover" Vietnam as a theme. Finally, the film was aired by New York's public television station, Channel 13 (WNET-TV), and has been seen frequently on the campus circuit.

By now Jane Fonda was known throughout the world as a radical actress or, in her own words, as "an actress with revolutionary politics." Her distinguished performances in *They Shoot Horses* and *Klute* (the latter just then going into general release) were not enough to lift

216

her up from notoriety. Her causes had been so numerous and seemingly so indiscriminate that Saul Alinsky, one of the most acerbic of America's radicals, said just before his death later that year that Jane "was a hitchhiker on the highway of causes."

But an attentive observer could see signs of discrimination. Something about certain members of the Black Panther Party alarmed her. She knew that they were exploiting her, which was fair enough, but they were also demeaning her behind her back. She was an easy target since she often spoke in haste without adequate preparation. Huey Newton made every effort to keep Jane's image "cool" with the Panthers, but then in March 1971 there was even a strain there. Huey told Bill Calhoun of the Lumpen rock group, made up of Panther members, that they should pack their instruments and join Jane on her tour of Army bases. The Lumpen's primary purpose was, in Huey's words, "not entertainment but political education through music and song." Jane knew nothing about this. The assumption seemed to be that anything the Panthers wanted her to do, she would do. Jane informed Newton that she had no intention of undertaking the cost of carting these half dozen musicians along on what was going to be a very expensive tour.

Earlier, the Panthers had asked Jane to personally finance a documentary about the Panthers, but when it came down to the point of Jane handing over to them thousands of dollars as the "budget" for this project, she balked, naturally enough. While not permanent, these strains left the door open for Jane to retreat from her total commitment to the Panthers or, as she preferred to put it, to see their cause as "interrelated" with others. At about this time she appeared on the Dick Cavett show and said:

> I guess that was one thing that I learned. Having been a liberal I dealt in terms of isolated issues. You know, there was the problem of racism; there was the problem of war . . . and a problem of poverty,

and I as a sort of do-gooder would try to help people. Then I discovered that in fact all of these things were connected. That you can't talk of war or peace without the problem of racism, without dealing with the problem of oppression, and that all of these things are really one and the same, and that the problem is not out there, it's here. It's touching my life; every one of us are victims of these problems that have created our system.

She was being booked so solidly by the GI coffeehouse circuit that she simply had no time to spare for the Panthers. She did not walk out on the Black Panthers; there was no time for them.

Jane was always just one jump ahead of becoming any one thing beyond being an actress and activist. She seemed impulsive, but she was not. She was as much on the move as any political careerist, but nearly everyone who met her was moved by her sincerity. It was as though the quicksilver conscience so visible onscreen in her father's performances had translated itself into living, personal form. Hank could put that conscience on the shelf between films, except for important causes in which he believed, but Jane seemed compelled to make it a working part of her psyche.

The saturation bombing of Hanoi and its environs in December 1970 had been so devastating and seemed so criminally irresponsible that Jane wanted to be an eye-witness to the consequences of this crime. On February 22, 1971, arrangements were made through the French lawyer Leon Matarosso, who made contact with representatives of the Democratic Republic of Vietnam in Paris. Matarosso had been on the staff of the Bertrand Russell War Crimes Tribunal and was on close terms with top-ranking members of the North Vietnamese embassy in Paris. The week of Jane's intended departure, probably because word had filtered back to the CIA in Washington that she had completed arrangements for such a trip, the American government announced that it was canceling all visas for travel to

North Vietnam. At least her adversaries were paying close attention.

At the time when Jane was having her powwows with the Indian tribes her father was busy in New York performing in a situation comedy series for the American Broadcasting Company called *The Smith Family*. Though sixty-five, he showed no signs of slowing down. Hank and Jane had worked out some of their differences, but whenever he thought she was being flagrantly exploited he told her so.

> I'm not unhappy that she's an activist . . . that she is as sincerely concerned as she is. I'm unhappy about some of the people she is listening to . . .
>
> But Jane won't listen to anybody else but Mark Lane. I don't agree with Mark Lane . . . I think she's been very badly advised by Mark Lane . . .
>
> Jane getting arrested was a bad rap. She had a suitcase full of vitamins which I put her onto from my doctor, who's a health man. You can't travel without taking a bagful, because you take twenty-four at breakfast, seventeen at lunch and nineteen at dinner. You put them in little vials, and they're unmarked, and when you come through the border and somebody sees it, he's got to be suspicious. I'm sure they'll know by now, as soon as they analyze it, they'll know it's vitamins, and then she's free.

Jane's arrest had worried Hank, and he was frightened for her far more than he ever had been in the past. He believed that the government was out to get her, a belief shared by Jane. He also felt that she was the naïve victim of her friends. Despite what Hank thought, Jane and Mark Lane shared a few headlines as he stood by her side and got her off. Lane's small success—it wasn't a complicated case and probably not one of political harrassment, given Jane's baggage full of pills—simply prolonged his association with Jane.

29

In the summer of 1971 Jane returned to her farm near Paris to prepare for her role in Jean-Luc Godard's *Tout Va Bien*, costarring Yves Montand. After her tours with FTA and her campus appearances against the war she was psyched up for her first truly revolutionary movie, but she also needed to renew her physical resources.

The idea behind the movie was biographical, drawn from Godard's notion of how Jane herself had been radicalized overnight by the student strike. In *Tout Va Bien* a young woman (played by Jane) is radicalized by a strike in a factory. Shooting began, and it seemed clear to Jane that an abstract idea did not make a movie. Soon she was looking as troubled as she had looked a decade earlier while putting *The Fun Couple* together. Jane found Godard to be without human feelings. Later, in 1974, talking to the film critic Molly Haskell, she described him as:

> somewhat fascistic in his methods, although a great technician. . . . Godard really hates people. Especially women. He never told me what was going on in *Tout Va Bien*, and when I realized, I wanted to leave, but he threatened to rough me up if I did. It was a terrible experience. Nobody takes him seriously in Paris now. But then . . . I thought it would be so great to work with Godard.

Jane's comments about Godard threatening to rough her up is astonishing, and one wonders if some of her remarks of this sort were not part of the near-paranoid state she was in as a result of government surveillance, and the frequent and often unexpected hostility she encountered at the time. The Godard "threat" also sounds like a line from the script of *Klute*, which she had finished less than a year before making *Tout Va Bien*. As for Godard's feelings, he believed that he had abandoned his former misogyny and was making an important profeminist statement. It was Jane's first portrayal of a woman journalist, but it was a trial run she would rather have done without. For Godard fans, it contains one spectacular scene in a massive supermarket with much of the excitement of his earlier traffic pile-up in *Weekend*, which in turn had no doubt been inspired by a similar scene in Laurel and Hardy's 1928 comedy, *Two Tars*.

She went to Italy to recover from the ordeal of Godard, convinced that no movie should be made without any redeeming entertainment value. While there, she met some revolutionary exiles from South America who convinced her that she was mistaken about political films—that film was the most powerful molder of opinion and should enlist in its vital area of the revolution the most talented artists possible; people like herself. She had a sacred trust, they said, to tell the real truth about America on film.

It was not much of a rest, and perhaps she was influenced by these arguments. As for Godard, even he mellowed as in 1980 he moved into his forties and made *Every Man for Himself*, a seemingly random but very shrewd look at three young people—two women and a man—living in an urban area of Switzerland; the movie has less connective tissue than any of Jane's splendidly entertaining films of the seventies, but it holds the viewer in ways that Godard was reaching for in *Tout Va Bien*. Perhaps she resented being used as a guinea pig.

It was the age of indifference. The sixties had contained too many riots, too many campuses stormed and shaken, too many flower children stoned out of their benevolent minds, too much bitterness, death, hypocrisy, simplistic reductiveness and general lunacy. Tempers had cooled; reform was put on back burners. It was in this dispassionate time that Jane Fonda emerged surprisingly unscathed, a survivor by a whim of history. By 1971 there were few Americans who did not agree with her about the war, although many would view her future trip to Hanoi as outrageous. But those who attacked her now were the radicals of the seventies, the extreme right.

In March, she was among the five actresses nominated for an Oscar. It was the second time she had been so honored, and by now she had heard so often the story that she had been cheated of that first award because of her politics and general activism that she believed it. *Klute* was not the major breakthrough film *They Shoot Horses* had been; it was another aspect or extension of the same tough-surfaced Fonda persona—the girl who is bright, sexy, tense, very much alive, a handsomely packaged ticking bomb rather than a glass of champagne. In April, on Oscar night, Jane showed her vast television audience and the spellbound industry crowd yet another face—gracious lady, the Vassar girl *retrouvée*. It was a face the public was to see often. When she won, she appeared onstage in simple black tailored slacks and a blouse. There was a pause and then she said: "There's a lot I could say tonight. But this isn't the time or the place. So I'll just say 'Thank you.' "

Relief was palpable. The storm had passed and everyone could settle back and applaud now, as they did not when she came down the aisle.

Hank could not avoid having mixed feelings about this honor to Jane. He was intensely proud—of that there was no doubt—but he also had an ego the size of the moon and he had never won an Oscar,* not even for *The Grapes of Wrath*, although he had been nominated

* At the 1981 ceremonies in Los Angeles the Academy of Motion Picture Arts and Sciences finally awarded Henry Fonda a special life achievement Oscar for having embodied the American spirit in films down through the years.

for that one and had lost out to his old friend Jimmy Stewart. Considerable adjustment in his feelings would be needed in the decade ahead as Jane's fame began to outshine his own. To the surprise of those who knew him well, he was going to delight in it.

In early August 1971 Jane flew from New York to California, where she was to join director Alan Myerson, an early associate in FTA, to play the girlfriend of a demolition-derby driver, played by another FTA partner, Donald Sutherland, who was also to be the movie's executive producer. The film was to be called *Steelyard Blues*, a poetic reference to the junkyard of scrap metal where the stock cars eventually end up.

Jane's derby groupie was far more amoral than her Bree Daniels; all the characters in the comedy were an affront to the establishment, which was the major point of the film. Jane was now in a period described by her years later as her "blacklisted years—three years or so." But since Myerson said that four studios were bidding on the production, perhaps it should only be called her "graylisted period." Certainly, however, until 1974 only a handful of film projects were made available to her.

Myerson was a good-natured antiwar activist with radical labor leanings, youthful in outlook, a good film "technician" (a word Jane used a great deal) and quite willing to commit himself to a project that was more fraternal than serious, although such future film heavyweights as screenwriter David Ward (author of *The Sting*), Tony Bill, and Michael and Julia Phillips were involved in its making. They would be shooting mostly in Oakland and at a dirt track near Santa Rosa. The choice of locations seemed to be more political in motivation than cinematic. Nearby Berkeley was a student antiwar center, "the Cambridge of the West."

Jane brought Vanessa with her and stayed at the Berkeley House Hotel during the first few days of shooting. She was still having her affair with Donald Sutherland that neither intended ever to become serious; he later said, "I'm always in love in some way with the women I work with in my films." With Jane, they had more than acting to talk about. They complemented each other very well: Jane, in Sutherland's presence, was the sober one, almost humorless, her feet solidly on the ground, while Don orbited around her in pursuit of this enthusiasm or that. They were too intelligent to consider marriage; Jane had said often enough that she never would marry an actor.

It seemed a matter of some urgency to Jane while in Berkeley to visit the Red Family, a radical collective on Bateman Street that owned or leased three or four houses in one block. The Red Family was an elitist group of activists, described by some as a radical version of high society. There were at least a dozen members living on Bateman Street, and they were then in their second year of communal living. The group had been founded by Robert Scheer, his wife Anne Weills—although their marriage was already in trouble and they had begun living in different houses—and activist superstar Tom Hayden, who soon moved in with Weills. The Red Family had won a certain notoriety even in shockproof Berkeley. Neighbors complained about the glare of security lights blazing all night long around the several Red Family houses; they also believed the collective to be heavily armed, a belief supported by stories written about them by sympathetic reporters.

When Jane visited the Bateman Street commune during a break in her shooting schedule, she found that Tom Hayden had gone—"expelled," she was told. Since she had met Hayden earlier that year during a campus rally at the University of Michigan, she was curious about the facts behind that. He had been much impressed by that meeting, since she did not look like "Barbarella"—a strange expectation from a man who should have been enthusiastic about her deliberate downplaying of her sexuality in *They Shoot Horses*. With Hayden's canny insight into people, he saw immediately that Jane needed a strong man to lean on. "She was skinny and nervous, eyes darting around. . . ." Jane, of course, had shed all the trappings of glamour, including her earlier penchant for beautiful men. Tom Hayden was undersized and far more blunt-featured than even Vadim had been. His nose was bulbous, and adolescent acne had pitted his face. He had a disconcerting habit of looking through people rather than at them. If Jane had learned to "act naturally and human" through a battery of devices including the Method, Tom Hayden had not learned to act at all. This did not make him more natural; it made him seem disinterested, detached, just *there*. Yet Hayden carried with him the aura of past glories and present commitment that made him interesting on historical grounds. Within less than a year, so would Jane, adding this status as at least an important footnote to her other attractions. If Hayden carried no weight as a charismatic personality, he came into a room like an astronaut. He may not have been to the moon and back, but he had been in places equally arcane and perilous. Jane was instantly attracted to this aura, and also found him witty. She later found that he was as addicted as Vadim to *Mad* magazine.

But the Red Family had nothing good to say about Hayden. Jane spoke with his ex-lover, Anne Weills, an attractive militant feminist who was supported in her move against Hayden by her estranged husband, Robert Scheer. Of that rupture Weills later said; "When I broke up with him [Hayden], it was not because I didn't love him but because he manipulated everyone—me, the men, the women, in the collective. He is the most manipulative, power-conscious person—obsessed with it—I have ever known." Jane, an old hand at it herself, could not see being manipulative as cause for banishment. She said nothing, and doubtless later agreed with Hayden's views on the break:

It was sick [he would say]. The resolution of the competitive rivalry between myself and Anne [he unconsciously puts himself first], with everyone else participating in the ritual killing of the father figure. What humiliation and what loss. The jackals of the movement, all those who lived to see idols destroyed, were out spreading the word.

Jane remained noncommittal. Although she may not even have used the word as a regular part of her vocabulary, she must have sensed that Hayden was practicing *Realpolitik*, and his quest for power, even over this collective, had injured some feelings. If the feminist Weills saw it as male chauvinism, since she was so deeply into feminism, that was her problem.

Hayden had driven south to Los Angeles in a battered Volkswagen, his ego bruised but apparently intact, in tears, with his stomach heaving, a revolutionary cut off from the revolution. He changed his name to Emmett Garity, moved into a dingy flat in Venice, a dropout ghetto left over from the sixties, and began making contact with the working class. He was soon enough making issues out of their concerns, and his wounds healed fast. Hayden moved from his base in Venice back onto the antiwar trail, abandoning the Garity alias, and very much Tom Hayden again.

Through most of her mother's stay in Berkeley, Vanessa was enrolled in the Blue Fairyland Nursery School, run by the Red Family; the name had been chosen by the collective's children. Although the children usually played indoors or in the back yard of the house of Robert Scheer, where the nursery was located, sometimes the preschoolers could be seen "marching" along Bateman Street carrying posters of Mao. Sometime in August, Jane moved from the Berkeley House Hotel to 3016 Bateman, a Red Family house, but propinquity did not lead to closer ties with the Red Family. She must have seen that if she were to stay there would be a showdown between herself and Anne Weills. Anne Butterfield Weills was a woman as strong, in a political sense, as Jane. She had been one of the three Americans who went to Hanoi in 1968 as a representative of the National Mobilization (to end the war in Vietnam) to escort three American pilots back to the United States following their negotiated release. Her estranged husband, Scheer, backing her up in every way, was very much in the hands of the feminists. He, too, was well known in antiwar circles, having helped found the Peace and Freedom Party. Jane abruptly decided to move on.

Jane flew East, where she took a suite with Donald Sutherland in the Chelsea Hotel on West Twenty-third Street. They both needed to unwind after the strenuous, tight schedule of *Steelyard Blues*. Early that fall, they were committed to go on a tour of Pacific army bases for FTA. There was at the time grave dissension within the FTA, and the charges against Jane and Sutherland were much the same as those that had expelled Tom Hayden from the Red Family. Country Joe McDonald called a press conference to denounce the two and tell the world why he was leaving the FTA shows. He said that the press had catered to Sutherland and Fonda.

> but the movement has been duped by them. Their place in the hierarchy is much lower than they think it is. . . . They've assumed a position of authority they don't have, and I'm not going to be any part of their ego trip.
>
> I want to demystify Jane Fonda and Donald Sutherland. They're novices. I think she's had a bad effect on the (GI) movement. She has created dissension. People are starting to look at her as leader of the movement, which she is not. Nor is Sutherland. . . . Jane insists on being the producer and on raising all the money and her secretary and press agent are the secretary and press agent for the FTA shows. No one else has any say. . . . I would have stayed with the show if it were possible to work out the conflicts collectively. But it's just one or two people making the decisions, and they wield complete control.

Fred Gardner, too, whose idea it was to form the FTA show organization and the GI movement, turned against Jane and her clique. He said in a newsletter to the *Second Page*, a counterculture newspaper in San Francisco:

The show does not fight imperialism. It does nothing but advertise organizations and projects that have utter contempt for soldiers. . . . It's full of missionaries and fakers. It's a movement that has never done—that scorns and vilifies—the slow hard work of building an organization that will take power and reorganize this society.

Jane said nothing to refute either McDonald's or Gardner's charges. She was developing a genius for silence at the right moment which was every bit as effective as her father's. And if she felt even slightly critical of Tom Hayden for his expulsion from the Red Family, it was wiped out by her own contained anger over these defections.

She was distracted at the time by other concerns. If she had taken nothing else away from Berkeley, she had resolved while there with sister Weills and the other militants to fight harder for the liberation of women from the straightjackets of the past. Her FTA producer, Barbara Gordon, set up an interview on "fascinating women" as part of a public television series known as *The Great American Dream Machine*. In a conversation with that program's Dassey Hagen, Jane observed:

We women think that we are in control of our lives, that we are defining ourselves, when, in fact, none of us are. Our lives are defined by men, directly by men—the men we live with, or the men we love, or the men we're married to, or the men we work for—and, indirectly, through television, film, radio and other media, which are controlled by men. . . .

Jane was venting some of her frustration over the fact, which she knew better than anyone, that men had shaped her life since birth. It was something she had inherited from her mother Frances, and she never would be able to shake it off completely. She would go on looking to one or another man for approval, for strength and, most maddening of all, for her own *raison d'être*, for a long time to come.

She spoke of the roles "fitted out for us," but said, "we have to gain strength to redefine these roles for ourselves." Then she moved from analysis to a frontal assault:

> We have certainly messed up the world about as far as it can go with men in the leadership role. I think the time has come . . . well, Daniel Ellsberg said it on the Dick Cavett show a while back, "We should start listening to women." And they *should*. Men are going to have to start listening to us.
>
> Where are the *women* cycle killers? Where are the *women* who lurk in the dark alleys to murder? Where are the *women* who sit around the SALT-talk tables and plan future nuclear wars? . . .

Jane acknowledged that she had awakened to her revolutionary spirit about feminism during the summer, although she does not mention how it came about there in Berkeley. She thought that women found her funnier than men did. Some men, she said, found her impossible, with no sense of humor. Still, she said that she was no "separatist." Was this a declaration that she was not about to become a lesbian activist like Kate Millett? There was a lesbian or two involved with the FTA shows; lesbian actresses would work with her in some of her films. Jane could not have cared less but, interestingly, she never did embrace the homosexual cause, lesbian or male, with any real fervor, although she was called upon by gay activists to put in an appearance on a few occasions. She believed in giving them their rights and certainly some of them were her friends away from the activist trail, but among the minority causes Jane championed, she gave the least time to gay rights. Homosexuality was still something of a taboo among those vast film audiences who were her real constituency, and increasingly in the years ahead, Jane would move in straighter and straighter circles, however radical their politics. Hollywood as a community was about a decade behind New York and San Francisco, with several bastions in between, in its acceptance of gay life-styles. It was true in the old big studio days when star William Haines was forced to retire from films because he refused a studio order to leave his lover; and it is true in the new Hollywood that is run by the radicals of the sixties who have become the movie moguls of the eighties. There is usually nothing straighter than a militant radical, sexually speaking. However, Jane's stance on this issue was very fluid and could change at any time. She always had been the champion of the underdog and the disenfranchised, and the puritanical purge of American morality was far along by the spring of 1981 under the manic guidance of the Moral Majority.* As rights for gays buckled in America along with black rights, Jane was known to be concerned and anxious.

* An ultraconservative political group that helped elect President Ronald Reagan and whose program opposed abortion, homosexuality and the feminist revolt.

30

Americans had been pushed beyond the point of endurance by the early seventies. The most expensive war in history was sapping the national economy and, far more importantly, the national spirit. It was a war nobody wanted anymore, not even the most hawkish of the men in Washington and those out in the jungles of Vietnam. It had been nearly twenty years since the French had retreated from Dien Bien Phu, and America had moved in that time exactly to the point that had caused the French to give up.

By 1972 there were few Americans who did not feel deceived by their leaders. Nixon and Kissinger had by then been announcing for nearly four years the withdrawal of American forces and an end to U.S. involvement. Their proclaimed goal was "Vietnamization," which ideally meant turning the land over to the Vietnamese a hamlet or a region at a time. Practically, it meant keeping the American war in Indochina going with the Vietnamese doing most of the fighting, supported by massive American bombing raids. It is difficult with hindsight to probe Kissinger's motives, but he evidently believed that by intensifying the bombing and the slaughter of innocent Vietnamese, the North Vietnamese would look to the American withdrawal with relief akin to surrender.

Everyone knows that nothing of the sort happened. The Americans were defeated for the first time in the two hundred years of their history, and they were defeated primarily because they were misled by every President from Kennedy on. Kennedy preached the gospel of preserving liberty everywhere in the world, which turned out to be not only impossible but a travesty (does freedom reside in death and total devastation?— perhaps, of a kind); Johnson insisted upon winning some sort of "peace with honor" and was so shocked when his mission collapsed that he backed away from the presidency; Nixon promised the world peace at last and "an early withdrawal." Perhaps Nixon meant it when it became his chief campaign issue, but Kissinger managed to enlarge the conflagration by drawing Cambodia into the net of total destruction. It may take the world as long to forgive the United States for its surprising new role as a destroyer of nations as it did to forgive the Spanish for expunging the Mayans and their culture from the Americas. But then again, America could be as lucky as West Germany and Japan, who lost an earlier war after barbarous attempts to win it and in due course emerged as among the most civilized and prosperous nations on earth.

Jane believed everything she was told by the North Vietnamese and their friends. Their goals ("to drive the Yankee imperialists from their country"; to unite their country—under the communists); their rhetoric; their tallies of battle casualties and prisoners of war—all were taken at face value and most were repeated by Jane on one occasion or another. She became their best propagandist, and declined to believe anything that came from the White House or the Pentagon. There was a time earlier when she had believed everything that the Black Panthers told her; basically Jane lacked the ability to detect a lie or an exaggeration if it came from a friend. She was told at one point that there were 339 American prisoners of war, and she repeated this figure in numerous speeches and interviews, including an appearance on the David Frost television show. It turned out that there were nearly twice that many when the list was published by Hanoi just before the men's release.

Jane thought that her Vietnamese friends lacked a

232

capacity for hatred, but any decent history of Vietnam would have informed her that it was only the South Vietnamese who had no gift for animosity (one of the reasons why they made such poor soldiers), who loved parties, singing songs and entertaining friends. The North Vietnamese were essentially humorless, miserly people, who spent their free time doing something constructive or political. It can be said now with some accuracy that they hated the Cambodians and those in their own country who disagreed with them. This feeling of hostility was in no way personal; it touched all of their enemies.

Jane's enemies in America were even more careless with their facts. Superpatriots often proposed that Jane Fonda stay permanently with "her friend Ho Chi Minh." Jane never in fact met the president of the Democratic Republic of Vietnam, who died in 1969, just as she was becoming active in the antiwar movement. A number of her French communist friends had met him, however, since he had helped found the French Communist Party in 1920. At least one historical figure who is much venerated by Jane's enemies helped Ho Chi Minh at a critical juncture in his rise to power. Chiang Kai-shek helped set up Ho Chi Minh as leader of an independent Vietnam, knowing perfectly well what his politics were. When the Allies landed in the south near the end of the Second World War, the Japanese overthrew the French colonial regime in Vietnam and set up an "independent" Vietnam run by local Vietnamese and under the nominal rule of Nguyen Emperor Bao Dai. To "secure" North Vietnam for the Allies, the Kuomintang under Chiang occupied a large part of the country for seven months or until eased out by the natives. Chiang's forces then withdrew across the border into China. With the situation thus stablized, on August 19, 1945, five days after Japan had surrendered to General MacArthur, Ho Chi Minh entered Hanoi with a thousand Vietminh cadres and proclaimed the birth of the Democratic Republic.

Bold moves are often collaborative things. Jane had

said often enough that she was first of all a screen actress. The history of Hollywood is one of cycles and trends precipitated by outer pressures. As the women's movement heated up and those unaware of Hollywood's past history as a reactor rather than a reflector waited for some strong feminist film, Hollywood predictably hardened in reply. Women could no longer carry films alone. The sole exception of Barbra Streisand only reinforced the point, since she was as tough in business matters as any man in films. Jane had reached a point of stardom where she could not enter a film deal as the "feminine interest." Added to this was the burden of being so controversial that there was a quasi blacklist working against her. She felt that the moment had come for the ultimate gesture.

In show business, singer Joan Baez was as militant as Jane and was almost totally involved against the war. From the beginning, though, she and Jane differed in their attitudes. Baez was a pacifist, and once wrote:

> The pacifist thinks there is only one tribe. Three billion members. They come first. We think killing any member of the family is a dumb idea. We think there are more decent and intelligent ways of settling differences. And man had better start investigating these other possibilities because if he doesn't, then by mistake or by design, he will probably kill off the whole damn race.

Jane believed that there were "just" wars. The war in which her father had fought, the war against Germany and Japan, had been a "just" war. It was, as Jane saw it, an honorable war, even unavoidable. Hitler was exterminating a race and had to be stopped. Now, for some insane reason, Americans were in the business of exterminating a people, the Indochinese, and had to be stopped. It was, to Jane, a dishonorable business. So Baez and Jane were in agreement regarding this particular war.

Americans had been venturing into North Vietnam

for a number of years, and the North Vietnamese government had become especially skillful at guiding these visitors through. There seemed to be no special duplicity, and no visible barricades; English-speaking escorts were invariably provided and, since American visitors were handicapped by little of no knowledge of the language and none at all of the terrain, they were entirely in the hands of their hosts. Now Jane was going to see for herself what it was like.

PART VII

No Retreat from Vietnam

31

Jane's flight to Hanoi in July 1972 seemed a spur-of-the-moment thing, but it had been carefully planned by Jane with officials of the Democratic Republic of Vietnam in Paris well in advance. Her friends were surprised because she told practically no one about it. One who was not surprised was her old friend from the antiwar trail Tom Hayden. He planned to be there himself.

"JANE FONDA IN HANOI," read the headlines throughout the world. It was big news because she was a big star who was known for sparking controversy. In Hanoi she was a showpiece and their best propaganda tool to date. There were carefully selected prisoners of war to visit, pilots, according to the most reliable word, *willing* to meet her. Jane said that there were seven prisoners of war who gave her messages for scores of people, including a woman working in an Orange County supermarket in California. These POWs urged the people back home to defeat President Nixon in the November election. Jane said, "They fear if Nixon stays in office they will be prisoners forever." She described the men as wearing purple-and-red striped uniforms and they were later seen in a silent color "home movie" shot by Jane of their meeting.

During her visit she seemed most upset by the American bombing raids on North Vietnam's dike system, and she seemed intent upon getting a strong message through to American troops then engaged in battle with the Vietcong. She made at least ten broadcasts over Radio Hanoi, and these broadcasts became a rallying point for charges of treason later brought against her. In portions of transcripts later released by the American House Internal Security Committee, Jane was quoted as telling the soldiers over Radio Hanoi:

> Tonight when you are alone, ask yourselves: What are you? Accept no ready answers fed to you by rote from basic training. . . . I know that if you saw and if you knew the Vietnamese under peaceful conditions, you would hate the men who are sending you on bombing missions. . . . Have you any idea what your bombs are doing when you pull the levers and push the buttons? . . . Should you allow these same people and same liars to define for you who your enemy is?

In one of her broadcasts monitored in Tokyo she allegedly said that the solution to the Vietnam problem must be based on the Vietcong's seven-point proposal that she described as "just and moral" and which meets "the aspirations of the Vietnamese and American peoples as well." She said that the United States must withdraw all its troops from South Vietnam and set a terminal date for this withdrawal and cease support for the South Vietnamese government. She emphasized that she wanted to "publicly accuse Nixon of betraying everything the American people have at heart, betraying the long tradition of freedom and democracy."

The broadcasts might have been more effective and caused less congressional stir if they had sounded more like Jane and less like an official brief. Later, following a visit in the countryside to a bombed village, she would recall the trip in the most vivid, personal terms:

> A swarm of young boys saw a white woman in the back seat and began to run alongside the car, shouting and waving. I had asked the interpreter what they were saying. "There's a Russian lady," he told me. Uncertain as to what their reaction would be, I

asked him to tell them that I was an American. When they heard this, they only hesitated for perhaps an instant and then redoubled their shouting and waving, running and jumping to see this American better. Perhaps the first glimpse of a friend from America instead of a plane.

Touring some bombed ruins, she again made her identity known

. . . and through gestures tried to express my feelings about destruction. . . . Then, trying to explain myself I said the Vietnamese word for peace, *hoa binh*, and pointing to myself, "American *hoa binh*," and "Nixon," making a face and giving a thumbsdown. They [some North Vietnamese soldiers] laughed and we all fell silent.

With Tom Hayden she visited Bach Mai Hospital, which had not yet been nearly destroyed by bombs. Many of the doctors were women, and Jane took photographs of them for a slide show she had in mind.

Among the American prisoners of war in Hanoi at the time of Jane's visit was Major Ted Gostas, of Cheyenne, Wyoming, who had been captured in 1968. He was not a model prisoner; he was, in fact, the sort of prisoner Jane herself had been on her single night in jail—observant, with something of a chip on his shoulder. In his words:

Now this thing about south and north Vietnamese. It is a moot point to argue. Sure, the south are so called VC [Vietcong] and the north are regulars. But I never knew the difference except that south wore black and north wore brown. But they are all the same. And I think that such distinctions made by the media are absurd. What difference does it make? They are all one and the same. Ask Joseph Conrad and he will tell you that in the *Heart of Darkness*.

I can't tell you about movements [as a prisoner] in the Asian Theater. Hell, north was south and east was west and I was in shock. A rocket had gone off in my room, man, how was I to know? But there were clues. I know I walked many miles.

I know I was on trucks for many miles.

I know I crossed mountains and rivers and streams and stepped on snakes.

I know the Chinese characters [in print] differ from Vietnamese characters so even did the uniforms differ for about a year. So I guessed I was in China. A week before I moved to Hanoi some [eye] glasses came to my eyes. They were made in China. I have them today. But where in China? I don't know. I say south because I vaguely remember it didn't seem like a long time to get to Hanoi for the last six months of my ordeal.

How I was transported out of China, I don't remember. 18 abcessed teeth were pouring puss into my stomach and my heart was experiencing awful times. God, we don't understand Asians. Kipling's East is East is true. Case in point, a man captured at the same time as I stepped on barbed wire. I sat next [to] him for nine weeks and watched a pin prick in the foot eat its way all the way through and emerge from the other side.

Jane Fonda entered his narrowed world suddenly and disturbingly:

. . . around summer's end [1972] . . . one afternoon a Cadreman [North Vietnamese regular] came to my cell and opened the door. I strode out into an "exercise court" (written thus because I never got to use it) and waited for his instructions. He was typical of the Cadre of the North, with pith helmet and red star encased in a blade of wheat.

"How do you feel," he asked.

"Sir?" I replied.

"How do you feel?" he repeated.

"The same."

"Well, I have some interesting news for you. Today we are honored in the Democratic Republic of Vietnam, for one of your famous film stars has come this day to visit us. She is the famous Jane Fonda and she has spoken to us this day in Hanoi. She has visited our glorious people and praised them for our struggle against American imperialism."

"Jane Fonda?"

"Yes."

"Well tell her to come here and see me."

"That is not possible, for there are many [POW] camps in Vietnam. But we have brought to you her writings of her speech. It is a glorious speech in support of our just cause."

He handed me a long sheet (legal size) of white paper. On it, in English, was a speech supposedly rendered that very day by Ms. Fonda. . . . I can't remember all of it. But I do remember it was a solid backing of the people of North Vietnam in their struggle and talked about the courage of the peasants in the fields. . . . I reacted to the speech, sir. I wept. I did not believe it. I felt betrayed. I felt that it simply could not be. I had seen a movie years ago when Henry was young. It was about Drums on the Mohawk or something. You know, "Leatherstocking" stuff. Well, Henry ran away from Indians chasing him with tomahawks. They poop out and he gets safely to reinforcements. How often I thought of that in prison. . . .

When Jane returned, she faced the crisis of her life. With help from the Justice Department, members of Congress were seeking her indictment as a traitor; they would fail because of the illegal nature of the war itself. Her own father disapproved of what she had done, although as the depth of the feelings against Jane became evident to him, he rushed to her support, saying that he resented people "who expect him to denounce her" and adding that although he did not agree with her thinking on certain issues, he loved and respected her for voicing her opinion.

Numerous radicals and humanitarians had gone to Hanoi already but only Jane Fonda would be likened to Tokyo Rose. Apparently the magnitude of one's fame increased one's liability to diatribes and possible prosecution. Jane told the press: "What is a traitor? I cried every day I was in Vietnam. I cried for America. The bombs are falling on Vietnam, but it is an American tragedy."

It could be expected that Jane's trip to Hanoi would provoke American Legionnaires, superpatriots and hundreds of thousands of the self-righteous. Indeed, their response was visceral. What was truly surprising was the criticism that arose from her "friends."

Jean-Luc Godard and his writing collaborator Jean-Pierre Gorin took particular exception to a photograph of Jane that appeared in the *L'Express* of Paris, in which Jane with mouth drawn down in anguish is listening to a Hanoi resident's complaint, over the caption: "Jane Fonda questioning Hanoi inhabitants about the American bombing." The two men were moved to produce a short feature entitled *Letter to Jane*, in which much of the footage is devoted to just that photograph, rather like Andy Warhol's *Empire*, during which we see the Empire State Building throughout the film's length.

Godard and Gorin's disappointment in Jane's behavior is repeated in a scolding manner on the sound track. They were offended principally because she put herself forward as the "star" of both this photograph and her investigative journey. Her *Tragic Pity* was paternalistic, and *Letter to Jane* calls to mind some words of Bertolt Brecht: "One must have the courage to say we have nothing to say." In the future, the filmmakers advised:

One must say, "I'm listening to the Vietnamese who are going to tell me what sort of peace they want in their country." And one must say as an American, "I'll keep my mouth shut because I admit I have got nothing to say about this. . . . I have to listen . . . because I am not a part of Southeast Asia."

The Frenchmen had a point, and there is even some evidence that Jane took their chastisement to heart. But a subdued Jane Fonda is an unnatural Jane Fonda. Her only true identity was as a star—not in the way of

Marilyn Monroe, but closer to the fashion of Lillian Gish or Gloria Swanson. Perhaps if we could blend the two women, taking the commitment to films of Gish and the various offscreen crusades of Swanson, we would come close to the mystique of Jane.

32

Jane's view of the world needed some support. Of course she was now getting some from an aroused and protective father; that had brought them closer. But she needed a man in her life. Radical feminists were quick to point out that this was Jane Fonda's great weakness. She would help them in every way she could but there was always that bottom line: she required a sustained relationship with a man. Tom Hayden had seen this very quickly. Call him shrewd or extrasensitive to others, he saw Jane's longing and moved into that void. Their radical friends were amused by the heat of their feelings for each other, but this crowd had not been around when Jane was with Timmy or Andreas or Vadim. She was a warm, responsive woman. Jane and Tom began living together in the latter half of 1972.

One recalls all those romantic high adventures made during and after the Second World War in which the Maquis or partisan man is holed up in enemy territory with a woman member of the underground. Tom Hayden had come to believe in engagement with the enemy—mostly members of the establishment—as the first step before hardening into positions and attitudes: plunge into revolution and then decide what the issues are. What you did created its own position. This was heady elixir to Jane, who had to be a little breathless as she raced from one desperate cause to another.

Hayden, just two years Jane's junior, had been brought

up in a lower-middle-class background by his mother, a school film librarian. Some of his radicalism has been traced by the writer Jack Newfield to his "overwhelming sense of the sinfulness of the affluent, 'quasi-fascist' society" to his roots in Roman Catholicism. Hayden later recalled:

> The school [affiliated with the notorious Shrine of the Little Flower of neo-fascist Father Coughlin in Royal Oak, Michigan] was Father Coughlin's but I didn't know that. I never remember a political sermon. . . . I do remember that they would make you kneel in a Christian position and then beat you to teach you a lesson. . . . It didn't work, not even in grade school. But those nuns were in robes and you felt you couldn't rebel. You felt all alone.

While Jane was growing up in the shadow of a national monument (Hank), Tom Hayden was doing the same in the shadow of a monument to bigotry (Coughlin). If we accept the fact that Henry Fonda represented the conscience of America and Father Coughlin the outer edges of American savagery, then we can see something of the attraction that these two activists, meeting again in the beleaguered city of Hanoi, had for each other. They knew many of the same people and had spent time in the same places.

It was in Berkeley that Hayden first joined other students demonstrating against the House Un-American Activities Committee. He had hitchhiked there from the University of Michigan campus, where he was a junior. "I became a revolutionary in bits and pieces," he said. That autumn, as editor of the campus daily, Hayden urged students to support those students in the South who were sitting in to enforce integration. He went South that year to observe the activities of the Student Nonviolent Coordinating Committee, and following his graduation that spring he worked full time with SNCC in Mississippi and Georgia. It was in McComb, Mississippi, that he personally felt the violence and wrath of the Southern redneck when one of them struck him during a voter registration drive. It was the same summer that other white bigots killed two white activists and one black, all, like himself, down from Northern colleges for the summer. That autumn, Hayden published a pamphlet about his experiences there, called "Revolution in Mississippi."

In December 1961 Hayden realized that all of this student activity needed a central clearinghouse and coordinated strength, and with thirty-five other young activists, he founded Students for a Democratic Society (SDS). The following summer, meeting at Port Huron, Michigan, he issued a statement that has become a classic manifesto in the New Left movement:

> We are people of this generation, bred in at least modest comfort, housed in universities, looking uncomfortably to the world we inherit . . . beneath the reassuring tones of the politicians, beneath the common opinion that America will "muddle through" . . . . is the pervading feeling that there simply are no alternatives, that our times have witnessed the exhaustion not only of Utopias, but of any new departures as well. . . .
>
> We oppose the depersonalization that reduces human beings to the status of things. . . . We see little reason why men cannot meet with increasing skill the complexities and responsibilities of their situation. . . . Human relationships should involve fraternity and honesty. . . . Human brotherhood must be willed.

The statement called for "participatory democracy," a government in which the individual would share "in those social decisions determining the quality and direction of his life."

The Port Huron statement and Hayden's role as first president of the SDS would make him the most visible young activist in America. While Jane was touring in *The Fun Couple* and shooting *La Ronde* and worrying about her bare ass showing on a poster on Times Square,

Hayden was taking graduate work at Ann Arbor in sociology and studying C. Wright Mills, especially his *The Power Elite*, which would become a kind of bible of the New Left.

There was more, much more, to his past than this. He had reached his apotheosis as a certifiable saint of the New Left upon being indicted as one of the Chicago Seven, when he was arrested for provoking riot on the streets of Chicago during the Democratic National Convention in August 1968. The Chicago authorities had been mistaken about the provocation: Hayden had planned the demonstrations along with Rennie Davis, head of the Mobe (Mobilization to End the War in Vietnam) and other activists. Indicted with them were pacifist David Dellinger, Black Panther cofounder Bobby Seale, Yippie founder Abbie Hoffman, Jerry Rubin, John Froines and Lee Weiner. The trial, under Judge Julius Hoffman, was a travesty during which Seale was bound and gagged, appearing with a cloth tied about his mouth as a silent defendant after several outbursts that inflamed Hoffman. They were all found guilty, but the verdict was overturned in November 1972 by a Circuit Court of Appeals. Hayden, the tireless organizer, pulled together all of their defense for their attorneys, "the most exhausting chore of my life," and published a book on the ordeal, *Trial* (1970).

Hayden was a fairly eloquent writer, his ideas reflections of his actions. He set some of them down in *Rat*, a counterculture weekly:

> There will be no way to mobilize action at the time [summer of 1968] without major initiative from below. . . . The growing consciousness of the Movement—its justified distrust of organized leaderships, its creation of "revolutionary gangs" or "affinity groups," its experience with the police and the streets—is sure to be a controlling force of some kind over the loose official hierarchies.

As Garry Wills later wrote, "These *were* our children in the streets [of Chicago]—indicting us." Hayden had been there leading them. He came to Jane a hero and a legend in his own time, and all at the precocious age of thirty-one.

33

One thing often overlooked in analyses of what makes America a unique experiment is the unpredictability of its passions and loyalties. If the original passion was profound enough, nearly anything could be forgiven; Charles A. Lindbergh is a good example, even though his later position in the pantheon of heroes was sustained as much by the eloquent writings of his wife as by anything he did or said himself. Senator Joe McCarthy fell into such disrepute before his death that his name would enter the dictionary as an "ism" signifying wrongful slander of political persons, while Senator Eugene McCarthy, who gave every indication of lifting that good old Irish name out of the mire and making it ring for all time as a symbol of pure-hearted political activism, has become only a footnote to the history of the nineteen-sixties. In films, revisionism cuts even deeper into reputations. Millions of movie fans go to see Marlon Brando perform today even in a truncated role such as those he played in *Apocalypse Now* and *The Godfather*, but they see him as a freak of commerce—he gets over a million dollars per film and every last fan knows this—rather than the great performer he used to be.

In the case of Jane's first excursions into radical politics, America itself was aflame from one end of the country to the other with a rage that had been building up since the time of the Bay of Pigs. Kennedy had been oversold, and Americans had to look back years later to his then thrilling declaration, "Let every nation know, whether it wishes us well or ill, that we shall pay any price, bear any burden, meet any hardship, support any friend, oppose any foe to assure the survival and the success of liberty," to see that it was the blueprint that led the United States straight into the shame and debacle of Vietnam, principally under Lyndon Johnson and Richard Nixon.

But it was Richard M. Nixon who was supervising America's continuing quest for "the survival and the success of liberty" in Indochina when Jane was awakened to the cruel joke that this quest had become. America's insistence upon "liberty" for the Vietnamese was a little like the hunter who pleads for all decent citizens to help him protect the white-tailed deer by killing them ("keeps them from starvation," "must be harvested to keep nature in balance").

Jane saw this in 1968 with a clarity few others did at that early stage. Perhaps she was a little precocious about her Vietnamese stance because she detested Richard Nixon so much. Their hatred for each other, as we have already seen, began in earnest sometime in 1970 when President Nixon became aware of this gadfly from the movies and gave orders for her to be placed under strict surveillance. Jane Fonda was, in Nixon's eyes, a spoiled rich girl, a "hellion" who smoked pot, appeared on the screen in the nude so often that she said *she was bored with it*, and according to a reliable report considered the word "shit" to be the most utilitarian word in the language. Jane, sensing her chief stalker with almost animal sensibilities, reacted in kind. Nixon was small-minded, ruthlessly opportunistic and dangerous; within months Jane was calling for his impeachment well before Watergate. She also discovered, years later, when Nixon's reputation was in tatters and it couldn't possibly matter to anyone, that he used expletives as strong as her own and with greater frequency. Nixon was, Jane told everyone, including television interviewers, a liar. She spent much of her energies late in the summer and fall of 1972 working for Nixon's defeat at the polls. "I wanted to blow the whole thing wide open," she said. She could not know then that it was better for him to win and be destroyed the following year than to lose.

It had all of the elements of classical Greek drama. The rebellious princess believes her country's war against the people to the north is wrong and an abomination, so she goes to the capital of the enemy and embraces them. She brings them flowers and there is great joy and celebration in the camp of the enemy. Then her own people begin to think as she does and there are riots against the king and uprisings everywhere. There is growing unrest among the troops. The king himself goes insane and begins destroying countries all around the enemy to the north. He believes the enemy to have fled there to these neighboring sanctuaries. His reason begins to fail him; he even looks under his bed each night.

At the time of Jane's first trip to Hanoi there were strong signs within Vietnam, among all the people of South Vietnam, that the myth of American altruism, of keeping the South free and liberated, was unsupportable by every evidence. A South Vietnamese youth said, "We students take note of the fact that on this side we have half a million foreign troops, while on the other side there are none." What had happened, as Frances FitzGerald so eloquently put it in *Fire in the Lake*, was that:

. . . The U.S. officials had enmired Vietnam. They had corrupted the Vietnamese and, by extension, the American soldiers who had to fight amongst the Vietnamese in their service. By involving the United States in a fruitless and immoral war, they had also corrupted themselves.

Miss FitzGerald later describes the military destruction of the country's agriculture and industry, so that there is literally nothing of the country left to save. "South Vietnam is a country shattered so that no two pieces fit together."

253

What strikes one as astonishingly coincidental about the parallel lives of Jane Fonda and Richard Nixon in the second half of 1972 is that they both attempted the riskiest venture of their lives at the same time. On June 17, the night of the second Watergate break-in, Jane was making final preparations to go to Hanoi. On July 6, when FBI head L. Patrick Gray III warned President Nixon that his own staff was giving him "a mortal wound" through their interference in the Watergate investigation, Jane was on her way to North Vietnam.

On Jane's return at the end of July conservative Americans everywhere—Nixon's constituency—were aflame with hatred and abuse for her. In late August, in Miami Beach, the Young Americans for Freedom reported that they had collected nearly five hundred signatures at the Republican National Convention for a Georgia veterans' petition for the prosecution of Jane as a traitor. In Washington, Richard Ichord, the chairman of the House Committee on Internal Security and a Missouri Democrat, declared that Jane Fonda had violated the criminal laws in making her Hanoi broadcasts, and stated that he was introducing legislation to prevent such trips as hers, forbidding American citizens from traveling to any part of the world where America was in armed conflict, unless authorized by the President.

Meanwhile the President himself was overseeing the payment of nearly half a million dollars to the Watergate burglars, as the lid on the break-in tightened. As Nixon tried to cover his tracks, Jane was publicly trying to undermine him. Her exhausting tours of the country in behalf of the Democratic candidate, Senator George McGovern, appeared to have done little good. Some McGovern people did not welcome Jane's support, feeling that her "traitor" label might damage him.

In December, before Nixon was sworn in for his brief, abortive second term, Jane stopped off in Stockholm on her way back from filming in Norway. While Jane was marching with some ten thousand Swedish anti-Vietnam War demonstrators, a woman in the crowd showered her with red paint. It spattered her face and

254

her clothes, but she took the assault in her stride and continued the march. They marched to the American embassy, which was guarded by several hundred policemen, some mounted and a number of them with dogs; there was no violence. Once again, Jane condemned Nixon, saying, "His conception of peace is to escalate the killing. The U.S. election did not give Nixon a mandate to carry on the war."

The seeds had been sown for Jane's future vindication. She was already a heroine on American campuses, throughout Europe and nearly all of Asia.

34

When the flow of scripts from Hollywood filmmakers suddenly slowed down, a deal was negotiated between Jane and an independent British firm to do *A Doll's House* with the most successful of the victims of the Hollywood witch-hunt, director Joseph Losey, who had to go to England to rebuild his career. All the auspices seemed favorable. A hero of the Old Left meets a heroine of the New; but trouble began almost immediately. Losey once said:

> My own predicament is that I'm constantly naïve about people. I seem always to go overboard—then I become disillusioned. I yearn for total reciprocity. I think that the most gratifying things in life are sexual, personal, and professional rapports. I am always searching for these rapports. But it's difficult, and rare, and mainly impossible.

In the past he had had the good luck to work with the playwright Harold Pinter and the actor Dirk Bogarde on a number of very successful films such as *Accident* and *The Servant*. There was a great deal of "reciprocity," nearly total rapport. Losey had heard nice things about Jane and expected the shooting of the Ibsen play on location in Norway to be a memorable experience.

And so it was, but chiefly as a nightmare. Jane and Tom Hayden arrived with her own screenwriter in tow: Nancy Dowd. That was ominous, but Losey, while he may have been alarmed, said nothing and began filming. Jane, Trevor Howard, Delphine Seyrig, David Warner and Edward Fox spent the better part of November and December 1972 at Roros, where it was already deep winter, attempting to infuse this strong drama with new, cinematic life. Jane would bring to the role of Nora a great deal of her own defiance, far bolder than Nora's curtain declaration. That the movie succeeded as well as it did owed much to Jane's sure professionalism and the loving attention to period and place for which Losey had become famous.

Where it fails is in the casting of David Warner as Helmer. One begins to feel that in whatever battles raged offscreen, Warner was the loser. He becomes more and more actorish as the movie progresses, while Jane grows more and more real. There is also some serious meddling with Ibsen's intent. Although David Mercer, an Englishman, is given credit for adapting the play to the screen, reports from Norway suggest that he was not to blame for attempting to make Nora's crime—that of forging her father's signature—less reprehensible by making her a nobler creature than Ibsen ever intended. This effort takes several forms: Nora is truly in love with the charmless and tyrannical Helmer; she is no longer a flirt but rather firmly turns aside Dr. Rank's declaration of his love for her almost as rudely as if it were a pass; and because she is this noble creature who can love an odious husband, she commits her crime in the name of that love, to save his life. Only the first and the last are Ibsen's and none of the rest works. Still, Jane gives us a charming, forceful Nora who manages to make credible even the most astonishing scenes and dialogue.

Edward Fox comes closest to Jane's success as Krogstad, the junior bank officer who knows the secret of Nora's forged note. Fox brings to the part an air of having been out in the world with other imperfect beings.

Mercer's efforts to open up Ibsen's play succeed in the early stages but fail as the movie proceeds. Jane later would describe Mercer as "an alcoholic misogynist English playwright" (which she apparently thinks trebly damns him). Like her father, Jane does not concern herself with such touchy points as slander when she is really worked up about someone. She went on to say:

All the men involved had decided that what Ibsen said about women didn't apply any more. I discovered that the male characters, who are somewhat shadowy, had been built up and the women were shaved down . . . except Nora—if you tie Nora's tubes, you've got nothing left. There was I, another woman, and Delphine Seyrig, and we were being called dykes, a gaggle of bitches.

They were supposed to give us two weeks of rehearsal, which they didn't. So there we were, and it was like the house was burning, what could you salvage? You grab your socks. We tried to get at least the most important things back in [which was the rub, according to Losey, since it was not Ibsen they inserted but Ibsen by way of Dowd and Fonda]. It wasn't that we sat around bitching. Actually, most of the men were drunk all of the time. And of course they interpreted anything we did as simply wanting more lines to say. They painted it as a conspiracy of dykes ganging up on "us poor men." Every day there would be some inscription on the camera about Women's Lib. The strangest thing happened: I found I had to become Nora with Losey, bat my eyelashes, and make it seem as though it was his idea. Every day I realized how valid the play was, as Ibsen's whole thesis was being acted out.

Losey never had the guts to confront me. On the contrary, he wrote me love letters, but he attacked women in lower positions. He tried to set us against each other. Then when it was all over, he gave these interviews in which he attacked me, called me cruel, and said I was disrespectful to the crew. Actually, I got along fine with the crew—the grip and electrician. It was just that I didn't want to socialize with all of them, because Tom was there and I wanted to be with him.

I was completely professional. I never came late and I always knew my lines. Losey would have preferred an Elizabeth Taylor, with tantrums and scenes. But a perfectly normal, well-disciplined actress who had some ideas about the play, that he couldn't handle. And this from a man who calls himself a progressive, a Marxist.*

Jane rarely attacked anyone this strenuously except a political figure. Losey concedes that there was a bloody clash of personalities. There are occasions when film productions break apart, the warring factions clearly defined, the battle lines drawn. John Huston's *The Misfits* with Marilyn Monroe and Clark Gable was such a casualty, the acrimony between Marilyn and the screenplay's author and her husband Arthur Miller spilling over everyone. The long drawn-out battle probably contributed more than anything else to Gable's death only days after the film was finished. It is peculiarly disabling to a movie when it is filmed far from home. Years later, Losey recalled that during the shooting of *A Doll's House*, there was often open hostility. He said:

> I don't know Jane Fonda very well—I wonder if anybody does. I have great admiration for her talent and some respect for her public positions. I think she is immensely attractive, and we had a bloody awful time on *A Doll's House*.
> I don't believe she has the slightest idea in the world who or what I am. I wonder if she has much more idea about herself.†

The crew—with the exception, as Jane noted, of the electrician and the grip—were unanimously behind Losey. It was the first and perhaps the last time Jane ever found a group of technicians so openly hostile, with so much resentment.

Mercer's opening sequence, entirely invented for the

* Interview with Molly Haskell in *The Village Voice*, issue of November 7, 1974.
† Letter to the author from Joseph Losey dated October 27, 1980.

movie, showing Nora skating in the late afternoon at a public pond with her older, more worldly girlfriend Kristina for company, is delightful. Even the expository scene between Kristina and Krogstad, tacked onto this scene, works, although here we begin to question the wisdom of attempting dialogue in Ibsen's idiom without his great strengths as a dramatist. Ibsen's work has been described by certain critics as mechanical in structure and some have even faulted his dialogue. Yet it is a common failing of some critics of Ibsen, Dreiser and Lillian Hellman to dismiss their dialogue as "utilitarian," an insignificant part of their "large, important themes." Ibsen has been rewritten by numerous film and stage playwrights besides Dowd and Mercer, but only Arthur Miller has managed to rework the plays with any success and that is because the two men are so similar in temperament. Mercer's (or Dowd's uncredited) hand is always visible when the dialogue is invented or rewritten.

There were frequent story huddles between screenwriter Nancy Dowd and Jane. There was a tug-of-war going on between the ladies, joined in their stand by costar Delphine Seyrig and Losey, who was guiding Mercer's hand. Jane, fighting for strong feminist underpinnings to Nora's final departure, believed that she had the backing of Ibsen's ghost. Losey, equally passionate, was doing battle to keep the original spirit of Ibsen's work. In his own lifetime, Ibsen had a few highly critical things to say about feminists who saw only that particular side of A Doll's House. And there is Tom Hayden's presence on location: could this master rhetorician be playing at drama or acting as a gray eminence while his future wife instructs Miss Dowd? It is all a very sad chapter, but an important one. If some suffragist in Ibsen's lifetime had gone this far, the playwright would have shot her and been acquitted on a plea of self-defense.

Losey's tampering is of a different sort and has little to do with "shaving down the women's roles." In his characteristic quest for a feeling of place, there are so many exterior scenes (sleighs through the streets, children tobogganing, train arrivals, etc.) that they seriously drain away the claustrophobic nature of Nora's predicament. It was much the same problem that confronted James Poe when he attempted *They Shoot Horses* as a movie. The walls cannot close in on Nora because she is out-of-doors so much. Losey must have seen this and decided that her walls were spiritual ones: but interiors of souls are hard to show on the screen, which is why we have so many second-rate film versions of almost every great novel ever written, although it must be said that Losey succeeds in depicting souls nearly as well as any other filmmaker this side of Bergman. Reality—of course Nora came and went a great deal—is served, but there is little sense of her spiritual confinement, her caged feeling, that is so integral to the stage play.

An issue was being fought out here that would be settled in the near future. In *A Doll's House* Jane was quite obviously seeking, and being denied, control over the films she made. The thing to do was to have her own producer who thought as she did or was pliant, and writers who would be comfortable with Jane Fonda at their elbows as they typed. Losey was too powerful for her, but her time would soon come.

PART IX

Old Friends and New Enemies

35

Throughout Jane's open opposition to Richard Nixon, she was buoyed by reassuring hands reaching out to her at every rally, and perhaps the flow of adrenaline and vitamins through her system. She had seen the world's misery, the oppression brought about by war, poverty and disenfranchisement. She had resolved to do something about it and, in the doing, had come out of her ivory tower and become one with the people. They accepted her as genuine. Jane Fonda not only became a rallying point for antiwar activists everywhere, but the range of her celebrity—she was the best-known American film actress in Russia—made people pay heed, even if they disagreed with her. Some of her friends believe that her years of antiwar activity helped shorten the war. If they are right, even to the extent of one less day's killing, then she deserves more than a footnote to the history of our time.

All Jane's appearances on the antiwar circuit were now being channeled through her Indochina Peace Campaign. In late December 1972 she had returned from Norway and the tribulations of *A Doll's House* to wind up the year with a series of rallies in Boston and Cambridge, Massachusetts, where campus militants had broken down the ivy-clad walls of Harvard permanently.

Jane never failed to appear wherever she was booked, no matter how foul the weather or how small the crowd. On the night of December 29 there had been a sudden freeze over slick highways. She was invited to speak informally to a group of Cambridge people at the home of Mrs. Alice Ryerson, whose husband ran the Ryerson Steel Works. Maryel Locke, a lawyer and mother of five sons as well as three stepchildren, strapped herself into her car and drove over glazed highways to the Ryersons' house in Cambridge. She found no more than twelve people there because of the road conditions. But Jane arrived, on the arm of Mike Ansara, long known as a liberal force in Boston and head of the local Indochina Peace Campaign. She did not seem especially upset to find such a small group. Jane sat crosslegged on the floor, and spoke for nearly two hours on what she had found in North Vietnam. To emphasize the fact that the Vietnamese were not anti-American despite the punishing bombing raids and their suffering, she said that they had put on a production of Arthur Miller's *All My Sons*. As Maryel Locke remembers it:

> I mostly remember her using her hands beautifully—she has long fingers—and her precise diction, and her knocking me out with her charm, her directness, her bothering to spend all that time with so few people. Afterward, she asked if people would donate money to a worthy cause and explained how they could get a tax deduction. I don't believe anyone gave her a check at that moment . . . the Ryersons did afterward. I asked her privately . . . about her films. She looked pained and said she didn't really like any of her films. When I pressed her for what to see nevertheless, she said *They Shoot Horses*. . . . I went out and helped scrape ice off his [Ansara's] windshield so they could drive off.

Mrs. Locke was so impressed and charmed by Jane that she volunteered to hold another fund-raiser on her own on January 2. It was held in a friend's art gallery, and about ninety people showed up, including a few of Jane's local supporters whom Jane had asked Mrs. Locke to invite. During Jane's talk a man stepped inside from the street with a camera poised against his cheek and began taking pictures of the entire audience; the gallery owner shooed him outside again. Jane, used by now to this harassment by the FBI, ignored the intrusion.

Jane and Tom Hayden still were the targets of a massive surveillance on the part of the FBI. Not only were they being photographed along with all their audiences—a form of intimidation that suggested to some who were caught by the agents' cameras that the government would have an interest in them, that they were "marked" people—but their mail was being examined. The mail checks covered not only their various residences but Hank Fonda's two homes, on East Seventy-fourth Street in New York and his newly bought Mission-style ranch house in Bel Air, California. Their phones were bugged and informants placed wherever possible within peace groups and militant parties, such as the Black Panthers. It became so pervasive Jane was eventually forced to inform all of those working for her organizations that they must be on the alert for spies in their midst. These counter-surveillance methods succeeded for the most part, although Jane and Tom began a suit for judgment and damages against the Department of Justice in the autumn of 1973 when the Nixon administration began to crumble. Richard Nixon, Jane's most intrepid enemy, would be too busy over the next year to bother with her, and the Department of Justice under John Mitchell was in deep trouble as well. The government settled the matter out of court and agreed to cease and desist.

The Locke rally went very well and afterward Laurence Locke, also a lawyer, buttonholed everyone present until he managed to collect $1800 in checks or cash. The Lockes had opened a joint law office that morning, where she planned to specialize in workmen's compensation and women's rights; this successful rally made their day and they were euphoric.

On January 21, 1973, Jane married Tom Hayden in her Laurel Canyon home. Hank and Shirlee Fonda were among the wedding party, along with Peter and his second wife, Rebecca Crockett. Peter had been divorced by Susan Fonda in June 1972. Jane announced after the ceremony that she was expecting Tom Hayden's child, which came as no surprise to anyone since she was quite obviously pregnant. Hollywood, recently so provincial, seemed not particularly shaken by the unorthodox rites. The youthful rebels had made their point in the nineteen-sixties and nearly every American town and village had seen an unconventional couple united barefoot—sometimes with the pastor unshod as well—wearing homespun, sackcloth or denim, or literally nothing at all. Jane and Tom's wedding was sedate by comparison.

Three days later, with no time for a honeymoon, the Haydens were back in the Boston area for another rally organized by Maryel Locke. Jane and Tom were staying in a "commune" set up by a white-collar activist group known as Nine to Five. Hayden was not especially gracious as Mrs. Locke waited for Jane to appear. In truth, he lacked most of Jane's social graces, which had been ingrained in her. Over the years ahead, and with Jane's prompting, he would improve as his ambitions deepened and broadened. Jane still had her *Klute* hairstyle and wore her usual uniform of dungarees and boots. Mrs. Locke recalls:

On the way out in the car [about forty minutes], she quizzed us about the people who would be there and what she would say, and she asked us to put the light on in the car so she could look over some notes. She also told us that she was trying to decide what to do about her career. Some of her new friends wanted her to stop acting and do more serious work, certainly not the kind of films she'd done before. We told her to keep being an actress, that these people consciously or unconsciously wanted to strip her of her power, and if she was not known as an actress, she would simply not command the attention she was getting for the causes she cared about. She said she had been doing *A Doll's House* for Losey and it was difficult.

Jane's "new friends" were members of Hayden's circle and their suggestion that she should leave the movies might have stemmed from Tom's own insecurity at the time. Soon enough all of them saw that what Mrs. Locke perceived was absolutely right: Jane was far more useful as a major star than she was out of the limelight.

Jane's speech before the group in Weston that night was typical of her antiwar oratory. The themes remained fairly constant, although she never gave the same speech twice: "The North Vietnamese have recognized that you cannot exist as a human being if you don't know who your enemy is. In order to survive, they had to give us a face." This statement was doubtless intended to counter the prevailing feeling, especially among the troops, that the enemy was "faceless—invisible."

She spoke of an old woman in North Vietnam who came up to her crying, and took her hand. "She was just so moved to meet an American woman. She asked me to thank all the Americans who were trying to stop the war. . . . This couldn't have been planned or staged; it happened too often. To see hospital after hospital, cultural centers, factories, schools in ruins, and then to be greeted by such an overwhelming expression of warmth."

We catch a glimpse here of the person the North Vietnamese saw in Jane: an important American, a star in films, come to give them reassurance that all Americans were not determined to kill them for no reason, to blow up their hospitals and their homes, burn their crops and scourge the countryside. Jane said that one Vietnamese told her, "If the people ever learn to hate, our cause is lost." She spoke of her vision of a people completely united in pursuit of a common goal: the right to determine their own future. This was, she said, unlike anything she had seen in America. It had changed her approach toward activism and living.

The Weston rally was held the night after the cease-fire was announced by President Nixon and three days before it was to go into effect. It might be expected that getting money out of the audience to help end a war which the President told the nation was winding down would be difficult. But Jane coaxed a thousand dollars out of them, chiefly through her persuasiveness and Nixon's lack of credibility. The only trouble was that the cash and checks were misplaced for almost a day. Laurence Locke, who did the hard-sell act of extracting the money, had handed it all to Jane in two plastic coffee cups pushed together. Forgetting what it was, Jane had put the money down, and the next day was on the telephone to the Lockes wondering where it was. The Lockes phoned their hosts, the Jack Higginses, who began a search of the wastebaskets with the help of their many children. The money was found in one of them and dropped off to Jane.

The act of clinging to a dream of enlightened Americans who had been changed by the experience of Vietnam would continue until it hardened into an impervious shell of faith that would resist even the future tides of history—the pillage of Cambodia by the Vietnamese, the refugee camps, everything. Jane went twice to Vietnam. "We're a cynical people," she would say. "It's in our culture. But I can't be cynical after that."

Jane's Indochina Peace Campaign now had offices in Los Angeles and Cambridge, Massachusetts. Its goals were to raise funds for medical aid to North Vietnam; to bring pressure on Congress to cut off economic support to the Thieu regime in South Vietnam; to secure the safe release of political prisoners of the Thieu regime; and to help educate Americans about the reasons for the war and the significance of the peace treaty. Jane would set up a film production firm as a kind of corporate spin-off of IPC. IPC Productions would eventually function on a commercial level and make films such as *Coming Home* (1978) for theatrical release, and through the astute management of Jane and her production partner Bruce Gilbert, it would become one of the most successful independent film companies in the world. Some of its profits would go into political ventures, but not all.

36

On January 27, 1973, the Vietnam cease-fire agreement was signed in Paris "in eerie silence," according to the New York *Times*, ending nearly twenty years of American involvement in Vietnamese affairs. The American withdrawal of troops was completed two months later. The strangest and longest war in American history was ended. The fighting did not end, though, for several days. An American helicopter sent north to bring a Vietcong delegation to Saigon was shot down before reaching its destination. Americans, too, were engaged in heavy fighting in isolated battles at Longhoa and other hamlets.

Jane did not seem impressed by the formalities, and pushed on with her appearances for IPC. She had assembled a forty-five-minute slide show on women in Vietnam. She narrated all showings live, telling her audiences that Ho Chi Minh linked the movements for women's liberation and Vietnamese revolutionary nationalism. He said, according to Jane, that neither could occur without the other. She regretted that in America so many women left the antiwar movement to take up their own cause. "It is limiting," she said, "to neglect to link up the war with the women's movement." When the Americans took over from the French, Jane charged, women in Vietnam were more brutally treated than before. They were raped as a matter of practice, and often were mutilated by the insertion of Coke bottles and live eels.

271

During her slide show tour the American POWs were released. It was a dramatic homecoming, seen by millions on television; extremely pale men with a fuzz of hair on their scalps, most of them with eyes dark-ringed by sickness and years of imprisonment. A few of them were lame, and one wondered if their injuries had occurred in combat or in prison. Then among the several hundred former prisoners of war. a number of them began telling government "debriefing" officers of torture. Air Force lieutenant colonel Kenneth North said that he was tied with wire, kicked and slapped around, then was trussed up and hit with rifle butts until he wished for death. His captors even tore up his Geneva Convention card outlining the rules for treatment of prisoners. Navy lieutenant Charles R. Zuboski said, "There was a constant denial of any intellectual pursuit. You had to do it in your head."

Jane was quick to denounce them, saying that one of the few ways we are going to redeem ourselves as a country for what we have done "is not to hail the pilots as heroes, because they are hypocrites and liars." Of the sixty hostile POWs, she told a slide show audience in April in Los Angeles:

> Who are these men? They are the oldest persons captured. Only twenty-nine of the 600 POWs have spoken of being "tortured." And they have the most to lose by not painting their captors in a poor light.
> Their whole future depends on loyalty to the U.S. military and to machismo. They can't say that it was the unspoken policy of POWs to collaborate with the North Vietnamese. They have to present themselves in a hero's image.

When Jane told a television interviewer, "History will judge them [the POWs] severely," a fresh torrent of outrage struck her. Secretary of Defense Eliot Richardson said that calling American POWs "hypocrites and liars" was an "egregious insult to all our returning prisoners." He said that he had personally visited with thirty-five to forty returned prisoners from Vietnam and their integrity and honesty were apparent to him. He added that a person making such a judgment was "badly motivated or simply fails to understand what he or she can plainly perceive." In Richard Nixon's only documented mention of Jane, he wrote in his diary on March 6, 1973:

At ten o'clock I met the first POWs I have seen. It was a very moving experience to see their wives and the two of them—gaunt, lean, quiet, confident, with enormous faith in the country, in God, and in themselves.

Apparently they had been exposed to enemy propaganda throughout and had never given in to it. For example, they were shown still photos of the big crowds demonstrating against the President. They, of course, heard tapes of messages from Ramsey Clark, Jane Fonda, and the other peacenik groups, but they had nothing but contempt for them.

In his *Memoirs*, Nixon went further. He said:

It was not long before the returning men had confirmed the widespread use of torture in the prison camps. Some were tortured for refusing to pose in propaganda photos with touring antiwar groups. Miss Fonda said that the POWs were "liars" for making such claims; one POW had his arm and leg broken because he refused to meet with Miss Fonda. It was during her trip to North Vietnam in 1972 that she broadcast appeals over Radio Hanoi asking American pilots to quit flying bombing runs over North Vietnam.

Jane proposed that the real heroes were the young men who refused to fight and those who resisted the military. She described the returning POWs as looking like "football heroes. . . . Look at the Vietnamese's emaciated bodies. Thousands will never be able to walk because of the cramped living in tiger cages. Those are tortured people. These football players are no more

273

heroes than Custer was. They're military careerists and professional killers."

It was not Jane's finest hour. There had been torture on both sides. After all the evidence had been given, that fact was irrefutable. It is possible she still does not accept this: she had committed too much of herself, too many bridges had been burned during her Vietnam crusade. Finally she did begin to take on the spiritual ferocity of Joan of Arc. The prisoners, she said, "forced the Vietnamese to be brutal. They tried to escape. If you try to escape from prison in this country and you're the wrong color, you get shot." She *believed* in the purity of heart of the Vietnamese people; she had seen their rubble and their dying, talked with their most eloquent spokesmen. These former POWs were trying to tear down the image she had so carefully assembled of a peace-loving, dedicated people. They had to be liars.

The furor continued unabated into the following year. "Mr. Speaker," Congressman Robert Steele (Republican, Connecticut) began: "I would like to nominate Academy Award-winning actress Jane Fonda for a new award: the rottenest, most miserable performance by any one individual American in the history of our country." Congressman Steele was still concerned about Jane's calling the returning prisoners of war "hypocrites and liars." His "nomination" was just rhetoric, but in the Indiana Senate a resolution was adopted censuring Jane and urging her to "retract and apologize."

Jane was not about to do any such thing. While conceding that American prisoners might have been tortured in North Vietnam when

guys . . . misbehaved and treated their guards in a racist fashion or tried to escape. . . . Some pilots were beaten to death by the people they had bombed when they parachuted from their planes. But to say that torture was systematic and a policy of the North Vietnamese government is a lie. And the guys are hypocrites. They're trying to make themselves look self-righteous, but they are war criminals according to the law.

Because of her blind faith in the Vietnamese, Jane conveniently forgets her own behavior while in the clutches of the law: she kicked and screamed and yelled profanities. Contrast this with the behavior of some of the American prisoners of war, almost equally rebellious in spirit but most of them wise enough not to scream and shout. The majority were not docile nor did they collaborate in any way with their captors, as Jane later implied. In wartime detention, survival and expediency are instincts of far greater force and universality than vainglorious courage or patriotism. The bravest are apt to spend much of their captivity in solitary with foul air, and when they curse their captors a rifle butt sometimes splits their heads open. This was true in the German and Japanese POW camps: it was true in North Vietnam. A colonel told one POW near Hanoi that he wrote in his report to the Pentagon that he needed no alarm clock in the prison, since he was awakened by the man's screams from the interrogation center. If Jane herself had been male and a prisoner of war in Vietnam (she would be the first to say that she would have refused any duty there in the first place), she might not have survived captivity because of her defiant attitude toward all authority.

And even now when all of the accounts of suffering have come in from the Boat People, Jane remains intransigent. If she recanted she would not be Jane Fonda, loyal to the last.

37

In late 1972 and early 1973, Peter Fonda was living with his second wife, Becky, and his two children on board a sailing ship he had bought with the earnings from *Easy Rider*. He was, he wrote,* an anarchist "who does not wish to be a citizen of the United States or Russia or China or France or England or any nation." This voluntary man without a country was most concerned about the alarming decrease in available oxygen, so necessary for survival:

> About thirty percent of our oxygen is manufactured by plants but the percentage keeps decreasing, for we've been cutting down the great forests left and right—to build carports, to make newspapers with, to make paper to wipe our asses with. We've been bombing the forests out of Vietnam. That country is now a wonderful sandtrap, and Spiro Agnew, if he wants to, can spend the rest of his life hitting golf balls out of Southeast Asian bomb craters.

He reasserted his atheism, but gave some specifics about his belief in reincarnation:

> This [decomposing] tree is giving itself back to the ground it came from, it is going back to where it was born. From this decomposing tree, other things will grow: insects and plant life and other insects that will

* *Gallery* magazine, February 1973.

feed off the tiniest ones you'll find there. . . . Here is reincarnation, for that tree is reborn. But the man or woman who wants to be reincarnated refuses to accept that future destiny as a tree or bug or worm— but that's where it's at. We are not separate from any of these creatures.

Peter would shortly abandon the life of a sailor for a landlocked one on a large area of land he bought in Montana.

In March 1973 Peter's latest film, *Two People*, went into general release. It was a story that Peter had nurtured for months and finally had persuaded Robert Wise to direct. It was about an American deserter from the Vietnam War (played by Peter) who meets a fashion model at loose ends (played by newcomer Lindsay Wagner, who later would win fame on television as the *Bionic Woman*). They fall in love, but their situation is impossible and he goes off to turn himself in. The movie opened to hostile reviews. Perhaps it was too early for such a film, but it was not helped by a weak script and an untried and uncertain leading lady. It was an important film, however, since it may have inspired Jane to option a script with a similar theme entitled *Buffalo Ghosts*, written by her screenwriter friend Nancy Dowd. The theme of *Buffalo Ghosts* would be carried over into the final shooting script of Jane's picture, rewritten by Waldo Salt and called *Coming Home*.

In early autumn Jane, Tom, a male companion of Tom's, their infant son Troy, and Jane's mother-in-law flew to Leningrad for the filming of Maeterlinck's *The Blue Bird*. Jane had only a cameo role—she would appear on screen for less than ten minutes—but she had not seen Russia since her visit with Vadim nearly a decade earlier.

It is not easy to describe a fantasy gone wrong; indeed, a fantasy which is no fantasy because we can see at once all the effort that has gone into it. Fairies don't fly on jet fuel, creating noise and an obvious path of pollution. *The Blue Bird* does not soar, unfortunately, it flops noisily and dies.

The film's director, George Cukor, says that he doesn't understand why the picture failed. If that is the case, then perhaps the director is more at fault than the script or the players. In looking back on the splendid career of Cukor (*The Royal Family of Broadway*, *A Bill of Divorcement*, *Dinner at Eight*, *David Copperfield*, *Camille*, *Holiday*, *The Philadelphia Story*, *Gaslight*, etc.) there is nothing to suggest that he is capable of fantasy, but then absolutely nothing suggested that Victor Fleming could create a classic in *The Wizard of Oz* in 1939. Cukor stages this film as he has staged all of his previous films, with stars in all the key roles and even some minor bits. If the story were *Dr. Zhivago*, all would be well, but we are here watching two small children in search of an elusive bluebird.

The pity is that this was the last gasp of real détente, a true partnership in film between the Soviet Union and the United States. Cukor's insistence upon having total control over this movie (perhaps to be expected when an American is put in charge of a foreign venture) has given it a Hollywood look except for the exteriors. I would not trust Hollywood with *The Blue Bird* at any time under any circumstances. Maeterlinck himself failed in Hollywood when he presented Sam Goldwyn with a bee hero; that sent Sam reeling from a story conference, his hands to his head.

The screenwriters literalized everything. They were unsure of themselves at every turn: they didn't seem to know if the picture was a musical or a child's fantasy or both. They had grandparents who had died dozing through eternity and singing about not having enough to do. The presence of half a dozen major stars of the American and Soviet screen and ballet matters not a jot. If it is anybody's film it is Elizabeth Taylor's, and she is miscast; as the woodsman's wife and the children's mother she is merely competent. In the role of Night, Jane is the more skillful actress but no more convincing than Taylor. With the flicker of an eyelash she delivers the line, "You know you're only allowed out on Halloween," to a clutch of freakishly costumed wretches who escape from the nether regions below Night's Disney-style castle. Our first glimpse of her piques our curiosity. She is wearing what must be the world's largest shower cap, or is it an umbrella worn on top of the head? It is in Jane's scenes that we are most aware of the deficiencies of the photography. Her craggy black castle walls seem nothing more than anthracite. The film cries out for a photographer as lyrical as Jane's good friend Haskell Wexler or Nestor Almendros who shot *Days of Heaven*. Jane spent six weeks in Russia shooting her ten minutes of film. There was much more footage shot, but Jane and Ava Gardner were both heavily cut in the editing. Neither complained, for by that time it was obvious to everyone that it would take a miracle to salvage the picture and nearly everything was tried by way of resuscitation.

Jane had not really come because of the part anyway. She owed Cukor a favor since he had been among the first to see her great talent—in another weak picture, *The Chapman Report*. And most of all she wanted to see Russia again. She knew that she was popular there: among *The Blue Bird's* stars, she and Elizabeth Taylor were the only ones who drew mobs of fans wherever they went. Cicely Tyson was relatively unknown and blacks were not warmly welcomed by the Russian people; visiting blacks were often considered arrogant, very possibly because they spoke in cultured tones, wore expensive clothing and expected decent and prompt service in Soviet hotels. Ava Gardner's fabled beauty and fame had failed to reach Moscow and Leningrad. But Jane's *They Shoot Horses* had been a major hit all over the Soviet Union, and most Russians knew that she had been to Hanoi. It is interesting to note, for Jane's detractors, that they didn't think that she was a communist. And Jane herself was soon to realize that there were no radicals visible anywhere around her in Leningrad. The Russian people didn't seem to want to talk politics; they were far more interested in where she bought her jeans. Tom Hayden was so shocked to find the Russians on the street so bourgeois in their attitudes that he and his friend quickly fled back home, leaving Jane with young Troy and Tom's mother.

38

In late 1973 a major film offer was tendered to Hank by Paramount. The script was from a Brian Garfield novel entitled *Death Wish*, and it concerned a man whose wife is murdered and daughter raped and driven mad by intruding New York hoods from the streets. The husband and father then launches a one-man vigilante crusade to rid the city of this scum by personally picking them off one after another. Hank, who still opposed vigilante justice with just as much fervor as he had in 1943 when he did *The Ox-Bow Incident*, turned down the part, and Charles Bronson went on to make the picture, one of Paramount's biggest-grossing films in 1974.

Instead, Hank chose to return to his first love, the New York stage, in a one-man show called *Clarence Darrow for the Defense*, a meticulously detailed character study of the legendary criminal lawyer by television writer David Rintels. The production opened on Broadway on March 26, 1974, to generally favorable reviews. A month later it closed to go on tour, and while still in his dressing-room backstage, Hank collapsed. He was rushed to Lenox Hill Hospital, where a pacemaker was implanted to stabilize his heartbeat; within two weeks he was released, walking unaided to his limousine. Jane was half a world away when her father's medical trauma began, concluding an adventure that had been planned weeks earlier. Events were moving so fast now that it was difficult to keep up with them, but Jane was trying.

The Nixon presidency was collapsing rapidly and rumors were circulating that he would resign. On April 1, 1974, with a little over four months of Nixon's White House days remaining, Jane, Tom Hayden and son Troy, then nine months old, arrived in Hanoi with the director and cinematographer Haskell Wexler to renew old friendships, see what progress had been made in rebuilding the country, and film their visit in a documentary to be called *Introduction to the Enemy*. In the journal Jane kept of her trip* she wrote:

> . . . it would be the longest stay for either of us. It was prime time for an extended visit; the country was once again rebuilding in the wake of war, and the South was facing the prospect of an interminable "new war" which had begun almost simultaneously with the much-heralded cease-fire. So we left Troy in good hands in Hanoi and proceeded on a two week journey south with . . . Haskell Wexler and a cameraman and a sound-man from the Democratic Republic of Vietnam. . . .

The film, she said, was being edited by Wexler for release through the Santa Monica-based Indochina Peace Campaign, highlighting moments of their journey from Hanoi to the liberated zone of Quang Tri Province.

Her affection for the North Vietnamese is close to the surface throughout this journal. She writes of their crash construction programs, such as twelve buildings, each holding sixty families, each with its own kindergarten and shops:

> Too much is needed too fast. . . . The catalog of reconstruction needs is total. This is the *third time* these same people have begun rebuilding their country in 30 years. . . . Following the bombing halt in 1969, they once again set about rebuilding but in 1972 Nixon resumed the bombing and this time nothing was spared.

* *Rolling Stone* magazine, July 4, 1974.

Jane was especially moved by the destruction of Bach Mai Hospital, which she and Tom had visited when many of the women doctors there were photographed for her slide show, *Women in Vietnam*. Now they learned that most of these women were dead, killed in the bombing as they tried to get the patients out. She mentioned orphans and torture victims from South Vietnam being sent North, where she believed they would get proper care. Nowhere did she concede that the North Vietnamese might have tortured or brutalized people or given anything less than love and gentle supervision to children.

> The streets of Hanoi are bustling and exuberant, and most of all there are the children; benign mobs of beautiful, happy-looking children who would follow us white-skinned guests in their country wherever we took a walk.
> There were almost no children in Hanoi when I was there in July 1972. Hundreds of thousands of them had been evacuated to the countryside and given shelter in the homes of the peasants.

A doctor left her own two children temporarily to look after Troy Hayden in a Hanoi hotel room during the twenty-four days the Haydens were in Vietnam. She wept when she really had to say goodbye to him. . . .

In this same mood of uncritical acceptance of everything about the North Vietnamese, Jane wrote that "one of the qualities the Vietnamese hold most precious is people's ability to change. The change is what's of greatest importance, not what used to be. Hence the acceptance of former Saigon officials into the liberated zones, prostitutes into important posts." Thus, in subtle ways, Jane disarms those who wait for the "blood bath." More tellingly, Jane describes her efforts at "exorcising" the effects of the alienated culture from which she came ("as an actress without a social consciousness, I was a promoter of that culture").

In contrast to the "children everywhere" in the North,

she wrote that there were nearly half a million prostitutes in the South. The American troops, she was told, brought obscenity and a huge drug problem to the country. And surprisingly, an artist told her that there were anti-hippie groups forming in the major cities because "in Vietnam they are decadent and counter-revolutionary."

Jane herself was obliquely praised when a poet mentioned how "isolated" the early American protesters were. "Then one had to really believe in the justice of your cause." Jane concluded:

> The Vietnamese, for all their suffering, know why they have fought and who their enemy is. They also know why they want to live. If we Americans can have the courage to look again at Vietnam and learn the lessons she has to offer, learning in the process who we are, then perhaps we, too, will find we have something to live for.

Introduction to the Enemy is notable for its lack of grimness. Haskell Wexler's color cameras show us a Vietnam that sparkles with sunlight much of the time; Jane's face is often beaming, and it doesn't matter that Tom Hayden often looks dour, because his is not a presence to hold an audience. We see rubble and devastation, but Wexler's palette distances us from feeling horror. Where it succeeds is in showing us some of the stoical patience of these people. As a positive view of the North Vietnamese, it succeeds totally; where it fails, unless some of the prints are defective, is that there is no translation of some of the important leaders' statements and they invariably speak only Vietnamese. One suspects that these leaders are highly critical of Americans, perhaps even inflammatory. There is always an English translator beside the others, if they do not speak the language themselves, so the poets, painters, actresses, even a few local government heads, such as one woman in a launch during a picnic along the river, speak of their lack of hostility, *always*

284

of the need to rebuild; they are *admirable* people always. And there are the women in jobs of every description. It is easy to conclude from this film that the war has brought about total women's liberation in North Vietnam.

39

The farcical tragedy of Watergate unfolded in the summer of 1973, and there were massive efforts on the part of Nixon and his underlings to contain it throughout the winter of 1973–74. For Jane it was unadulterated bliss, not because her country's leaders were found to be criminals, but because Nixon was at the top of the ladder among the world's rogues, in her view, and now his own men were sawing away at the lower rungs so that he would wind up in the mire with a couple of dozen lesser officials.

On August 9, 1974, Nixon resigned just hours ahead of his impeachment, more humiliated than any President in the history of the American republic, including both Andrew Johnson and Harding. The "imperial presidency" had come to an end. Only Nixon and Kissinger* escaped prison.

The effect of all this on Jane's career was nothing short of magical. She had told everyone that Nixon was a criminal years before his fall; she had told the world that the war in Vietnam was an international crime long before the consensus of the American people affixed that label to it. Jane's "graylisting" period was at an

---

* Yet even Kissinger's reputation suffered. During the long Watergate investigation, it was revealed that he had routinely wiretapped his own staff. Apparently he was a man who trusted no one. The legacy of Watergate, ironically enough, was that the American people no longer trusted politicians.

end. As the last of the Watergate conspirators rode off to the slammer, Jane Fonda was flooded with film offers from every major studio in Hollywood.

The effect upon radical politics and on the lives of both Jane and Tom Hayden was equally exhilarating. The American establishment was shaken, much of it so devastated that it would be years before most Americans could accept the truth—that even Presidents can be crooks. Jane was so immersed in politics when her stock shot upward again in the film industry that she had to say no to nearly everything. She was helping Tom pull together a political party, a clutch of independents to defeat Senator John Tunney.

In April 1975, Tom Hayden announced that he would run against Tunney in the primary. They had support in places Tunney scarcely bothered with—the Chicanos, a holdover from their help to farmworkers' union chief Cesar Chavez, when Jane picketed supermarkets to boycott lettuce, grapes and other produce; the students, who backed Hayden as one of their own; and show business, from rock stars Linda Ronstadt and James Taylor and actor Jon Voight. In the end Tom lost, although he got something like 40 percent of the vote. But Tunney's seeming invincibility was destroyed by the Hayden race and he lost that autumn to S. I. Hayakawa, who ironically had taken a hard line against the students during their takeover of San Francisco State College when he was president there. Such are the vagaries of politics.

Jane and Tom both decided at that point (early 1976) that she must get back into films quickly, and for big money. By this time they had moved into a modest Santa Monica house where they would remain. Her film earnings would soon be in the millions once she produced her own pictures under the banner of IPC, which heretofore was only in the film-strip and documentary business on a free rental basis to colleges and organizations.

She accepted the female lead in a comedy called *Fun with Dick and Jane*, with George Segal, who had won a reputation as a kind of latter-day William Powell after his success in *A Touch of Class* (1974). In all of her comments about the film Jane would point out its "message" as being the overselling of consumerism in America. Dick and Jane Harper are living in a posh suburban home with every last comfort when he suddenly loses his job. The truth is that they don't own anything: it is all bought on credit. When their payments stop flowing out, the creditors close in, even rolling up their lawn and carting it off. With the bank about to foreclose and put them out on the street, they decide to become fashionable thieves. They find that they have a genuine gift for it, and successfully rip off drugstores, the phone company, and eventually Dick's former boss, when they blast open the company safe.

Any Jane Fonda fan would have known that she could do such a role in a walk after her earlier *Period of Adjustment* and *Cat Ballou*. But Jane had so recently been billed shrill and obnoxious in the media, the public at large was not prepared for her elegant comic style. She was a revelation as Jane Harper; they had forgotten her sardonic wit (she had been gone from comedy for years!), the way her elongated finger could wrap itself around a cocktail glass, the sexy pose she could assume as she perched on some piece of furniture, her chorus girl's legs crossed. The message of the film was that Americans who are drowning in easy credit can stay afloat simply by turning to crime and continue to gorge themselves with luxury foods, live lives besotted by creature comforts such as heated pools, indoor gardens and exotic toys for their children (the Harpers have one—an odious son). Jane was something more than expert as a comedienne; she lifted this predictable farce to human credibility. *Fun with Dick and Jane* brought Jane back to the mainstream of American films with an impressive splash.

With her comedy successfully launched and commitments piling up, Jane, the Vassar dropout, took a few days off to accept a brief speaking tour of college campuses with Tom, promoting their Campaign for Economic Democracy and urging more public control of corporations and an end to tax loopholes. At the University of Central Michigan she condemned a large chemical company for industrial pollution and the corporation promptly suspended all grants to the school. She told another group of students that she had wasted her school years and urged them not to make the same mistake. Her tour reinforced her growing conviction that college students of the seventies were suffering through "the age of nothingness" and "the Goodbar syndrome," drawn from the movie, she said,

> in which a young woman's obsessive sexual appetite ends in tragedy, her life devoid of any meaning. . . . There is a sense that you don't matter, which I think is the most dangerous, pernicious thing of all. And what that adds up to is that you kind of draw into yourselves. You not only draw away from political and social involvement but I'll wager that not many of you have very many deep relations . . . we've become afraid to feel.

40

One would like to believe that the dramatic events around which the movie *Julia* is built really happened. Probably the key to the truth of the matter lies in Lillian Hellman's prefatory sentences in *Pentimento*, from which this "true story" was taken:

> Old paint on canvas, as it ages, sometimes becomes transparent. When that happens it is possible, in some pictures, to see the original lines: a tree will show through a woman's dress, a child makes way for a dog, a large boat is no longer on an open sea. That is called pentimento because the painter "repented," changed his mind.

Making herself a heroine of the Resistance movement against the Nazis was doubtless an old fantasy of Miss Hellman's. Tough, "scrappy," a companion and lover Dash Hammett once described her, and antifascist, she must have resented the fact that throughout this period she had American ties, contracts in Hollywood, and a decent man who needed her with him in New York and Hollywood. But while we can believe in the character of Julia, in the fact that she once existed and did these things—we can even believe in her death at the hands of the Nazis—it is more difficult to accept Lillian Hellman herself as a character under these circumstances. With the death of her old friend Dorothy Parker in 1967 following on that of Dotty's husband, Alan Campbell,

Hellman must have repented the more prosaic facts of her trip to Europe with the Campbells, and placed herself square in the middle of this dangerous mission—the act of smuggling a great deal of currency concealed in a cossack-type hat into Berlin to purchase exit visas for "maybe a thousand" Jews and others. Alternatively we can take this very contrived espionage plot another way. Perhaps Julia or someone in the Resistance movement did ask Miss Hellman to be a courier of some currency into Berlin. She told Dorothy Parker about it soon afterward but kept it from Alan Campbell, who was known to be a gossip. It was risky and it was successful—done and filed away in the mind as of no great moment.

The background of the story is important because with *Julia* Jane would begin a new phase of her career: taking dramatic events from recent or current history and making big, entertaining movies of them. One followed on the heels of another: after *Julia* in 1977 came *Coming Home* in 1978 and *The China Syndrome* in 1979. Of the three, the least credible is *Julia*. Lillian Hellman is a major American playwright, far too often dismissed for her plot contrivances, and critics who do this are missing the whole point of Hellman's significance. She has a genuine gift for taking abstract political or moral ideas and turning them into gripping drama. Excluding *Julia*, she is an acute observer of her times and usually a shrewd critic of herself. *Julia* seems almost wholly synthetic, a work of bad fiction; still, it provided Vanessa Redgrave with a solid role and Jane with a very real challenge.

As playwright Lillian Hellman, Jane is unfortunately not very credible. The substance just isn't there—through no fault of Jane's. She lights a great many cigarettes and smokes a few of them; she balls up a good many sheets of paper; she treats her friends Dotty Parker and Alan Campbell as though they were baggage she wished she'd left behind in New York—principally, it would seem, because they get in the way of her mission for the Resistance movement.

291

Lillian Hellman is as hard as a diamond, but she and someone equally tough, such as Dorothy Parker, could neutralize each other and become warm, affectionate friends. One suspects that Dorothy Parker is treated so shabbily in *Julia* because the screenwriter, Alvin Sargent, did not know that Hellman and Parker were the closest of friends, indeed as close as Hellman was to Julia. Hellman could have told him something of this durable friendship, and it is a mystery why she did not.

Despite the movie's shortcomings, *Julia* was skillfully staged in a big, old studio way by its director, Fred Zinnemann, and produced by Richard Roth in London and Paris and on location in England and France. Coming as it did at about the same time as *The Turning Point*, which also starred two major actresses, *Julia* helped to break down the decade-old resistance to female stars carrying a picture. It seemed less a victory for feminism than audience apathy to any more "buddy" films. Howard Hawks was dead; John Ford was dead; their successors were finally given the news that jolly macho hijinks were not certain winners at the box office.

While *Julia* was shooting at Elstree Studios, Jane, Tom and young Troy met Afdera Fonda on a London street near Afdera's flat. They embraced warmly and both remarked on how little the other had changed. But these were just civilities. Afdera saw in Jane a mature woman—angular, graceful and looking more like her father than ever. And Afdera had changed, too. She was far more subdued than when Jane had last seen her, and was now a handsome middle-aged woman who still retained a charming trace of youthful vivacity. Afdera invited them back to her flat for some home-cooked spaghetti, and the reunion came off well enough. Afdera did not expect to like Tom Hayden, but he surprised her with his quick mind. "I could see why Jane was drawn to him," she recalled.

Jane's contact with Vanessa Redgrave, while never broken, would become more and more infrequent following their film together. Redgrave was now, as Jane had been in the early seventies, semiblacklisted. Her last major film for commercial release, *Agatha* (1978), in which she had played a young Agatha Christie, had done only fair business, more the fault of the script, which was high on style and low on drama. Since that time, she ran for a seat in the House of Commons as the Workers Revolutionary Party candidate and won fewer than four hundred votes, and made a documentary film, *The Palestinians*, in which she danced defiantly holding a gun. Her actress sister Lynn was quoted as saying, "I love her a lot. . . . She's one of the great eccentrics." But in 1980, all of this controversy flared anew.

In autumn 1979 Vanessa Redgrave, who was radically pro-Palestinian, was hired by a television motion picture company to play the role of the half-Jewish cabaret singer Fania Fenelon, who saved herself at Auschwitz by becoming a kapo.* Even Arthur Miller, who wrote the script, was dismayed by the producer's choice, and there were protests and disturbances throughout the production. But her performance was praised everywhere, even by many Jews.

Vanessa and Jane were not wholly out of touch, but Jane had been doing some revisionist work on her image in the late seventies, some of it in the interest of sustaining a film career that had reached the very top plateau of stardom and the rest to ensure that Tom Hayden's political ambitions were not imperiled. They needed to draw a veil of discreet silence over both their pasts.

By this time Jane seemed to have moved light-years away from her militant "Hanoi Jane" days. Like Redgrave she had acquired a grandeur about her, but quite unlike Redgrave she was not going to embrace any cause that could shred her present reputation if she fell into the wrong clique. Jane had been saved by the tides of history, washing pure all of her many demonstrations of

---

* Kapos were concentration camp inmates who collaborated with the Nazis and were given preferential status, saving them from the gas chambers. Fania Fenelon became the conductor of the Auschwitz orchestra, playing symphonic music for the new arrivals off the death trains to allay their fears.

loyalty and affection for the people of North Vietnam. For the majority of fans and audiences it no longer mattered whether or not she still felt that affection. The lid had been shut tight on Vietnam, at least for Americans. It was not a subject anyone chose to sit around and discuss over a few drinks, and it had become, like religion, too delicate a matter for casual conversation.

It seemed unlikely that Redgrave's career could be saved by the erosion of support for the cause of Zionism and Israeli expansionism, despite growing sympathy in surprising places for the PLO. Only her art could save her, and following *Playing for Time*, it seemed possible that it might.

41

The Hollywood in which Jane was now rising as a power to reckon with was quite unlike the old Hollywood in which she had been raised. Not only had the studios collapsed in the old-fashioned sense of having stables of stars, writers, directors and so on, but the old studio heads were gone, replaced by cadres of young people, mostly former radicals like Jane herself. There were former Yippies in positions of authority and more former members of SDS than you could count at every level of movie making. Still, in 1978 Jane did not have enough clout to get *Coming Home* financed and distributed, and it wasn't until she enlisted the support and backing of the producer Jerome Hellman that everything came together. But Jane was the one who persisted, who never relaxed until her production company (IPC) had the movie in the works and on its way to the screen.

That had taken quite a bit of doing. Jane must not have forgotten the script about a Vietnam deserter which her brother Peter had made (entitled *Two People*) back in 1973, and while his film had failed, Jane was determined that *Coming Home* would not. Meanwhile, screenwriter Nancy Dowd had been working on her *Buffalo Ghosts*, which was set in the Midwest and told of two former high school sweethearts—the roles eventually played by Jane and Jon Voight. In the original screenplay, when Jane's husband returns from a tour of Vietnam, he has changed, as has his wife, who now feels a profound horror about the war, having befriended a paraplegic veteran, whom she recognizes as her old boyfriend, in a nearby army hospital. Later, without having met the husband, the paraplegic goes away, and the husband, his values and life turned upside down by a meaningless war, drives down the wrong side of a divided highway to his death.

The final shooting script was turned over to veteran screenwriter Waldo Salt, who was responsible for *The Midnight Cowboy*, and Robert C. Jones, who made the husband far more conventional and understandable, and more of a stereotyped hawkish American officer. They gave the wife and the paraplegic a torrid love affair, a relationship that would completely alter the attitude of the wife, Sally, toward the war and much else. The story's sympathies, once divided between wife and husband, were now altogether with the wife since the husband had become less important and more wooden. Like *The Best Years of Our Lives* (1946), the final draft of *Coming Home* concerns itself chiefly with change and readjustment, and like the Robert E. Sherwood script of that film it is a love story told honestly without evasion but with considerable compassion—except where the husband is concerned.

Hal Ashby approached Jack Nicholson to play the paraplegic, and he considered Bruce Dern or Jon Voight for the role of the marine major. When Voight read the script he said he would do anything to be in the picture but he preferred the role of Luke, the paraplegic, eliminating Nicholson from consideration (he had a number of prior commitments anyway), with Dern falling into the role of the major. As finally pulled together in the Salt version, it was a part Dern had played numerous times before, that of the cold, quirky fall guy.

Producer Jerome Hellman and Jane's producer, Bruce Gilbert, now had a movie production in motion, with distribution and financing set by United Artists. Much of their final good luck stemmed from the early reports coming in on Francis Ford Coppola's *Apocalypse Now*, then filming in the Philippines, which was shaping up, according to advance word, as the greatest war film of all time.

Ashby was a man very much at home with other counterculturists. He went barefoot a good part of the time, let his hair grow down to his shoulders and had been an antiwar activist at heart although he had never done much about it. "Maybe Hollywood is bothered by their conscience," he said of the series of films on Vietnam at the time. "Maybe they feel they sidestepped it. It's a very interesting question and I wish I could give a definite answer as to why. I mean, I even asked myself the same question when I decided to do the film."

Jane proposed hiring the cinematographer Haskell Wexler, who had shot and directed her striking documentary *Introduction to the Enemy*. Wexler had a genius for making the viewer very aware of color, while downplaying it as a distraction to the drama. He had worked with Ashby before when the director had done a warm and homely film portrait of Woody Guthrie from the folk singer's book *Bound for Glory* (1976). Ashby had won for himself a good-sized cult of fanatics with *Harold and Maude* (1971), his love story between a twenty-year-old boy with a death wish who falls in love with an eighty-year-old woman. Not so incidentally, he had shown a real feeling for servicemen's camaraderie in *The Last Detail* (1974). His most successful film had been the comedy *Shampoo* (1975) for Jane's old friend from her starlet days, Warren Beatty. Ashby was not, however, the first director approached for *Coming Home*. John Schlesinger was asked to do the film, but he had just suffered one of his few failures in *The Day of the Locust*, set in Hollywood during the 1930s, and at the time he was fighting shy of tackling another American subject.

Ashby's contributions to *Coming Home* are not small ones. He persuaded Waldo Salt to take a great deal of rhetoric about the war out of the dialogue, making Sally and the paraplegic, Luke, almost inarticulate. In fact, they communicate best in bed. It is during the scene of their first night together that they quicken into life for most audiences. The old missionary position seems not to work and the impression is strong that Luke may have been rendered impotent by his war injuries. There follows a strong suggestion of mouth-clitoris contact, Wexler's photography being wonderfully subtle. The sexual venturesomeness grows out of Luke's need to prove that he will not allow any dysfunction to impair their lovemaking.

Much of the best footage in the film may well have been the result of a kind of collaborative improvisation. When the shooting date came around, which was inflexible because Jane had already signed a contract for Alan Pakula's western *Comes a Horseman*, there were critical scenes missing from the script, including the ending. Jane said to Ashby: "Have you ever started a film knowing no more about what we're going to do than this?" Ashby had to say "No." Jane looked at him and said with a grin, "I hope it works." The loose construction worked better in the shooting than a tight script ever would have. The confrontation scene in the beachfront apartment Sally has rented, when her husband Bob, returned from the war, takes out a rifle and the audience expects that somebody is going to get killed, was all done without a script. The three actors improvised in front of a tape recorder and then Ashby sat down with scriptwriter Robert C. Jones—Salt had suffered a mild heart attack—and built the scene from that material.

The ending gave everyone the most trouble and it is the only false note in the picture. Salt ended his version by having the major flashback to Vietnam and then go berserk, using his rifle to take hostages; with the police and helicopters closing in on the church steeple to which he has fled (the memory of Merian C. Cooper's *King Kong* is a revered one among filmmakers), he flashbacks again and winds up killed on the freeway (with a deep bow to scenarist Miss Dowd). All of this was shot, but it clearly didn't work for reasons of familiarity and much else. So Ashby finally ended his picture by having the husband commit suicide by wading into the ocean and swimming out to his death. It fails for older movie fans since it is precisely the way Fredric March took his life at the end of *A Star Is Born* (1935).

Much has been written about the strong nature (for ordinary movie-goers) of the nude love scene. Apparently Jane was not worried about it, although as Hal Ashby reflected, she might have been concerned that people might say, "I always knew that's what she did runnin' along with the Black Panthers like she must have." Ashby explained that these critics would say these things regardless of what's on the screen.

Coming Home succeeded on several levels—as a war film about America's most unpopular war; as a love story; and as a reflection of the mood of America in those critical times, especially in its taste in music. *Coming Home* has a ceaseless background of rock music, often loud enough to make you strain to hear the dialogue. And, not least, *Coming Home* swept the Academy Awards in 1979. Jane won as Best Actress, for the second time; her leading man Jon Voight won as Best Actor, and the film was nominated as Best Picture, but lost out to another film on the Vietnam War, *The Deer Hunter*, a movie ideologically opposed to *Coming Home*. So the triumph was mixed—since Jane had urged everyone to stay away from *The Deer Hunter*, which she and many others believed presented a hawkish view of the war, a charge vigorously denied by its director, Michael Cimino. In her acceptance speech, Jane insisted that the film could not have been made if it had not been for the faith and support of its producer, Jerome Hellman. She was being extraordinarily modest, since she had been the crucial element in pulling all of that together.

The pressure of success was now very strong. Jane could afford to do only the films she wanted to do, but they had to be solidly entertaining—no more Godards for her. That pressure was equally strong on Tom Hayden, who with Jane's money was emerging as the only New Left politician with the financial backing necessary to make an impact on the national scene.

Over the next year Jane would make three films ranging from mediocre—*Comes a Horseman*—to extraordinarily significant—*The China Syndrome*. She is fascinating to watch in all three, and in only one of them, *California Suite*, is she called upon to do a typical movie star turn. In this last film, she plays Hannah, divorced from her immature Hollywood writer husband, played by Alan Alda, and sharing custody of their sixteen-year-old daughter. Forced to shape a series of Neil Simon one-liners into a character, Jane succeeds magnificently. "I can't wait to get out of here," she tells her ex-husband, Billy, referring to Hollywood. "It's like Paradise with a lobotomy." She hasn't seen him for nine years and tells him, "You look like a fourteen-year-old boy," and "You have changed. You've gone clean on me." To which Billy replies, "I gave up my analyst. I went sane." Where Jane succeeds so well is in showing the tension beneath all the acid wit. She is afraid of losing her daughter to this "blond life" and in the end she does, but gracefully.

Comes a Horseman had an unusually quiet release for a Jane Fonda picture. This Alan J. Pakula film was allowed to expire after a few weeks of making the rounds in autumn, 1978. Her first western since *Cat Ballou*, it was more of a pleasure to make than to watch, and Jane was able to ride off some of the tension that had built up over the weeks of shooting *Coming Home*. Since the latter picture went into release all over again following the Academy Awards, it effectively blocked Pakula's mistake from the public memory.

PART X

Rehearsal for Doomsday

42

On March 28, 1979, a state of confusion and general emergency began at Three Mile Island, Pennsylvania. A valve had snapped shut in the nuclear power plant there, cutting off pump water, and a "small" radiation leak had occurred in reactor number two, with radioactive steam escaping into the atmosphere.

By the next morning everyone in the three counties—Dauphin, York and Lancaster—nearest to the nuclear site knew that the accident was near-disastrous and could get much worse. There was talk of a *meltdown*, a word many people had never heard before but which, according to some experts, could render much of central Pennsylvania an uninhabitable ghost land with barricades around it. Schools were shut down by the *nuclear accident* (two more words new to most of us)—and remained closed throughout the following week.

George Orwell once wrote that there was a "great redeeming feature about poverty; it annihilates the future." Here at hand was the rich and not too surprising irony of the nuclear age: *it* now seemed capable of annihilating the future. What a surprise it was to many to discover that their homes, their land and possessions were no longer truly theirs. They could be wiped out tomorrow or the day after that by a technical miscalculation. Metropolitan Edison, known as Met Ed, operators of the plant, kept repeating that there was no danger, that the radiation in the atmosphere was at a very low level. The governor at first echoed these remarks, but by Friday, March 30, he was warning all pregnant women and preschool children out of the immediate area, wholesale evacuations were occurring, and buses were going up and down the streets of Middletown and other communities within a five-mile radius of the plant, picking up stray evacuees without transportation. Churches and auditoriums some miles away began filling up as makeshift dormitories. Evacuation instructions urged parents not to pick up schoolchildren but to proceed to their designated asylum, where all families would be reunited. Young men as distant as the cities of York and Lancaster quietly began moving out of the area, some with families, though many not even married but not wishing to risk having their genes damaged and imperiling their future hopes.

The site itself was so hot that the utility company had asked for volunteers to go inside to begin the difficult job of cooling down the reactor. An army of experts had been sent in from outside, and the Nuclear Regulatory Commission had a folksy spokesman, Dr. Harold Denton, on the job explaining the dangers and the possibilities. Despite his ability to dissect the eye of the hurricane so tolerably, his tone of voice was remarkably like that of the captain of a commercial airliner informing his passengers that "there is a small fire in engine number two . . . no cause for alarm." Such voices will announce Doomsday, of that we can be sure.

One resident in four from the three counties involved was leaving; three out of four from the five-mile radius of the site. Although at first there was a shocking lack of official instructions for such a catastrophe, by the weekend, people were told to pack one suitcase each with necessities and that they would be given a four-hour warning alert before any evacuation. The Nuclear Regulatory Commission (NRC) announced that "consideration might be given to evacuating the population in the ten- to twenty-mile area if engineers were to try to clear the gaseous bubble from the reactor core." More trouble. The ailing reactor was now belching up a huge bubble of gas that confounded the experts. Suddenly there was an ominous silence on the public relations front; no more reassuring pap. Even Met Ed was holding its corporate breath. It was during those two or three days of numbing anxiety that the Nuclear Age cracked asunder; all the hopes for cheap energy went glimmering in those deserted town streets surrounding Three Mile Island.

Jane had returned to her Santa Monica home from St. George, Utah, where final location work was done on Sydney Pollack's *The Electric Horseman*. She was sick with concern about the plague of cancer throughout the St. George area caused by nuclear fallout from bomb tests more than fifteen years earlier, an epidemic believed by most experts to have grown out of just low-level radiation. Thousands of grazing sheep in Utah had died more than ten years previously, also mysteriously, to the consternation of officials.

So Jane had come into the antinuclear movement fully committed after her weeks in St. George and, more than a year before that, struggling to bring the Karen Silkwood story to the screen. Miss Silkwood had been exposed to radioactivity while working in a plutonium plant, developed a wasting illness and sued for several million dollars. On her way to meet a reporter to talk about her case, her car was forced off the road by another driver, an action many swear to have been homicidal, and Miss Silkwood died. Her family was awarded $10.5 million in damages, the largest such award in history.* Unfortunately, Jane's company, IPC, had run into difficulty getting legal clearances to the Silkwood story, a necessity in any dramatization.

Almost as deeply committed to warning the nation of nuclear perils was the actor Jack Lemmon, who had made two documentaries, one on the dangers inherent in proliferating nuclear plants and another called *Plutonium: An Element of Risk*. When the script of *The China*

* The award subject to possible reduction when reviewed by an appellate court.

Syndrome, about a nuclear disaster, was first brought to him by actor-producer Michael Douglas, in Lemmon's own words:

> I flipped. Now a whole year went by [1977–78] and I literally did not work because I was afraid that if I did something else and this finally did jell that I might lose it on a physical conflict. So I just took the chance . . . and then the next step was when they got the bright idea of Jane coming in because it was obviously material she would be sympathetic with. Her part was written as a man and it was [originally] going to be played by [Richard] Dreyfuss. Dreyfuss gets all fouled up with various things . . . and then somebody, Michael or whoever—but God bless 'em— somebody said, "Wait a minute. What about Jane Fonda to play the Dreyfuss part?" Which threw me for about thirty seconds and then I said, "Migod, that's brilliant!" But first I thought "Hollywood strikes again! We've got to get a girl in there."

After the signing of Jane and her company as coproducer, director James Bridges, who had done *The Paper Chase*, was approached, but the prospect of handling stars of the magnitude of Jack Lemmon and Jane frightened him. Finally Jane persuaded him that she was not formidable, and he came aboard.

Although the movie had been in the works for three years before the Three Mile Island disaster, the man who created it was forced to bow out with a credit line and a scripting fee. *The China Syndrome* had been written by Michael Gray, who had studied to become a nuclear engineer. "Everything that happened in the script had already happened in various plants," Lemmon said. This was thanks to Gray's initial fears that had derailed him from a nuclear physics career into screenwriting. Lemmon explained:

> What we did was to have those sequences all in one plant. You've got a fifty-million-dollar control room, and it is true that at one time they almost flooded

one of the plants because a ten-dollar needle got stuck. It would be no more than your speedometer suddenly going out . . . this had happened. Then the riveting thing. And falsifying X-rays. I'd love to know how many times that's happened. Exactly like the Alaska oil pump. They turned the damned thing on and oil began leaking all over Alaska. And what did they find? The same X-ray used over and over again.

Bridges managed to bring his genius for creating and sustaining suspense, so obvious in *The Paper Chase*, to a Hitchcock-like perfection in *The China Syndrome*. The essential difference between the two filmmakers in this instance was that in a Hitchcock film the audience is always in on the secret: we know there is a bomb planted in the room, but the men in the room do not. In the nuclear plant film, no one seems to know why the accident happened and the suspense is in the race to pinpoint the cause and stop the chain of events before a meltdown. Bridges was also a writer, and he rewrote large sections of the film, tailoring the part of the investigative reporter to fit Jane, who went into frequent huddles with him over details. For example, it was her idea to have a lethargic, oversized pet turtle as a bedmate. Bridges was, according to Lemmon,

a sneaky director . . . one of the best directors I've ever worked with and gives less direction. One little piece of direction, but to accomplish that, I would have to change something else in the beginning . . . very subtle but it made a difference. One key unlocks more than one door when he gives you the right key. He's also been an actor. There's a great plus to that. It doesn't make you a better director except . . . you understand the actor's problems.

They shot all of Lemmon's scenes first because he had an inflexible date to go into rehearsal for Bernard Slade's *Tribute* on Broadway. These were also the toughest sequences to film since they were nearly all set in the huge control room, the only fixed set in the film, and consisted mostly of dialogue.

Conviction was the key to the success of this unorthodox thriller. Audiences had to believe in what was happening despite the alien jargon, the computerized control room, and the vast unknowns that could not be explained in detail. Close scrutiny of the movie reveals that one character holds it all together, that of Godell, the man in charge, played by Jack Lemmon, who said:

> They won't know I'm around, but I'm going to hold this little mother together. I was pleasantly surprised that it was as effective as it was. . . . It was fascinating to me because at least fifty percent of his dialogue nobody's going to understand, fascinating from the actor's point of view, to make that interesting, to somehow convey, because I did feel and I was correct, as did Jim, that it's not important that they understand *what* he's talking about, what is important is that it scares the hell out of 'em because they know something's wrong but they're not capable of understanding it.

Perhaps one of the major parallels to Three Mile Island was this fear of the unknown. The long-range effect of the disaster that was unfolding near Harrisburg would be not only in the threat posed to the young or the unborn but also in the emotional ravages of having no guide, and no disaster program, the psychological stress of remaining caught within range of this technological giant gone wild. Only the very rich could flee and that part of America is predominantly middle-class. This stress would leave many thousands of residents with permanent mental scars.

A cloak of secrecy concealed the initial panic among Met Ed's executives. They had reason to be alarmed: while they all had been briefed on safety procedures in the event of a mishap at the plant, apparently *no one ever had considered the hazard the plant posed to adjacent populations just by being there.* It was revealed during hearings months afterward that they knew almost at once that the reactor cover had been exposed by the accident and that the gravest of possibilities—a meltdown—could occur. They said nothing to the NRC until long after the twenty-four-hour deadline for such reports, specifically breaching a standing regulation.

A Mrs. Horner, a woman living in Falmouth one mile from the site, said:

> It's a monstrosity . . . that thing down there. They [the utility company] don't know what it will do to us. They have misled us all along. The government told us it was safe. But now we find out they have had problems they never told us about. We never wanted that plant there in the first place.

She could see the ominous, massive cooling towers of Three Mile Island from her front lawn. Most of her neighbors had fled their homes and gone into Red Cross or church dormitories miles away. She went on:

> My son called and advised us to pack all our things and leave. He wants us to move out of here for good. But we can't. We're not young people. . . . We're not that well off. We can't pack up and take off because things aren't all right with Metropolitan Edison. . . . I don't think they know what is going on. I was hanging my wash Wednesday morning, air was coming downriver. They didn't bother telling us what they were doing. If I was affected, then it happened Wednesday. . . . Our son advised us not to drink the water and to take as many showers as we could [to] wash off the radiation.

Some of the media coverage was irresponsible: NBC-TV broadcast a "News Update" on Saturday, March 31, saying that the gas bubble was nearing an explosive state and that a mass evacuation was imminent. A few more suitcases were packed by residents, but by now they were getting used to the danger—the "blitz syndrome"; in the terrible stillness after an air raid, you felt no relief, just a respite. You got on with your life. And so it was near Three Mile Island.

When, on the third day of the crisis, a cloud of radioactive gas spewed from the stricken reactor, it seemed evident that the "experts" were now venting the dome to reduce the bubble, deliberately contaminating the atmosphere in a last minute effort to avert an epic disaster. Local people could only guess at what was happening.

Secrecy, too, surrounded the shooting of *The China Syndrome*. Michael Douglas explained to the others on the film: "We've got to do a lot of dealing with . . . power plants. Without dancing around, let's not look for trouble—'This is The China Syndrome Company; we'd like to visit your nuclear plant.'" They first decided on a working (cover) title of *Eyewitness*. Then, for a while it became *Power!* The studio, Columbia Pictures, took this opportunity to press for a permanent change. As Jack Lemmon remembers it:

> First of all, they [the public] won't know what syndrome means, which is true, unfortunately, as I remember way back when I first started to do ecological documentaries and people were saying "What the hell is ecology?" . . . and then they'd see China and say well, it's about China and Intrigue or a political film because Jane is in it.

The production company tried to keep a closed set and no interviews were granted for several weeks. This was especially difficult for Jane, who was considered "good copy" by every reporter on the Hollywood beat. A few leaks occurred since there was extraordinary curiosity about what she was up to. Movie columnist Army Archard was allowed on the set in early July 1978. It was around this time that Jane stumbled and broke her ankle as the movie moved its final stages, but she was away from the studio for only a week. Her sole complaint was that she had to maintain a slender figure, "and it's killing me. But those gals [journalists and TV reporters] are all that thin." She always had been a compulsive eater, and keeping in trim was a continual battle, particularly when she was unable to take exercise.

Lying in their teeth, the producers told the power companies: "We aren't going to kick nuclear energy in the ass." Thus Douglas and Bridges got access to the Trojan nuclear reactor in Oregon; they visited the facilities at San Onofre and Diablo Canyon, and did location shooting at Scattergood, a gas-burning plant that looks much the same as a nuclear plant. Despite all their precautions, word began to leak out at Scattergood about the slant of the film before they had finished there. When Jane arrived one morning, Lemmon recalls: "There were an awful lot of hardhats out there screaming, 'Go home, you pinko. etc.' We were worried all day long, looking around to see if people were dropping wrenches."

The film was released the second week of March 1979, two and a half weeks before Three Mile Island. Commenting on the crisis afterward, Michael Douglas said, "I've never had an experience like this. It goes beyond the realm of coincidence. . . . It's enough to make you religious." Lemmon exclaimed:

Thank God it was out! If it had come out afterward, I think it would have lost some of the impact. We expected a lot more criticism from the pronuclear critics and public and we didn't get it . . . nowhere near as much as we expected. The few that did, of course, shut up totally the minute Three Mile Island happened. The power companies did everything under the sun to hurt this film. They sent out four hundred lengthy letters to the major critics around the country, saying "You will shortly see a film that is anti-nuclear this and that. It is filled with lies and inaccuracies, nothing but propaganda. Basically, they are going to alarm the American public unduly, and it is a disservice to the people of this country and the world," being very strong and definite about it, admitting that they had never seen it. You know, they're lobbying.

311

One power company executive who *had* seen it said—before the accident—that it was without "scientific credibility" and "in fact, ridiculous." The Edison Electric Institute commented, "Radioactive steam would be captured by the reactor's containment dome." When the dome at Three Mile Island failed to "capture" its steam during successive leaks, the Institute fell silent.

Members of the film company mutually declared a moratorium on any discussion of the accident, fearful of doing anything that might seem like exploitation of a tragedy. Jane was the first to speak out; she was too indignant to remain silent. Radioactive iodine was turning up in Pennsylvania milk, since dairy herds around the reactor site were all affected by the slow sifting to earth of the airborne isotopes. Health officials declared the milk safe for human consumption but few believed them. Much of it was hauled away to distant processing plants to be made into powdered milk. Nine months after the accident, an announcement would be made by Pennsylvania's Health Department that in Lancaster County, which lay across the river from the closed power plant, the rate of hypothyroidism in newborn infants, which can lead to mental and physical retardation, was five times higher than the state average.

On September 24, 1979, Jane and Tom Hayden launched their political tour of the eastern half of the United States at Three Mile Island; they had come to test the country's reaction to their own political philosophy as programmed into their Campaign for Economic Democracy. As Jane had done with the North Vietnamese, the blacks and the Indians, now she identified with these new victims of low level radiation. She said that she was "moved" about speaking to an audience in the stricken area. "I cannot even conceive what it's like to be in your position, and my heart goes out to you." The accident stunned her, she said, "but on the other hand, I'm not surprised. It was absolutely inevitable that there would be an accident somewhere, sometime. And I'm sorry"—and her words rang with conviction and emotion—"it happened to you. And I hope it doesn't get any worse."

The couple's main appearance in the area was at a rally in the Penn Harris Motor Inn in Camp Hill. Outside the motor inn's ballroom some forty American Legionnaires and their wives picketed the entrance, but their only audience was a crowd of several hundred who had been turned away because there was no more room inside. As the crowd entered, one of the younger veterans shouted, "She's using you! We're anti-Jane Fonda because she's a traitor to our country. She gave propaganda speeches in Hanoi while our boys were being tortured." But he was shouted down by another young bearded veteran, Robert Shaeffer of Harrisburg, "I'm a veteran [of the Vietnam War] and that's not what I think. I'm just for total peace and disarmament. I just think she was a person who had some money and some influence to go over there and help stop the war." Jane felt compelled to comment to the audience on the pickets. "I consider myself a good American. My ancestors' home was burned by the British two hundred years ago. I am an American. . . . I got angry during the Vietnam War and I've been angry ever since." The antinuclear crowd applauded her wildly.

And so they continued on their $150,000 trek across the East, South and Midwest—from New York to Detroit and on to Des Moines. In every city auditorium the response was the same: the house would be packed, tension would rise, and then there they were, swept inside and down the aisle by a platoon of bodyguards and cameramen. The audience would stand, applauding, for a better look and there would be audible gasps of astonishment at the real-life Jane Fonda, so glamorous and powerful and yet so determined to be simple and unaffected, to be one of them.

43

Bitterness against Jane's wartime adventures seemed to have died out as the seventies drew to a close. And then, unexpectedly, there it was again as vicious as ever. Governor Jerry Brown had appointed her to the California Arts Council, a prestigious post that sounded harmless enough. Jane and Tom had worked hard for Jerry Brown ever since he defended her against resolutions to brand her a traitor on the floor of the California Senate back in 1973. Now her critics in that body surfaced again, and the old charges were renewed as her confirmation was voted down. In August 1979, Jane Fonda was turned down for the Arts Council for "acts of treason" during the recent war.

Jane's friends rallied around. Her leading man from *California Suite*, Alan Alda, led a crusade to nip this revival of "McCarthyism" in the bud, but the Senate was unrelenting and Jane finally dropped out of contention. Even her former journalist friend Peter Collier attacked her in *New West* magazine, labeling the move to save her from a "witch-hunt" a travesty, and asking if Jane was to be considered "the Hollywood One" (as opposed to "the Hollywood Ten" who went to prison for contempt of Congress). So, despite her preeminence as an actress, it seemed that certain old and abiding hatreds would never really die. Some memories might be short, but these forces could lash out at her at any moment, and she would never be secure from them.

Jane had chosen not to answer such charges in the past, but this unexpected surfacing of old enemies caught her by surprise, and she said:

> I think it is shocking that a large majority of our Senate chose to inject politics into what should have been a discussion of my merits as an artist to represent the arts community in California. They excoriated my name and my reputation in the most vicious terms on the floor of the Senate and without offering me any chance to answer their charges.

Jerry Brown was incensed and said these senators "lacked the guts to let her at least come before the Senate and speak her mind." He called their moves "disreputable" and "dishonorable."

One senator, speaking for many, said that Jane could clear herself if she would apologize to those persons who suffered because of her visits to Hanoi. Jane retorted that it was

> out of patriotism that I went there. . . . That's why I made *Coming Home*, to try to communicate the horror of that war. . . . It may take a hundred years for history to be written and for people to understand that those of us who entered the war [*North Vietnam*] did so out of a tremendous care for this country and did not betray those men who were there, but it's very difficult. Six years is not a long time, I realize. And the mass psyche needs to feel that we were right in being there. And I may die before that need goes away. But it will go away one day and I hope it does, because if it doesn't we could get involved in another Vietnam somewhere else.

Throughout 1979, a great deal of pressure had been put on Jane to disavow the present government of Vietnam, the heirs of Ho Chi Minh, because of their indifference to the suffering of the so-called Boat People. Her position seemed to be that she would not turn her back on her friends in what used to be called *North*

Vietnam. Later she edged away from this corner by saying that she was not going to become an apologist for North Vietnam.

The Boat People were, of course, the victims of the sorting-out process of "desirables" and "undesirables" that always seems to accompany authoritarian regimes. Many of them were ethnic Chinese, the "Jews" of Asia. Some were Cambodians who had fled across the border from the murderous Khmer Rouge, still fighting a guerrilla war from mountainous enclaves against the occupying forces of the new Vietnam.

Jane broke politically with singer Joan Baez over this issue, since Baez made at least two journeys to the Boat People transit camps scattered about the Far East and sang at benefits to raise money for their relief. But Jane and Tom contributed money to that same relief fund and helped organize a rally in Hollywood for the cause; probably the pressures on them to do so were too great not to yield this much.

There was a time when Jane echoed the beliefs of the person closest to her at the time, and it was very hard to keep up with her; but not anymore. She now had almost unshakable convictions about some matters. One of them seemed to be that Tom Hayden was little short of a saint, that his concerns for working people and the disenfranchised were genuine and were not simply politically motivated. If Hayden subtly guided her into this belief, who can ever truly know? All American Presidents in recent history have had wives with a staggering amount of confidence in their ambitious husbands, including Jane's old adversary Richard M. Nixon. They also have had concern as great as Jane's; it was not for nothing that Pat Nixon suffered a stroke.

Joan Baez followed a lonelier course. Without any political ambitions to consider, she visited the political prisoners held by the Democratic Republic of Vietnam, and she was so shocked by the gross violations of their human rights by the government she had once supported (Baez had visited Hanoi on several occasions during the war) that she drafted an open letter of protest and her supporters found eighty Americans to sign it with her. The letter condemned the Democratic Republic of Vietnam for these violations. Jane was approached but refused to sign; Baez understood and declined to get into any feud over the matter. She knew that she was and always would be pro-peace, and she said that Jane was pro-Vietcong.*

The autumn of 1979 might have overwhelmed anyone but Jane. Before launching with Tom the Road Show for Economic Democracy, Jane opened a body-fitness salon in Beverly Hills called Jane Fonda's Workout. She told reporters that she wanted to invest her wealth in things she believed in, and working out was something she herself did three times a week; she did not want to invest in corporations, which were targets of her rage on frequent occasions. If Workout was a success, which it was, there would be branches (there were), and then she also said she was considering going into auto repair shops, since the public was so frequently ripped off there.

Her romantic comedy for Sydney Pollack, *The Electric Horseman*, opened around the United States, and she plugged it whenever she could. Her leading man, Robert Redford, turned out to be a perfect foil for her veneer of reserve. In the movie, they updated the old Tracy-and-Hepburn relationship, sparring and pulling back before falling into each other's arms. Instead of the old basic male-and-female skirmish, the film depicted commercial exploitation vs. environmentalist concerns (will they get the stallion Rising Star out of the clutches of the breakfast-food company and into freedom on the plains or not?). Nearly everyone seeing the movie knew in advance of the stars' private involvements with solar energy and the Indian rights movement—although it must be said that Redford's commitment to the Indian

---

* Joan Baez interviewed by Geraldo Rivera on ABC-TV.

cause was far deeper than Jane's early powwows—so it was a little like the mating of two champions. Director Pollack for the most part let his stars do their specialties, without imposing any strong viewpoints of his own. He said: "The thing I like best about *The Electric Horseman*, which is not a great film by any means, is you don't see a lot of directorial muscle in it. And I like to let films alone, let them tell themselves, which is the hardest thing in the world to do." In this sense, Pollack is very much like William Wyler, who maintained a rigorous neutrality in directing such masterpieces as *The Best Years of Our Lives*, *Dodsworth*, *The Letter* and *The Little Foxes*, although Pollack does not admit to being influenced by him.

A country singer called Willie Nelson, a grizzled 100-proof-voiced Texan, was invited to costar in the film as Sonny Steel's (Redford's) manager. Since Nelson had been named Entertainer of the Year by the Country Music Association, the combination of Nelson, Fonda and Redford was certain to guarantee a great deal of advance interest. With no acting experience, Nelson breezed through the part, relying on his many years as a guitarist-singer to guide him. He said:

> Reading lines is like singing songs . . . without the melody. It's all lyrics. The goal is the same, to make people identify with you and react emotionally. . . . I know the words to more than two thousand songs, so I guess I'm a pretty quick study. Nervous? No. But remember that I play a character a lot like myself, a man who has spent his whole life around cowboys and horses.

Temporarily removed by several hundred miles from most of her causes in St. George on location, Jane directed some of her restless energy into forming a small dance class, mainly to keep members of the company and herself in good shape. She had never allowed herself the luxury of relaxation with nothing to do; at least not within anyone's memory. She kidded herself about it by telling friends that she was "basically lazy."

The film was favorably received by the critics, none of whom was very excited although most agreed that it was a pleasant time killer. If it had an environmental message—corporate exploitation, said Jane—at its heart was Hallie Martin's (Jane's) awakening to long-suppressed romantic urges after being alone for a while in the empty desert night with Sonny. By Christmas, *The Electric Horseman* was the most popular film of the season.

The Hayden-Fonda Road Show blitzed through fifty cities, zeroing in on energy and corporate irresponsibility. Hayden's goal seemed to be to lay the foundation for a future national coalition of progressive groups. Jane was the main attraction and everyone was curious to see her, especially her enemies, who often picketed in front of the campus auditoriums and hotel ballrooms where they would appear; they were Catholic War Veterans, members of the American Legion, or simply disaffected individuals carrying hand-printed placards, mostly referring to "Hanoi Jane" or her antiwar crusade.

Tom and Jane put in eighteen-hour days and collapsed in strange motels each night, where they often watched themselves on the late television news. Several dozen newspaper reporters followed them around, and some of them remarked later that they surprisingly came to like Tom more and Jane less. Up close, Jane seemed coiled a little too tightly; Tom was more relaxed and able to roll easily with the questions. With the public, almost the reverse was true. Jane brought her electric presence to the evening and the auditorium, wherever it was, was hypercharged with it; while Tom brought his rhetoric and while he was applauded when he would shout, "People are willing to profit from the potential poisoning of their children," he started no hearts racing. Since he had gone out more or less solo, although accompanied by the most visible activist in the world, no coalitions were formed or even hinted at along the way. A week after their departure they were old news, a little like last week's weather. It was an expensive publicity spectacular that made their campaign goals— for solar power, control of corporations by "the little people," rent control, nothing roaringly radical. In fact, the tour threw a spotlight on the softening of two left-ists who seemed to be wading into mainstream politics without making any serious waves.

They appeared on *Meet the Press*, on *Good Morning America* and on television personality shows beyond number. Nearly every national magazine gave their tour a spread, and they received front-page coverage in news-papers wherever they appeared, with follow-up editorials, frequently hostile, in their wake. It was good advance publicity for *The Electric Horseman*, which Jane had not intended, or so she said, since hundreds of thousands of people got to see her locally either in person or on television. If Jane and Tom were looking for traces of a national groundswell for their movement, the trip must have seemed a major disappointment.*

Jane's sincerity seemed genuine to everyone; Tom's convictions less so. Few trust politicians anyway, and here was a turncoat. It helped that Jane's eyes were always on him as he spoke, despite the fact that she must have heard those words a thousand times. They also looked comfortable together, which helped. And of course that was part of the show. "I don't mind that my scripts overlap into reality," said Jane at one point, "and this tour might overlap into theatricality. But when I express my concern I'm not pretending." She was believed.

This all seemed to be leading up to something more than a run for the United States Senate, and even Jane did not deny that she thought Tom would make a great President. If the thought of one of the first Americans into Hanoi who was *not* a prisoner of war sitting in the Oval Office is too much for most people even to con-

---

* The CED has had numerous local successes, notably in the area of rent control.

template, think of Richard Milhous Nixon walking with Mao through the Great Hall of Peking. Nixon, the great friend of Chiang Kai-shek, was two or three decades later breaking bread with Mao, the man who ran Chiang out of mainland China; and when in disgrace Nixon considered the Chinese people (the *Red* Chinese) as among his most loyal friends and planned to return to visit them.

Jane's millions, from her films and various enterprises, were fueling this political phenomenon, and some of her friends who had been converted to the cause were coughing up substantial tax-deductible sums. She and her father may have complained about what a "lousy" choice the American people made in choosing Ronald Reagan as President, but they both knew, and certainly Tom did, that an actor in the White House could go a long way toward paving the way for an actress as First Lady.

While the Pollack comedy was being edited for release, Jane had director Colin Higgins doing research in the field (of female secretaries) in Cleveland, where Jane had made contact with an organization called Working Women, in Baltimore and in Boston with her old group called Nine to Five. Eventually, the latter would lend its name to the film itself. Higgins's assignment was to seek out, among other things, answers to the question: How would you dispose of your boss? Gun, poison and the hangman's noose were high on the list, and two of these found their way into the plot of the film in a fantasy sequence. Lily Tomlin, probably American television's greatest gift to comedy since Imogene Coca, was invited to costar, and Jane had the brilliant idea of asking the country singer Dolly Parton to play the boss's gal Friday. who manages to keep one step ahead of him in the race around the desk.

Nine to Five may well turn out to be the most successful film Jane ever made, and some of the reasons for this are readily apparent. It is a great audience picture. Dolly Parton, in her first movie role, not only has a huge following, but is very good in her part. Costar Lily Tomlin has the wittiest and juiciest role in the farce, and it is her best performance in theatrical films since *Nashville.*

For all of these reasons the movie is not to be dismissed lightly. Produced solely by Jane's company, IPC, it virtually guarantees that Tom Hayden's political future will be as heavily financed as any in the country.

As for the movie itself, it is better directed, by Colin Higgins, than Jane's earlier farce, *Fun with Dick and Jane,* but the script has less wit and is far more predictable.

It may give America's women nine-to-fivers a lot of laughs, but it has no real message for the militant. Since Jane and her producer, Bruce Gilbert, were as close to the screenwriters, Patricia Resnick and Colin Higgins, as most producers ever get, one must assume that Jane was being extraordinarily generous with Parton and Tomlin. She has given them the best parts and all of the really funny lines. Jane's Judy Bernley seems to be in a perpetual daze, except for a fantasy sequence in which she stalks her boss, Mr. Hart, with what looks like an elephant gun. Lily Tomlin's Violet makes the farce work. She even makes us believe that she could mistake a box of rat poison for "Sweet and Skinny" or whatever the coffee sweetener is that she puts into Mr. Hart's cup. Her stealing the wrong corpse out of a hospital emergency room is slapstick almost as fine as vintage Laurel and Hardy.

The answer can only be that Jane had no intention of making *Nine to Five* her film. At some point during the development of her movie on women who work, she decided to go for the money, and she has succeeded beyond her wildest expectations. She doesn't even keep a shred of sexual interest in herself, but gives it all to Dolly, who has the only bedroom scene in the movie—with her own husband, who looks like a fullback. Dolly's Doralee Rhodes may well be a superior example of a star turn by one of country and western's legendary figures, but it suggests even more strongly than did singer Bette Midler's dramatic tour de force, *The Rose*, that she has a bright future in the movies.

The critical notices were mixed and Jane, surprisingly, fared less well at the reviewers' hands than either Parton or Tomlin. She is not a very convincing secretary. Could it be that she can't bring the same passionate concern to the plight of sexually harassed secretaries that she brought to the antiwar cause or nuclear protests, Indian rights or even the future well-being of a horse?

PART XI

Genetic Iconography

"I do in life exactly what I do when I act. I go through this extroverted, exhibitionistic period—as an experiment. It has got to be the prime motivation of every actor—this need to express yourself sort of fictionally because you don't have confidence in your real self."

44

The summer of 1980 was the hottest in some sixty-odd years all across America, and more than 12 million people died from heat-related causes. It was also the summer of the longest actors' strike in history, when members of the Screen Actors Guild held out for a share of television rerun money. They finally won, but before they did Jane joined her father and Katharine Hepburn on Squam Lake in New Hampshire for the filming of *On Golden Pond*, a Broadway success which Jane had bought for her IPC company. Jane's purchase of this play for her father and herself was the final affirmation that things between them were again much as they had been when she was a toddler and growing up, except that now her fame and power had eclipsed his. Henry Fonda, film icon, had spawned an icon unlike any before her in movie history. The company stayed at the Brickyard Mountain Inn, which had a cluster of cottages along the lakeshore. Hank and Kate Hepburn were strangers since, despite years of working in the Hollywood studios at the same time, they had had different bosses. Kate was intrigued by Jane and as comfortable as an old shoe with Hank. She had always been the puritan rebel, but Jane had had the chance to be a rebel when puritanism was in rout.

Within less than five years, Jane had achieved almost legendary power within the film world and only a little less on a political level. This power was peculiarly American, because outside the United States her fame was that accorded to a great talent, slightly eccentric in her views and life-style. In America, she had moved beyond Clare Boothe Luce in her celebrity as a public figure whose origins were also in show business. There are no simple answers as to just how this came about. Bruised by Watergate and the debacle of Vietnam, America had learned to tolerate contrary views, for they just might turn out to be right.

Tom Hayden had never quite made it as a legend. Lacking the color and dark wit of Abbie Hoffman and the political glamour of Jerry Brown, he looks uncomfortable in white shirt and tie. His politics must be concentrated on the proles, since he is so obviously one of them. Ironically, his only drawback there is the growing aura of power and even queenly status of his wife, Jane Fonda. Her success, while fueling his ambitions, might in the end undermine him.

Josh Logan watched this legend he had launched as she handed a Tony award to her father on a New York stage. "She's Sarah Bernhardt!" he thought. And so she may well be. But Jane stood in no one's shadow, neither Bernhardt's nor Henry Fonda's. Her father may have been a national monument and now a movie icon, but Jane was indisputably regnant in Hollywood. No film queen of the past had risen from such a dynastic past, nor spread herself through her fame into so many corners, many of them tight. Fame was for her money in the bank, and she referred to it frequently as an empress might her chest of jewels or her colonies. It was not vanity, but hard common sense.

Certainly, Jane was for the seventies and eighties what Bette Davis had been for the thirties; Kate Hepburn for the forties; and Marilyn Monroe for the fifties; if any star reigned in the sixties it was Barbra Streisand, by default. Other actresses were equally gifted—Jane Alexander, Faye Dunaway, Jill Clayburgh, Diane Keaton, Ellen Burstyn—and away from Hollywood Vanessa Redgrave was not only as gifted as Jane but more exciting to watch, a fact that was immediately clear when

328

they appeared on the screen together in *Julia*. It was Redgrave one watched in all of their scenes together, but then Jane always had been generous with fellow actors.

Jane and Hank were now closer than ever. Nearly always supportive of his children when they were in trouble, he was now, especially with Jane, frankly adoring. She was in the Bel Air mansion a great deal, if only on the run. Perhaps she needed that elegant countrified ambience to compensate for her own plebeian house so close to its neighbors in Santa Monica.* But it was more than that. They both must have sensed that in whatever time remained to him, they would give as much love as possible to each other. So much had been in the way all those years ago.

On Golden Pond had opened as a stage play on Broadway in late February 1979. It could well have been written in the late thirties or anytime in the forties. It was in the tradition of *Our Town*, *Mornings at Seven* and even *The Glass Menagerie*, although none of its characters could conceivably be labeled neurotic as crippled Laura was in Tennessee Williams's drama.

Like Hank's much earlier, comedy-drama, *Generation*, *On Golden Pond* had a great deal to say about the strains between the generations, especially fathers and daughters, but Ernest Thompson's new play covered a much wider range of human experience than that. Its principal theme was the sadness that comes when people slowly awake to the inevitable fact of dying, but it is about neither illness nor death. If anything, it is a play brimming with hope for the human race. The author was a neighbor of Jane's in Santa Monica. Not quite thirty, he was an actor with a passion for playwriting, supporting himself by long-running appearances on afternoon television soap opera. Since it went so much against the grain of the times, his play was not first

---

* In 1982, they moved into a brand-new solar house as elegant as any in the film colony. Jane also has an "escape hatch" at a ranch in Laurel Springs, California, which she purchased for in excess of a million dollars to use as a retreat and children's camp for the CED.

mounted as a Broadway offering, but had a brief run off-Broadway at the Hudson Guild

Unanimous rave reviews from the critics prompted the producers, the actress Greer Garson and veteran Broadway impresario Arthur Cantor to bring it to Broadway. Jane bought it for IPC with the intention of costarring with Hank as his daughter. Her interest was more than simply the sound notion of acquiring a critical success. The daughter, Chelsea, is something of a rebel and a marital misfit. Her relationship with her father, Norman, has been bad since childhood, and she confesses to her mother, Ethel: "I . . . can't talk to him. I've never been able to. . . . Maybe someday we can try to be friends." To which her mother replies with some asperity: "Chelsea, Norman is eighty years old. He has heart palpitations and a problem remembering things. When exactly do you expect this friendship to begin?"

"I don't know. . . . I'm afraid of him."

The Golden Pond where the action takes place is a lake in New England. The Thayers, Ethel and Norman, have a lakeside cottage, spending their summers there for the past forty-eight years. Norman is as crusty as Hank; he is given to moodiness and fits of melancholy, lately centering around his strong feeling at eighty that he will soon expire; he is blunt-spoken. Chelsea is forty-two, exactly Jane's age then, and has refused ever to have any children because she thinks her own childhood was so disastrous. Jane declined to have children for a very long time for much the same reason. When the play begins she is about to arrive with her new lover, Bill, a California dentist with a fourteen-year-old son, who travels with his father on such outings because his mother doesn't want him.

Chelsea and her lover leave young Billy with her parents when they take off for a European holiday together, which turns out to be a wedding trip. The boy draws the old man out of his melancholia and they have a delightful time together. When the couple returns from Europe, Billy has acquired grandparents of the quirky sort that only he, who has moved from one trauma to another as a child, can fully appreciate.

Jane and her producer, Bruce Gilbert, pulled all of the elements of the production together with the same care they had lavished on all their other films going back at least to *Coming Home*. Mark Rydell, who had turned singer Bette Midler into a powerful actress in *The Rose*, was brought in to direct. Although Frances Sternhagen, a skillful and intelligent actress, had created the role of Ethel, one could hear the bravura echoes of Kate Hepburn's steely nasality in her last "big" speech to Norman, following what appears to be a severe and frightening spasm of angina:

> You've been talking about dying ever since I met you. It's been your favorite topic of conversation. And I've *had* to think about it. Our parents, my sister and brother, your brother, their wives, our dearest friends, practically everyone from the old days on Golden Pond, all dead. I've seen death, and touched death, and feared it. But today was the first time I've felt it.

The long actors' strike had shut down nearly every television and film production on both coasts. Jane and her producer-partner managed to achieve a compromise and the shooting went on after a brief pause. Jane Fonda had that kind of power.

45

The setting sun was dazzling on the waters of the Pacific seen from the street in front of the Haydens' house near the Santa Monica shore. A teenage skater zipped down the block to the turn next to the shore road and swung around in circles there, back and forth, back and forth. The houses are crowded close together, and Jane and Tom's is weathered but functional—an ugly house in a desirable location. The day may well come when a coast highway will blaze through the block.

John Lennon had died the previous month, murdered by a crazed man in his middle twenties with an identity conflict and rage in his heart. Jane and her contemporaries were in mourning, but while "Strawberry Fields Forever" can move her to tears she was already with Vadim when the Beatles burst upon the scene. Yet if she related to any of the Beatles, it was to Lennon. He believed as she did; their causes were the same, including the final one of family togetherness. They had both known the wrath of the American government, had both been busted on drug charges, hers trumped up by over-zealous authorities; even their defiant expressions in the slammer were similar, although behind the anger Lennon's eyes reflected a peace with himself that Jane's did not. Each had gone into a private world while famous as though they had climbed for a few moments into a fold of Glory's robe.

In early January 1981, Jane and her family were

recovering from a scare over Christmas when her father suffered a sudden irregularity in his heartbeat and had to be hospitalized. New medication brought the crisis to an end, and Hank went home again*, but it put a damper on their long-planned skiing holiday at Sundance, the resort created by Jane's old friend and costar Robert Redford.

Her physical-fitness salon, Workout, in Beverly Hills was heavily booked, and Jane was frequently seen working out there very early in the morning, both because she wanted to and because her presence lent a personal touch to a new business operation in a highly competitive field.

On the political front, there seemed to be a deliberate and extensive attempt on the part of conservatives everywhere to ignore her. But at home in California, that was very hard to do. Quiet plans were afoot to expand the Campaign for Economic Democracy although the Haydens had to feel some frustration over Tom's failure to build a broader constituency since his election to the California State Assembly.

There may be future convulsions and surprises, more FTAs and "GI movements"—absolutely certain if America is turned into an armed camp bent on confrontation with the communists by the archconservatives in power. Jane Fonda will again go on the peace circuit, rallying the people. But one thing we can count on: Jane Fonda will continue to mature as an actress. Perhaps that's what the other agitation is really about, getting it all together from her own discontent.

In a way, Jane Fonda never has returned from Vietnam. She is still out there on the road to Quang Tri Province. Just as Robert E. Lee never returned from Appomattox, nor Virginia Woolf from Bloomsbury, Jane remains in the public mind lithe and smiling as she moves through rubble. That is a myth, of course, compounded of Jane's fierce loyalties and the work of the media. Jane is also an actress with a mystique of power

*Henry Fonda died of heart disease on August 12, 1982.

333

and inherited genius. History has been extraordinarily kind to her; events and attitudes have been inclined to vindicate her. The same thing happened centuries ago to Joan of Arc, but unfortunately she had already died at the stake.

History's darling is also a woman and a mother. Family matters are important to her, and she seems determined to keep these separate from all the rest of her. In addition, there is a serenity about her in all public encounters that suggests what writers on Zen call "immovable wisdom," or, as Takuan wrote: "There is something immovable within, which, however, moves along spontaneously with things presenting themselves before it."

With the possible exception of her steadfast loyalty to the government of North Vietnam, she has always allowed her good sense to correct past errors, even to acknowledge them. "Did I say *that?*" she asks. Her family is fortunate; such persons are very rare.

BIBLIOGRAPHY

Across the River and Into the Trees by Ernest Hemingway, Jonathan Cape, London, 1950.

The All-Americans by James Robert Parish and Don E. Stanke, Arlington House, New Rochelle, New York, 1977.

The Autobiography of Bertrand Russell (1944–1967), George Allen & Unwin, London, 1969.

The Best and the Brightest by David Halberstam, Random House, New York, 1971.

The Black Panthers by Gene Marine, New American Library. New York, 1968.

Close-Up by John Gruen, Viking Press, New York, 1968.

Conversations in the Raw by Rex Reed, World Publishing Company, New York and Cleveland, 1969.

Ernest Hemingway: A Life Story by Carlos Baker, Scribner's, New York, 1969.

Filmlexicon degli Autori e delle Opere, Edizioni di Bianco e Nero, Rome, 1958.

Fire in the Lake: The Vietnamese and the Americans in Vietnam by Frances FitzGerald, Atlantic-Little, Brown & Co., Boston, 1972.

The Fondas by John Springer, The Citadel Press, Secaucus, 1970.

The Grapes of Wrath by John Steinbeck, Viking Press, New York, 1939.

Haywire by Brooke Hayward, Alfred A. Knopf, New York, 1977.

Helter Skelter: The True Story of the Manson Murders by Vincent Bugliosi with Curt Gentry, W. W. Norton & Co., New York, 1974.

"Holden Caulfield at 27" by Rex Reed, article in Esquire Magazine February, 1968.

The Italians by Luigi Barzini, Atheneum, New York, 1964.

Jane: An Intimate Biography of Jane Fonda by Thomas Kiernan, G.P. Putnam's Sons, New York, 1973.

Josh: My Up and Down In and Out Life by Joshua Logan, Delacorte Press, New York, 1976.

Kissinger by Marvin Kalb and Bernard Kalb, Little, Brown & Co., Boston, 1974.

Lee Strasberg: The Imperfect Genius of the Actors Studio by Cindy Adams, Doubleday, 1980.

Memoirs of the Devil by Roger Vadim, Harcourt Brace Jovanovich, New York, 1977 and Editions Stock, Paris.

The Memoirs of Richard Nixon by Richard M. Nixon, Grosset & Dunlap, New York, 1978.

Mission to Hanoi by Harry S. Ashmore and William C. Baggs, G. P. Putnam's Berkley Medallion, New York, 1968.

Nixon Agonistes: The Crisis of the Self-Made Man by Garry Wills, Houghton Mifflin Company, Boston, 1970.

Pentimento: A Book of Portraits by Lillian Hellman, Little, Brown & Co., 1973.

Prevent the Crime of Silence by Ken Coates, Peter Limqueco and Peter Weiss, Allen Lane, The Penguin Press, London, 1971.

Revolutionary Suicide by Huey Newton, Harcourt Brace Jovanovich, New York, 1973.

The Seesaw Log: A Chronicle of the Stage Production by William Gibson, Alfred A. Knopf, New York, 1959.

Sideshow: Kissinger, Nixon and the Destruction of Cambodia by William Shawcross, Andre Deutsch Ltd., London, 1979.

A Special Rage by Gilbert Moore, Harper-Colophon Books, Harper & Row, New York, 1971.

Steppenwolf by Hermann Hesse, Penguin Books Ltd., Harmondsworth, Middlesex, England, 1965.

Strange Interlude by Eugene O'Neill, Horace Liveright, Inc., New York, 1928.

The Tales of Hoffman: From the Trial of the Chicago Seven, edited by Mark C. Levine, George C. McNamee and Daniel Greenberg, Bantam Books, New York, 1970.

"Tom Hayden's Manifest Destiny" by Joel Kotkin, article in *Esquire* magazine, May 1980.

Vietnam by Mary McCarthy, Harcourt, Brace & World, New York, 1967.

With a Cast of Thousands: A Hollywood Childhood by Jill Schary Zimmer, Stein and Day, New York, 1963.

INDEX

340

343

347

349

351

353